T0200580

Researching Virtual Worlds

Methodologies for Studying
Emergent Practices

**Edited by Ursula Plesner and
Louise Phillips**

Routledge
Taylor & Francis Group

NEW YORK AND LONDON

First published 2014
by Routledge
711 Third Avenue, New York, NY 10017

Simultaneously published in the UK
by Routledge
2 Park Square, Milton Park, Abingdon, Oxon OX14 4RN

*Routledge is an imprint of the Taylor & Francis Group,
an informa business*

Library of Congress Cataloging-in-Publication Data

Researching virtual worlds : methodologies for studying emergent
    practices / edited by Ursula Plesner & Louise Phillips.
        pages cm. — (Routledge studies in new media and cyberculture ; 14)
    Includes bibliographical references and index.
    1.   Virtual reality—Social aspects—Research—Methodology.
I. Plesner, Ursula.   II. Phillips, Louise (Louise J.)
    HM851.R459 2013
    006.8—dc23
    2013005373

ISBN: 978-0-415-62444-2 (hbk)
ISBN: 978-0-203-10464-4 (ebk)

Typeset in Sabon
by Apex CoVantage, LLC

Contents

Figures and Tables

Acknowledgments

The development of the main themes of the book and the interest in researching virtual worlds as socio-technical ensembles emerging in ongoing practices and specific situations emanate from a collective, collaborative and interdisciplinary research project, "Sense-Making Strategies and User-Driven Innovation in Virtual Worlds: New Market Dynamics, Social and Cultural Innovation, and Knowledge Construction" (2008–12). The project was based at Roskilde University and Copenhagen Business School under the leadership of Professor Sisse Siggaard Jensen, one of the contributors to the book. We would like to thank Sisse Siggaard Jensen and all the members of the research team for fruitful meetings and productive collaboration. We would also like to thank the Danish Strategic Research Council (KINO committee) for funding the project (grant no. 09–063261). Finally, thanks to our reviewers and colleagues who have given valuable feedback on the chapters and to Emil Krastrup Husted for assistance with the preparation of the manuscript.

1 Introduction

Approaching the Study of Virtual Worlds

Ursula Plesner and Louise Phillips

A field of practice and scholarship has developed over the last ten years around "virtual worlds"; initially it was mostly concerned with defining what the information technological platforms known as virtual worlds were or could become (e.g., Bainbridge 2009; Heudin 2004), but it has increasingly focused on their role in practice and the complex socio-technical arrangements to which they belong (e.g., Heider 2009; Sonvilla-Weiss 2009). The present book engages in discussions of how we may understand emergent practices in and around virtual worlds with a focus on the crafting of methodologies that pinpoint the connections between technological elements and affordances, peoples' engagement and sense-making, and discursive patterns and visions. A central point of the book is that if we recognize how methods perform (Law and Urry 2004), it is necessary to pay attention to how the methods we use in the study of virtual worlds contribute to enacting them as particular phenomena. This book about methodology, then, is not about what virtual worlds are, or how particular methods are best suited to study them, but about how virtual worlds emerge as objects of study through the development and application of various methodological strategies. When virtual worlds are not considered objects that exist as entities with fixed attributes independent of our continuous engagement with them and interpretation of them, a possible consequence is to work with a very open approach to virtual worlds. In this introductory chapter, virtual worlds are referred to as complex ensembles of technology, humans, symbols, discourses, and economic structures, ensembles that emerge in ongoing practices and specific situations. Such a formulation is less a definition of virtual worlds than it is an approach to an amorphous field. This entails that engagement in research on virtual worlds can be expected to address a large variety of empirical phenomena relating to virtual worlds, going beyond how they are built, what takes place "inside" them, or how people use them.

The more fixed definitions of virtual worlds that can be found in the virtual worlds literature have direct implications for how it is conceivable to approach a study of them and which elements it seems relevant to focus on. This follows from highlighting specific characteristics of the IT platform.

For instance, virtual worlds have been defined as "crafted places inside computers that are designed to accommodate large numbers of people" (Castronova 2004, 4), a wording that points to the "placeness" of those worlds and to their potential social uses. They have also been conceptualized as "[a] synchronous, persistent network of people, represented as avatars, facilitated by networked computers" (Bell 2008, 2), a definition which highlights the individuals engaged in social interaction. Both these definitions resonate with the idea of "virtual worlds as places of human culture realized by computer programs through the Internet" (Boellstorff 2010, 126). Yet another attempt at pinning down the meaning of virtual worlds defines them as "[I]nternet-based simulated environments that emulate the real world and are intended for users to inhabit and interact within them through avatars" (Hua and Haughton 2008, 889). This definition points to the mirrorlike aspects of virtual worlds and hints at the potential correspondence between phenomena inside and outside virtual worlds. Finally, a common way of defining virtual worlds is to enlist several characteristics that must be fulfilled in order for us to identify something as a virtual world:

> The online journal Virtual Worlds Review defines a virtual world as 'an interactive simulated environment accessed by multiple users through an online interface.' Six essential features are prescribed: shared space (multiple users), a graphical user interface, immediacy ("interaction takes place in real time"), interactivity ("the world allows users to alter, develop, build, or submit customized content"), persistence ("the world's existence continues regardless of whether individual users are logged in"), and socialization, or a sense of community. (McDonough et al. 2010, 9).

All these definitions point to relevant aspects of the IT platforms labeled "virtual worlds," and to their specific affordances (Gibson 1986; Hutchby 2001). However, rather than aiming to contribute to refining definitions of virtual worlds—that is, what virtual worlds *are*—the aim of this book is to offer methodological strategies for capturing the situated practices in and around virtual worlds and hence treat virtual worlds as phenomena that are constituted in situations and practices and that emerge as particular objects of analysis in the research process.

SITUATIONS AND PRACTICES OF ENGAGING WITH VIRTUAL WORLDS

Some of the IT platforms central to the empirical investigations in the chapters of this book are Second Life, Habbo Hotel, City of Heroes, and the OpenSimulator Developer community. But the chapters are not simply studies of the characteristics of these platforms and the activities they afford. Instead, they share the assumption that, as an object of analysis, any virtual world is a moving target, and our knowledge about them is highly dependent on the work we put in to defining and delineating them. As a consequence, all chapters direct their attention to the processes of researching virtual worlds in a continuous interplay with the actors and technological elements that co-constitute these worlds. The chapters aim to open up the concept of virtual worlds by examining how they are made and remade through specific practices where technological affordances, symbolic entities, and social and interpretive processes become intertwined. Although the chapters develop different methodologies and thus different vocabularies, many of them articulate this ambition. For instance, in Chapter 7, Reinhard and Dervin ask what happens when the agency of the person engages with the structures of the virtual world. And in Chapter 3, Strand insists that we refrain from starting with a fixed definition of the technology in question (virtual worlds, three-dimensional [3D] Internet, or the Metaverse); rather, we should begin our empirical investigations by looking at the very practices, situations, and events in which a particular phenomenon occurs, asking openly what appears and what emerges.

The aim of this book is to make a distinct contribution to *methodological* discussions in the field of virtual worlds research—and studies of new media technologies more generally. It is not to add to the large number of books on virtual worlds that seek to *explain* virtual world technologies and practices and to apply various theoretical perspectives to *capture the specificity* of virtual worlds. Most of these books pay relatively little attention to *methodologies for the study of virtual worlds*. There are notable exceptions to this—for instance, a volume by Boellstorff et al. (2012) on the use of ethnographic methods in virtual worlds, and the extensive review of methods in which Bainbridge (2009) discusses a range of methods that can be applied *within* virtual worlds. For instance, Bainbridge details how experimental methods can be used to test reactions of people acting through their avatars to scenarios such as environmental catastrophes, conflict resolution in war zones, and so on. He also describes how observations can be used to study collaboration, the social consequences of bad behavior, or the implications of experimental architecture. To take a third example, he outlines how quantitative methods can be used to measure social dynamics in-world. In all these cases, what is presented are methodologies for studying practices *within* virtual worlds, whereby the researcher is "inside" them, for instance, embodied in an avatar. In contrast, the chapters of this book seek to engage methodologically with both online and offline phenomena and practices. This ties into the authors' shared approach to virtual worlds as elusive objects of analysis that are co-constituted through actors' and researchers' engagement with one another and with particular situations and practices relating to virtual worlds.

RESEARCHING VIRTUAL WORLDS AS ENSEMBLES OF TECHNOLOGY, HUMANS, SYMBOLS, AND DISCOURSES

The distinction drawn above, between online and offline, may be a way of talking about particular empirical domains in focus, but no sharp distinction between the two is upheld in the methodological contributions of this book. Few virtual world researchers operate with an understanding of 'the virtual' and 'the real' as two different domains. Virtual worlds, it is argued, are *both* virtual and real (Schroeder 2002, 2012) and the virtual is not the opposite of real. As Schultze (Chapter 4) states, such a distinction belongs to a representational view of reality. In her view, the online/offline distinction is out of sync with empirical observations of experiences of entanglement. Thus, to understand empirical phenomena in and around virtual worlds, we should avoid distinguishing *a priori* between physical and digital materiality. Although this type of methodological ambition is discussed to varying degrees in the following chapters, the whole book can be seen as part of a tendency to dissolve the in-world/out-world dichotomy in the study of virtual worlds (see also Plesner, Chapter 2), both on a theoretical and a methodological level (Lehdonvirta 2010; Taylor 2006). The contribution of Ruckenstein (Chapter 5) in this endeavour is to interrogate the question of how virtual worlds are interwoven with economic value pursued in corporate practices by ethnographically studying uses of a virtual world along with studying the technological development processes in the company behind that virtual world. Yetis and colleagues (Chapter 8) have a similar interest in how a virtual world is developed by stakeholders with various affiliations, with a focus on the resources they bring to the development work and the particular parts of the virtual world that are cultivated by them.

The book's contribution does not consist in reiterating the obvious, that a dichotomous way of understanding virtual worlds may be problematic—but in presenting specific methodologies that can be used to generate multi-faceted accounts of the situations and practices that bring virtual worlds into being. To make this contribution, several chapters construct virtual worlds as complex ensembles of technology, humans, symbols, discourses, and other elements and devise methodologies that capture the interwovenness of these elements. Thus, they seek to address the challenges described by Lehdonvirta (2010) who criticizes much scholarship on virtual worlds for holding onto an image of virtual worlds as independent "mini-societies". As he writes, "[t]hus far, the typical strategy for authors (myself included) to deal with this has been to treat the caveats as links or interaction between the real world and the virtual world. This strategy attempts to address the issues while still clinging on to the dichotomous model." Many chapters of the present book transcend the online/offline, virtual/real divide through multi-sited and multimodal research strategies, which move between sites relating to the creation and recreation of virtual worlds, focusing on practices in specific situations. In this way, they try to capture how technology, humans, symbols, and discourses are linked together in practice.

RESEARCH METHODOLOGIES FOR CAPTURING EMERGENT PRACTICES

"To capture" how technology, humans, symbols and discourses are linked together in practice and to describe these practices as "emergent" are of course not straightforward, neutral operations. In this book, we do not consider the previously described ensembles in and around virtual worlds as phenomena that are "out there," waiting to be captured, and we do not consider the phenomena "as emergent" in and of themselves. Rather, we conceive of virtual worlds as emerging phenomena insofar as they are co-constructed, such as in the practices under study. When this book engages with the theme of emergence, it is not to take the dynamics of emergence as a given (Corradini and O'Connor 2010). Rather, it is to focus on how objects are brought into being and transformed in co-construction processes in social interaction, including in our research practices. Across all the chapters, methodologies are presented that provide analytical lenses for studying how objects and social categories—such as virtual worlds, presence, and virtual worlds architecture—emerge from, and are reproduced and transformed in, processes of researching, designing, engaging in, and communicating in and about virtual worlds. The underpinning interpretative—and broadly social constructivist—assumption behind the book is that objects emerge from the situated and context-dependent co-production of meanings among the participating actors in social interaction. Adopted here is a postfoundational perspective on knowledge production, positing that the subjectivities of researchers and researched, research objects and research-based knowledge also emerge out of those meaning-making practices (Bourdieu and Wacquant 1992; Finlay 2002; Law 2004). This perspective leads to a common interest across chapters in how subjects and objects of research mutually constitute one another. It also lies behind the collaborative approach to research taken in several chapters, whereby practitioners in virtual worlds are engaged as partners with scholars in the co-production of knowledge.

With this book, we aim to present a range of methodologies for use in research on virtual worlds and other phenomena that could be constructed as "emergent practices." To this end, each chapter illustrates the use of one or more methodologies, reflecting, among other things, on the following: the interplay among metatheory, theory, methodology, method, and empirical case; the co-constitution of methodological approach and object of study; the specific methods for data production and analysis; the strategies applied to investigate emergent practices in a variety of situations relating to virtual worlds; and the strengths and limitations of the methodology or methodologies as approaches to studying virtual worlds and other complex, emergent phenomena. And, taken together, the chapters provide scholars and students with thorough discussions of the advantages and weaknesses of different methodological approaches to studying virtual worlds as socio-technical ensembles emerging in ongoing practices and specific situations.

It has been argued that emerging phenomena require new methods. For instance, the *Book of Emergent Methods* by Hesse-Biber and Leavy (2008) asserts that researchers increasingly find themselves looking beyond conventional methods to address complex research questions, and describes alternative uses of traditional quantitative and qualitative tools, innovative hybrid or mixed methods, and new techniques facilitated by technological advances. It is tempting to approach a relatively new media platform like virtual worlds as a phenomenon demanding new methods. As Williams, Rice, and Rogers write, "Although we consider possible research methods for new media as mainly extensions of existing methods, we propose that the new media researcher should consider alternative methods, or even multiple methods, and to attempt a triangulation of methods" (1988, 15). It seems sensible to remain open to the possibility of mixing more traditional and more experimental methods, but basically, the contributions of this book do not construct virtual worlds as an entirely new frontier in research methodology. Virtual worlds do have specific affordances, but much of what takes place in and around them is integrated with other technological elements and platforms, and remediates objects, practices, and events from other domains. Therefore, they can be said to present us with well-known types of methodological issues in new ways. Jensen's chapter offers an example of how methods inspired by visual anthropology and video interaction analysis can be combined to capture the situated practices and sense-making in relation to particular projects in virtual worlds. The author integrates considerations of both the visual, the situational, the interpretive and the material in her development of the video interview method, because "the video interview method presupposes that the experience and sense of being there is constitutive to human engagement with virtual being. This sense, and the actual and situated realization of it, is a phenomenon hard to explore through retrospective methods such as qualitative interviews or to capture in video observational studies of action and interaction, if applied separately [. . .] In video observational studies, in contrast, we can follow some of these actions from an external perspective" (chapter 6, 158). In this way, the chapter addresses some of the new affordances of virtual worlds, drawing on well-established methods in combinations tailored to new types of empirical phenomena.

A discourse of change, newness, innovation, and emergence surrounds new media platforms such as virtual worlds in both research and practice, and it can be argued that this demands a certain caution on behalf of new media researchers. It requires an openness toward recognizing the role of the past in the present, considering the stability underlying changes and remembering the usefulness of well-known methods in combination with methods that are closely tied to the affordances of new media technologies. So we should keep reminding ourselves that emergence and new practices are, at one and the same time, products of our analytical gaze and features of virtual worlds.

To recapitulate, it is central to our book to reflect upon how methodologies and specific methods contribute to constructing an emergent phenomenon in particular ways. As Strand (Chapter 3, 64) puts it, "[d]rawing on science and technology studies, [. . .] all methods can be understood as creating translations—that is, particular (and perhaps technologically mediated) ways of seeing and analyzing the subject matter. Particular methods mediate the object of study, rendering it visible for science in particular ways." With this reflexive approach to methods and methodologies for studying virtual worlds as emergent practices and relations, the book has an ambition of providing inspiration not only for the study of virtual worlds but also for studies of other emergent phenomena. The point is to supply readers not with definitive ways of tackling the complexities of emergent phenomena but with a broad foundation for their own reflexive consideration of those complexities.

METHODOLOGIES OF THE DISCURSIVE/MATERIAL

In the following chapters, a broad spectrum of perspectives and methodologies is presented: Actor-Network-Theory and post-Actor-Network-Theory, performativity theory, ethnography, discourse analysis, Sense-Making Methodology, visual ethnography, multi-sited ethnography, and Social Network Analysis. The book shares with other methodology books (McKenzie, Powell, and Usher 1997; Miller and Fredericks 1996; Potter 1996) the goal of demonstrating diversity and variety in terms of methodology and disciplinary focus and the goal of developing practical methodological strategies that are epistemologically coherent and subject to critical reflections on the part of the researcher. The distinct contribution of *Researching Virtual Worlds* is to illustrate the use of the previously mentioned range of methodologies in relation to an emergent object of research such as virtual worlds while emphasizing the need for ongoing critical, methodological reflections.

Along interdisciplinary lines, the methodologies discussed in the book straddle the fields of media and communication studies, sociology, science and technology studies, design studies, IT studies, and ethnography. This indicates that they are connected, in various ways, to two movements in social science and media and communication studies—the linguistic turn and the material turn. The inspiration from the linguistic turn can be seen in several chapters' analytical focus on discourses, imaginaires, sense-making, and the articulation of visions relating to virtual worlds, whereas the importance of the material turn can be discerned in analyses of distributed technological arrangements, digital objects, and the physical settings of research and engagement with virtual worlds.

In a sense, most chapters combine the two orientations by focusing on how the structures, affordances, or objects of specific virtual worlds make sense to users, builders, or other individuals who encounter them or on how the articulation of visions or imaginaires make a difference for the development of technological elements of virtual worlds. For instance, Reinhard and Dervin (Chapter 7) focus on individuals' ongoing attempts to cognitively bridge gaps in understanding that are considered necessary activities in emergent and ever-changing environments such as virtual worlds that are made up of a number of artifacts, symbols, characters and their equipment, and technical affordances and constraints. Jensen (Chapter 6) focuses on users' interpretations and reflections while observing the manipulation of artifacts and bodily responses and the expression of emotions. Ruckenstein (Chapter 5) not only applies a discourse oriented perspective to understand how the creation of value for both the companies behind and the users of virtual worlds are linked to discourses of prosumer capitalism, but also bases her analysis on ethnographic research that allows her to focus on the material practices and objects that shape the virtual worlds platform and the uses of it. Chapter 3 by Strand offers another example of the intertwinement of the discursive and the technological by proposing that an object of analysis such as presence in virtual worlds should not only be analyzed as a characteristic of the technological platform but can also be understood as a discursive entity, an "imaginaire," that productively participates in the creation of virtual worlds.

The sense-making and discursive approaches draw attention to the production of meaning in relation to virtual worlds—both with regard to the interpretative practices of individuals engaging with virtual worlds and with regard to how discourses are articulated in and around virtual worlds and how those discourses are connected to wider social and normative structures. In that sense, they highlight the individual, cultural, and political resources that are brought into—and become formative of—virtual worlds.

A common characteristic of the socio-technical approaches to virtual worlds is that their object of study is not defined in advance but emerges as socio-technical networks composed of heterogeneous elements through the empirical investigation and analysis. They share a relational ontology and an inspiration from Actor-Network-Theory to methodologically "follow the actors" to see which linkages they make to other actors in practice. Hence, they present a sensibility toward the emergent, guided less by preconceived theoretical ideas or constructs than by the diverse range of phenomena, topics, and technologies introduced by the objects/subjects of study.

The final chapter of the book (Yetis, Teigland, and Di Gangi) stands out from the others by presenting a primarily quantitative methodology, demonstrating how different lines of thinking within the social sciences and media and communication studies may inform a study of virtual worlds as—in the wording introduced earlier—socio-technical ensembles emerging in ongoing practices and specific situations. To capture aspects of the human agents who assemble these worlds, and the resources they bring into maintaining them, the authors apply an innovative combination of methods that, in various ways, construct stakeholders and stakeholder contributions as objects of analysis.

CASE STUDIES AND A RANGE OF METHODS

All the studies presented in the book are case studies because the aim of the book is to discuss how we can shed light on the ongoing practices and specific situations in which virtual worlds are made and remade and to reflect upon how they emerge as objects of study in various research practices. As it is common in case studies, given their aim of producing rich empirical material about the object of study, most authors have applied a range of methods. These include, among others, (online and offline) participant observation, interviews, video interviews, document analysis including analysis of blogs and web texts, video recordings, photo dairies, reception experiments, and word bust analysis.

The use of the overarching methodologies and the specific methods are illustrated and reflected upon in studies of a diverse range of practices and social and organizational settings: the construction of virtual buildings and cityscapes in socio-technical networks; the design and use of a virtual space for launching music; identity issues in relation to individuals and their avatars inhabiting an S/M community; the interplay between economic structures and the emergence and use of children's virtual worlds; the interaction of virtual world users and animated objects in virtual work settings; different users' varying engagement with different types of virtual worlds; and stakeholders' investment of time in a virtual open source community. By detailed critical reflections on how these varied practices and settings were approached using particular methodologies and methods, the chapters demonstrate how, through the development and use of creative, cross-disciplinary, epistemologically justified methodologies, we can study virtual worlds as ensembles of technology, humans, capital, symbols woven together with interpretations, and emergent practices.

THE CHAPTERS' CONTRIBUTIONS

The second chapter, drawing on socio-material approaches, is authored by Ursula Plesner and is entitled "Virtual Worlds as Emerging Cyber-Hybrids: Accounting for the Travel between Research Sites with Actor-Network-Theory." The title points to the chapter's ambition to highlight the distributed character of innovation in virtual worlds and the methodological strategy of "following the actors" to produce data. The object of analysis is not practices in relation to one particular type of 3D space, but the socio-technical networks (Bijker and Law 1992) in which innovation processes concerning virtual worlds are embedded. The chapter contributes to the research literature that aims to dissolve the inside/outside, online/offline, virtual/real dichotomies by presenting a methodology that encourages us to consider digital objects, discourses, political demands, and other entities as equally valid entities for inclusion in research on virtual worlds. The chapter operates on a meso-level of analytical reflection, highlighting choices in the research process and discussing how these relate to the empirical data. It pays special attention to the analytical takes that have been central to its construction of the story of innovation in and around virtual worlds and to the processes of naming and thus constructing objects of analysis.

In Chapter 3, Dixi Louise Strand similarly addresses the questions of how a distributed virtual/real phenomenon can be accessed empirically and how a methodology can capture a set of complex practices, unfolding both online—in a virtual space—and in a set of globally distributed homes and offices. The chapter interrogates the phenomenon of presence in virtual worlds. However, rather than starting with a fixed definition of the object of study, she examines the practices, situations, and events in which the object of study appears, asking openly what occurs and what emerges. The methodology is based on post-actor-network-theory, and integrates the analytical concepts of imaginaires, and assemblage in order to conceptualize and analyze presence not as an a priori characteristic or an inherent feature of virtual worlds but rather as a set of dreams and expectations, and as a very practical accomplishment. The chapter reflects on the challenges of the case study method in studying the design and use of emergent and distributed technologies in networked organizations, where locating and delineating exactly where the case study begins and ends is not a simple matter. The case study is conducted through the methods of interviewing, participant observation, and document analysis. Throughout the chapter, Strand presents detailed reflections on how these methods produce particular insights. Rather than providing a total overview or mapping of general patterns, the methodology produces a juxtaposition of sites and situations, and the analysis focuses on selected moments and the specific arrangements and situations in which presence appears and unfolds.

Chapter 4 by Ulrike Schultze adopts a perspective based on the theoretical lens of performativity in order to explore empirically how people, as cyborgs, perform identities in virtual settings through or with their avatars. Its methodological reflections are based on a view of virtuality as a social accomplishment as opposed to an inherent property of Internet technology (Slater 2002), and the chapter reflects on the analytical implications of this view. It is argued that cyborgian identity should be regarded in performative terms as fundamentally entangled social and material (both digital and physical) components and that real life– and virtual life–boundary-drawing practices are central to engagements with virtual worlds. To understand the practices by which distinctions between on- and offline identities and actual and virtual reality are produced and stabilized, Schultze presents an interview method that is based on the production and discussion of virtual worlds users' photo diaries, illustrating significant moments from their time spent in virtual worlds. In its combination of visual representations, written text and verbal interactions, the method leverages multiple modes of communication in an effort to elicit the diversity of the diarists' experiences (Elliott

1997). Also, the material conditions of incidents (e.g., the configuration of the space, what postures people held and how they were positioned vis-à-vis objects and others, what people were wearing) which are frequently left out of textual diary descriptions, become part of the record. In this way, the role of (digital) material resources and material practices, that is, how (digital) artifacts were used and what meaning they were given in the performance of identities, are made objects of analysis.

Chapter 5 develops a framework for analyzing the processes of creating virtual worlds, with a focus on how companies' search for profit and users' engagement in social relations online are constitutive of new modes of cultural production, distribution, and consumption. Here, Minna Ruckenstein draws inspiration from the concept of prosumer capitalism in which individuals contribute to the economy, making online worlds possible and profitable. The methodological framework draws partly on a discourse-centered perspective in order to explore historical accounts and thereby people's aims and desires in relation to the creation of the virtual world Habbo Hotel, and it draws partly on actor-network-theory in order to capture the dynamics of human and nonhuman relations and thus to gain an understanding of the material underpinnings of virtual worlds. The framework also emphasizes other aspects of materiality by incorporating an ethnographic method which focuses on the interaction between people and digital objects. Ruckenstein demonstrates how the social dynamics in virtual worlds can be explored through a methodological framework that takes the emergent qualities of human–object relations into account and directs attention to how virtual worlds are brought into being through chains of interaction between people and digital objects. Through its methodological framework, the chapter shows that online activities are not disconnected from offline practices and social relations and it also extends this discussion to the economic dynamics of Habbo Hotel and virtual worlds, arguing against the idea that "the virtual economy" is somehow qualitatively different and separable from "the economy." The argument is that the production of economic and social value that is supported through virtual worlds is an inherent part of monetary transactions and emerging worlds of sociality.

In Chapter 6, Sisse Siggaard Jensen presents and illustrates a video interview method that she has developed in order to analyze human entanglement with technology in actual use situations. The methodological framework is based on visual anthropology and ethnography, video interaction analysis, and situational analysis as well as the concepts of situatedness and assemblages. The specific methods are designed to produce and analyze visual and spatial data, with the aim of gaining insight into how human actors with avatars engage with virtual situations and thus participate in processes of organizing or reorganizing virtual worlds. The methods consist of video recordings that capture action, emotion, and movement from an external perspective and of in-depth qualitative interviews that provide actors' interpretations and reflections in relation to the recorded situations. The video interview method is illustrated through an account of the production of empirical material in a particular situation where employees in a public institution engage in a meeting in the virtual world, Second Life. It is shown how the situation is organized and reorganized by the interaction between human actors and scripted media animations. The chapter's contribution is to offer a methodological approach centering on visual material and digital objects that can be used in order to follow the dynamic processes of change which are typical of virtual worlds and which are generated by residents' co-construction of the environment.

In Chapter 7, CarrieLynn D. Reinhard and Brenda Dervin present Sense-Making Methodology (SMM) as an approach that can capture how users engage with media products such as virtual worlds in situations of engagement. The chapter reports on a qualitative case study experiment designed to allow for a systematic comparison of sense-making processes with different types of virtual worlds. The empirical material was produced in experimental sessions of novice users' engaging with a gaming virtual world and with a social virtual world. The chapter introduces SMM interviewing as a both highly structured and open-ended interview method and describes how it includes qualitative measurements of users' sense-making processes both during and after the media reception sessions. During the sessions, participants were asked to discuss their reactions to the media product via talk-aloud protocols. Reinhard and Dervin demonstrate the systematic and very detailed coding of the interview material, again inspired by a specific SMM method. They conclude that SMM is well suited to providing an understanding of the nuances of how users negotiate the affordances and constraints of various virtual worlds in co-constructing an experience that they can evaluate as being good or bad or as entertaining or not. It is argued that the understanding of sense-making processes at a micro-level provides a window through which it is possible to grasp general issues regarding the reception of virtual worlds.

Chapter 8, by Zeynep Yetis, Robin Teigland, and Paul M. Di Gangi, introduces a methodological framework drawing on both qualitative and quantitative methods of data collection and methods of analysis. It reports a case study of the OpenSimulator Developer community and sets out to explore how stakeholders interact with one another to obtain resources and to develop the public good for the community. The theoretical framework of stakeholder theory directs attention to the role of different actors in establishing and upholding virtual world communities, and Social Network Analysis is used to quantitatively measure relations among stakeholder groups. The empirical material consists of interviews with members of the community and the results of scraping (i.e., extracting information from) relevant online sites and mailing lists. The study is longitudinal, relying on data from the first four years and three months of the community.

Yetis, Teigland, and Di Gangi show that one can obtain an idea of the structural composition of a community through the production of network graphs, and that stakeholders' position in a network can be assessed through a calculation of their individual scores in network analyses. The combination of interviews and textual and social network analyses points to the differing contributions, resources, norms, values, goals, and time frames of active participants in the community. In conclusion, they argue for the value of applying multimethod data collection and analyses on various platforms in research on emerging phenomena related to virtual worlds.

SUMMING UP AND LOOKING FORWARD

The chapters serve as examples of the development of methods and methodologies that may address virtual worlds as complex ensembles of technology, humans, symbols, discourses, and other elements. When read together, they clearly illustrate how virtual worlds emerge as particular objects of study through the development and application of various methodological strategies, and as such, they illustrate the importance of a reflexive approach to how research on virtual worlds plays a part in enacting them. This introduction has argued for an open approach to virtual worlds that allows for an inclusive production and analysis of empirical material. Now, these types of aims and contributions open up for new agendas. If we choose to work with an understanding of methods as performative and virtual worlds as complex emerging objects of analysis, there is a need to develop more coherent methodological frameworks for approaching virtual worlds. Also, if we recognize that virtual worlds have particular affordances, virtual worlds research demands much further theorization and methodological reflection to create appropriate mixed-methods approaches that address both the technological aspects and the interpretive aspects of assembling and engaging with virtual worlds. It might also be beneficial to pay more attention to the concept of affordances than we do in this book, because this concept directs attention both to the features of the technological platforms and to how these are perceived and mobilized by actors (Kaplan 2011). The concept of affordances has become widely used in media studies and elsewhere, and, with the basic premise that a material object has affordances that are relative to the observer (Gibson 1986), it is in congruence with the previously described approach to virtual worlds and may inform analyses that bridge the domains of the technological, the individual, and the organizational. Finally, whereas the chapters do present us with a wide range of empirical examples emphasizing the miscellaneous nature of virtual worlds, the chapters can only give us a glimpse of what takes place in and around virtual worlds. We hear about how 3D environments are created virtually to give users a spatial perception of physical building projects; we visit a music laboratory where avatars dance while they explore newly released music; we meet Angela in a throne-like chair enjoying the company of her two male submissives. Moreover, we get to check in at the virtual Habbo Hotel and join children engaging with virtual objects; we get to see reactions to the world of superheroes and villains; we get involved in the weekly meetings of a library project at which an animated chair and a virtual dog are key actors. Finally, we become acquainted with an open-source community where entrepreneurs, academics, business people, and hobbyists collectively pursue both individual and mutual gains. But because the focus of this book is on methodologies, we only get snapshot impressions of the empirical richness of the cases, and the fine-grained analyses of empirical material will have to be pursued in other outlets. There continues to be ample room for analyses of the processes of assembling and engaging with virtual worlds, in particular in times of convergence where we might expect virtual worlds to become increasingly intertwined with other technological platforms.

REFERENCES

Bainbridge, William Sims. 2007. The scientific research potential of virtual worlds. *Science* 317 (5837): 472–76.

Bell, Mark W. 2008. Toward a definition of virtual worlds. *Journal of Virtual Worlds Research* 1 (1): 1–5.

Bijker, Wiebe E., and John Law. 1992. *Shaping technology/building society—studies in sociotechnical change*. eds. Wiebe E. Bijker, W. Bernard Carlson, and Trevor Pinch,. Cambridge, MA: MIT Press.

Boellstorff, Tom, ed. 2010. *Online worlds: Convergence of the real and the virtual*. London: Springer-Verlag.

Boellstorff, Tom, Bonnie Nardi, Celia Pearce, T. L. Taylor, and George E. Marcus. 2012. *Ethnography and virtual worlds: A handbook of method*. Princeton, NJ: Princeton University Press.

Bourdieu, Pierre, and Loïc Wacquant. 1992. *Invitation to reflexive sociology*. Cambridge, UK: Polity Press.

Castronova, Edward. 2004. *Synthetic worlds: The business and culture of online games*. Chicago: University of Chicago Press.

Corradini, Antonella, and Timothy O'Connor, eds. 2010. *Emergence in science and philosophy*. London: Routledge.

Elliott, Heather. 1997. The use of diaries in sociological research on health experience. *Sociological Research Online* 2 (2). Accessed April 6, 2013. http://www.socresonline.org.uk/index_by_issue.html.

Finlay, Linda. 2002. Negotiating the swamp: The opportunity and challenge of reflexivity in research practice. *Qualitative Research* 2 (2): 209–30.

Gibson, James J. 1986. *The ecological approach to visual perception*. New York: Taylor & Francis.

Heider, Don, ed. 2009. *Living virtually—researching new worlds*. New York: Peter Lang.

Hesse-Biber, Sharlene Nagy, and Patricia Leavy, eds. 2008. *Handbook of emergent methods*. London: Routledge.

Heudin, Jean-Claude. 2004. *Virtual worlds: Synthetic universes, digital life and complexity*. Boulder, CO: Westview Press Inc.

Hua, Guangying, and Dominique Haughton. 2009. Virtual worlds adoption: A research framework and empirical study. *Online Information Review* 33 (5): 889–900.

Hutchby, Ian. 2001. *Conversation and technology—from the telephone to the Internet*. Cambridge,UK: Polity Press.

Kaplan, Sarah. 2011. Strategy and PowerPoint: An inquiry into the epistemic culture and machinery of strategy making. *Organization Science* 22 (2): 320–46.

Law, John. 2004. *After method—mess in social science research*. London: Routledge.

Law, John, and John Urry. 2004. Enacting the social. *Economy and Society* 33 (3): 390–410.

Lehdonvirta, Vili. 2010. Virtual worlds don't exist: Questioning the dichotomous approach in MMO studies. *Game Studies* 10 (1). Accessed April 6, 2013. http://gamestudies.org/1001/articles/lehdonvirta.

McDonough, Jerome P., Robert Olendorf, Matthew Kirschenbaum, Kari Kraus, Doug Reside, Rachel Donahue, Andrew Phelps, Christopher Egert, Henry Lowood, and Susan Rojo. 2010. *Preserving virtual worlds final report*. Urbana: Illinois Digital Environment for Access to Learning and Scholarship.

McKenzie, George, Jackie Powell, and Robin Usher. 1997. *Understanding social research—perspectives on methodology and practice*. London: Routledge.

Miller, Steven I., and Marcel A. Fredericks. 1996. *Qualitative research methods—social epistemology and practical inquiry*. New York: Peter Lang.

Potter, W. James. 1996. *An analysis of thinking and research about qualitative methods*. London: Routledge.

Schroeder, Ralph. 2010. *Being there together—social interaction in shared virtual environments*. Oxford, UK: Oxford University Press.

Schroeder, Ralph. 2002. *The social life of avatars—presence and interaction in shared virtual environments*. London: Springer-Verlag.

Slater, Don. 2002. Social relationships and identity online and offline. In *The handbook of new media*, ed. Leah Lievrouw and Sonia Livingston, 533–46. London:SAGE Publications Ltd.

Sonvilla-Weiss, Stefan. 2009. *(IN)VISIBLE—learning to act in the metaverse*. Vienna: Springer-Verlag.

Taylor, T. L. 2006. *Play between worlds: Exploring online game culture*. Cambridge, MA: MIT Press.

Williams, Frederick, Ronald E. Rice, and Everett Rogers. 1988. *Research methods and the new media*. New York: Free Press.

2 Virtual Worlds as Emerging Cyber-Hybrids

Accounting for the Travel between Research Sites with Actor-Network-Theory

Ursula Plesner

Virtual Worlds are not only digital spaces for play or social interaction but are also increasingly developed for use in professional communication (for instance, medical training, conferencing, and production). For example, in the field of architecture and construction, individuals and companies are engaged in the innovation of advanced virtual models of buildings and cityscapes, using Second Life, the game engine Unity, or advanced simulation (nongaming) software. The idea behind such models is to give clients the possibility of entering a virtual world or environment and become active participants in the shaping of given projects. Some have visions of letting clients influence the building of their own properties; others have visions of user-driven innovation in connection with city development projects. Such uses of Virtual Worlds platforms in professional communication are not well established. Rather, they can be considered innovations in the making. It can be fruitful to talk about "cyber-hybrids" in order to capture how Virtual Worlds based on physical localities become altered virtually and materially as part of a developmental process. As emergent objects of study, it is a challenge to pin down their elements and to delineate what they are—but this is a feature they can be said to share with Virtual Worlds broadly that are not settled technologies but temporary outcomes of technological advances driven by collaboration across the gaming industries, academia, Information and Communication Technology (ICT) industries, and so on and by increasing technological convergence between different platforms.

When we try to define what kind of object of study a virtual world is, one place to start could be through defining what we mean by "virtual" and what qualifies as a "world." However, this tends to direct our focus of attention to particular sorts of 3D online social spaces. Rather than having one type of three-dimensional (3D) space as the object of analysis, this chapter is concerned with how virtual elements and worldly elements are part of larger socio-technical networks (Bijker and Law 1992). It is shown how elements of Virtual Worlds are bound up with a range of other—heterogeneous—elements, such as political demands, technical standards, and aesthetic objects (Plesner and Horst 2012a). The analytical approach is inspired by Actor-Network-Theory (ANT; Latour 1991, 2005). To demonstrate the value of this framework for the study of *elements of virtual worlds*, the chapter discusses an empirical study of virtual buildings and cityscapes. The study is based on a multimodal and multi-sited research design, using different methods and spanning several sites to produce empirical material. The discussion of the study concentrates on the strategy of "following the actors" for producing data, whereby the focus is on how actors and objects are related to one another in networks. This strategy is based on ANT's principle of symmetry. Concretely, the principle of symmetry implies that all types of entities are deemed relevant for inclusion in the analysis as long as other entities connect to them—that is, refer to them, use them, or are affected by them. In the conclusion, it is pointed out that the methodological advantage of ANT is this empiricist, symmetrical orientation to the empirical material, whereas the weakness is its inability to produce authoritative, general accounts of what larger phenomena such as Virtual Worlds are. In the following account, elements such as politics, aesthetics, and software development are highlighted but are not conceived of as macro-actors (Czarniawska and Hernes 2005) or as stable elements that structure innovation potentials. Instead, they are considered to be sets of micro elements and processes interwoven with the elements of Virtual Worlds.

THE VIRTUAL WORLDS METHODS LITERATURE AND THE INSIDE/OUTSIDE DICHOTOMY

Rather than looking at collaboration about architecture *within* Virtual Worlds (Chase, Schultz, and Brouchoud 2008; Fruchter 1999), the present chapter approaches elements of Virtual Worlds without constructing an "inside" or an "outside" of them, by following how elements are connected around them—elements that could otherwise be conceived of as belonging to an inside or an outside. In this study, the naming of the objects as cyber-hybrids is intended to point to this analytical focus.

To date, Virtual Worlds have been approached methodologically from a wide range of perspectives—for example, formal experimentation, observational ethnography, and quantitative analyses (Bainbridge 2007). It is noteworthy that in his rather extensive review of methods, Bainbridge sticks to discussions of methods that can be applied *within* Virtual Worlds. For instance, how experimental methods can be used to test avatars' and/or people's reactions to scenarios such as environmental catastrophes and conflict resolution in war zones, among others. Or how observations can be used to study the social consequences of bad behavior, collaboration, or the implications of experimental architecture. Or how quantitative methods can be used to measure social dynamics in-world. In contrast to this, this chapter is part of a tendency to dissolve the in-world/out-world dichotomy in the study of virtual worlds (see also Chapter 1), on both a theoretical and a methodological level (Lehdonvirta 2010; Taylor 2006). The theoretical and methodological inspiration stems primarily from socio-technical approaches to the study of science and technology. Before accounting for this approach in more detail, an attempt is made to synthesize similar current developments in the Virtual Worlds methods literature.

The attempt to dissolve the dichotomy between "the real world" and "the virtual worlds" has been made from within various scholarly traditions. Drawing on Anselm Strauss's concept of overlapping social worlds, Lehdonvirta (2010) describes series of overflows between virtual worlds, various other forums on the internet, as well as families and workplaces. He criticizes much scholarship on Massively Multiplayer Online (MMO) games and Virtual Worlds for holding on to an image of, for instance, games as independent "mini-societies." As he writes, "[t]hus far, the typical strategy for authors (myself included) to deal with this has been to treat the caveats as links or interaction between the real world and the virtual world. This strategy attempts to address the issues while still clinging on to the dichotomous model" (Lehdonvirta 2010, online). Jenson and De Castell have studied the transference of skills between the real world and video games, addressing the relationship between humans and things. They argue that the transfer of skills is quite evident when people engage in video games that relate to real world activities such as singing, dancing, skateboarding or even shooting in first person. Recognizing that video games transfer skills drastically changes the way we ought to perceive MMOs from viewing them as mere entertainment to acknowledging them as being *"artificially intelligent spaces where people collaborate, problem solve, read, strategize, communicate, participate and act together"* (Jenson and De Castells 2008, 42). The ambition of dissolving the inside/outside dichotomy has led other scholars to use as inspiration Actor-Network-Theory's (ANT) rejection of the inside/outside and of the micro/macro distinctions of social analysis (Latour 1999). For instance, in an ANT study of literacy networks (in school classrooms and an MMO game), it is argued that we should move beyond distinctions based on contexts such as "in school" versus "out of school," and it is suggested that the networks in the school and in virtual worlds resemble one another (Leander and Lovvorn 2006). Virtual Worlds, here, can be seen as obvious—but not isolated—sites to study the transformations of identities in larger networks. Another study used participant observation of how people move around within virtual cities and reflected upon the relation between interaction in a virtual city and physical space (Christiansson et al. 2011). In the following section, I describe other uses of ANT for the study of Virtual Worlds, and I introduce my own methodological approach. My approach is based on two basic principles of ANT, the principle of following the actors and the principle of symmetry.

ACTOR-NETWORK-THEORY AS A METHODOLOGICAL APPROACH TO THE STUDY OF VIRTUAL WORLDS

ANT is a sociological theory with particular methodological implications. The basic assumption is that social phenomena consist of networks of a multitude of human and nonhuman, social and technical elements, and to understand those phenomena, we need to study how networks are assembled. In line with this, the present chapter proposes to think of architectural cyber-hybrids as socio-technical networks, composed of heterogeneous entities (Law 1991) such as technologies, ideals, aesthetics, and economic models. *Sociotechnical networks* is another term for actor networks (Latour 1991, 2005), and I use both terms synonymously here. Both terms imply a research strategy of following the gradual establishment of assemblages of elements into more solid parts of reality. The ideal is to create detailed, empirical accounts based solely on the identification of links or relations between actors, nonhuman and human, and this has created the methodological imperative to follow the actors and to explore how each actor is linked to other actors. ANT's principle of *following the actors* has been applied to studies that trace emerging phenomena in virtual spaces. For instance, it has been followed how the negotiations of professionals inside and outside of virtual settings have led to innovation (Gonçalves and Fiqueiredo 2009). In this chapter, the methodological imperative does not lead me to reflect on actors' relation to one another in depth, but to show how the process of following the actors continuously reshapes the process of researching Virtual Worlds. Elsewhere, I have argued for validity based on the principle of inclusivity (Plesner 2012). A validity of inclusivity is attached to a particular kind of qualitative research in which the attempt to follow the actors and to consider all types of elements for inclusion in the analysis are the primary drivers. Following the actors is a methodological principle meant to ensure that the empirical material is allowed to direct the researcher's attention to other relevant empirical material. Obviously, any decision to include particular elements into an analysis is, ultimately, the work and responsibility of the researcher, so it becomes a challenge to write accounts that lay open how connections between elements are made analytically.

This issue of inclusivity is linked to another challenge—that accounts created based on the previously described principle are inherently messy (Law 2004), because of their preference for complexity over clarity and order. One potential problem with messy accounts of complexity is that in their attempts to let the empirical material speak, they are in danger of not being explicit about analytical steps. To tackle this issue, the following account underscores the connections between research sites and analytical choices, and thus shows the specificities of the work that goes into assembling particular versions of reality.

The process of researching how elements are assembled into networks also implies an agnostic and symmetrical approach (Callon 1986). In the present case, this means an open exploration of the elements that innovation in relation to the professional use of spatial communication in Virtual Worlds might consist of. A central objective is to avoid imposing a priori ideas about the types of elements it is important to look at. In other studies of Virtual Worlds, the symmetry principle has led to the argument that to understand games and virtual environments—and peoples' interaction with them—we need to consider them assemblages of an almost endless number of human and nonhuman actors. For instance, Virtual Worlds games are assembled from events, agents, and practices—for example, the interactions between players, virtual artifacts, reviews in magazines, and HTML codes that make games work (Cypher and Richardson 2006). It has also been shown that the innovation of creative business models in virtual networks can best be understood as socio-technical settings in which both humans (like employees, board members, and clients) and nonhumans (Internet portals and companies) are given equal analytical attention and counted as crucial parts in a network (Costa and Da Cunha 2009). In addition, a study of intelligent agents (a software program that makes avatars act) encourages us to abandon the separation of humans and technologies on the grounds that "non-language-bearing actors" are also carriers of culture, power, and values and have the power to intervene in people's lives. Hence, we must "re-embody the disembodied agents" (Wise 1998). This symmetrical way of thinking can also be seen in attempts to reconsider where thoughts or intelligence are situated, for instance, in arguments about the distribution of intelligence across persons and objects in an emerging virtual culture (Shaffer and Clinton 2006).

The principle of symmetry—that is, the ambition to avoid distinguishing a priori between human and nonhuman actors—has given rise to reflections about agency and to the use of the analytical concept "actant." An actant is an element in a network that makes a difference for other actors in the network:

> *any thing that does modify a state of affairs by making a difference is an actor—or, if it has no figuration yet, an actant. Thus, the questions to ask about any agent are simply the following: Does it make a difference in the course of some other agent's action or not?* (Latour 2005, 71)

The inclusion of other agencies than humans in sociological analyses is not an attempt to take away the agency of humans and grant it to other kinds of forces, but rather is recognition of the fact that humans do not act in a void. Instead, they are linked to all sorts of elements in long chains, and insofar as these elements "make a difference," they have agency. ANT's idea of nonhuman agency has been explored in relation to game studies, and it has been argued that it is productive to pay attention to the agencies of simulation and artificial life software. Many game technologies have become so complex that it makes more sense to conceive of them as actors with values and intentions than as dead technologies (Giddings 2007). In the present chapter, the principle of following the actors leads me to focus on elements such as discursive patterns, physical sites, game engines, and so on. Given the ambition to achieve symmetry, I could have focused on an endless number of elements, but the purpose is obviously not to be *all*-inclusive, but to open up the material through an analytical sensibility toward the interwovenness of humans and nonhumans, and to avoid "the twin pitfalls of sociologism and technologism" (Latour 1991, 110). As Latour argues, we are never faced with either objects or social relations, but with chains of associations of humans (H) and nonhumans (NH): "Of course, an H-H-H assembly looks like social relations while a NH-NH-NH portion looks like a mechanism or a machine, but the point is that they are always integrated into longer chains" (Latour 1991, 110). Precisely this point helps us to dissolve the outside/inside and macro/micro dichotomies that we might otherwise be tempted to draw on in the study of Virtual Worlds.

To recap, the point of a methodology inspired by ANT is to create accounts that describe emerging cyber-hybrids in a way that captures the open-endedness of technology. This allows us to see elements of Virtual Worlds as bound up with a range of other heterogeneous elements, such as political statements, technical standards, aesthetic sensibilities, organizational practices, professional training, hardware, software, robots, clients, planning tools, and materials (Plesner and Horst 2012a). Technologies, as Bijker and Law (1992, 7) put it, "are not purely technological" but rather heterogeneous and contingent.

The ambition to follow the actors and adhere to the principle of symmetry had consequences for how my study of innovation in and around Virtual Worlds was constructed and evolved, as illustrated in the following analysis. The analysis shows that, as a consequence of this ambition, the object of study changed continually throughout the research process.

EMPIRICAL STUDY AND METHODS

My studies were part of a larger, strategic research project that stipulated the focus on innovation and market creation in relation to Virtual Worlds. A lot of inspiration and data have come from seminars, workshops, and conferences held under the auspices of the project.[1] My interest in professional communication led me to focus first on innovation in Virtual Worlds for use in architectural communication, then on innovation in Virtual Worlds for use in professional communication more broadly.

The research process began with a broad survey of the field that pointed to sites of innovation and sites where innovations in Virtual Worlds were showcased and discussed. In the analysis, I describe in some detail how this led to the production of new types of empirical material that ended up consisting of (1) interviews with architects or other building industry professionals using Virtual Worlds for communication (about 10 one-hour interviews), (2) interviews with innovators in other industries using Virtual Worlds for professional communication (about 10 one-hour interviews), (3) ethnographic studies of innovation in a company developing Virtual Worlds for architectural communication (about 120 hours of observations, together with interviews and recordings of meetings), and (4) textual material such as dialogues on blogs and email exchanges, images, strategy documents, webpages, and other company documents. As the analysis demonstrates, the production of this empirical material was a result of the method of following the actors (Latour 1987) which implies that actors in the field were allowed to direct my attention towards sites to study. The basic assumption behind this method is to focus on the way in which actors themselves *assemble the world* (Latour 2005), rather than assembling it for them, analytically.

The ethnographic studies were conducted in Denmark; one-third of the interviews in the United States, one-third in Denmark, and one-third in other European countries. But, importantly, a large part of the textual material was also found on the Internet which emphasizes that innovation in and around Virtual Worlds happens in a space that crosses national (and other) borders. To understand circulating, nonsettled, and nonstandardized technological innovation, it seemed that there was no single obvious site to investigate. This was the rationale for a multimodal research design and a multi-sited production of empirical material.

Elsewhere, the empirical material has been analyzed with a focus on, for instance, particular discursive patterns, particular actants, competing configurations of technological solutions, and collaborative knowledge production (Plesner 2012; Plesner and Horst 2012a, 2012b). The following text is not a detailed analysis of one such specific empirical phenomenon but operates on a meso-level of analytical reflection, highlighting choices in the research process and discussing how these choices relate to the data. It illustrates that methodology is about taking decisions in an undecidable terrain, in this case, especially, when it comes to choosing the actors to follow.

ANALYSIS: INNOVATION IN AND AROUND VIRTUAL WORLDS

The following analysis describes my moves from research site to research site, giving accounts of each site and making it explicit why those moves were made. It pays special attention to the analytical takes that became central to the construction of the story of innovation in and around Virtual Worlds and to the processes of constructing objects of analysis.

Tracing Visions . . .

Research site 1: The research project reported here began in the office. It began with an interest in professional communication and the assumption that Virtual Worlds would be obvious sites to develop for professional communication among people dealing with space and the built environment, for instance, architects. Knowing very little about this aspect of Virtual Worlds which are generally better known for their entertainment or social functions, I began to search the academic literature and the internet, and soon came across the mentioning of experiments with architecture in Second Life. Searches on "virtual worlds" and "architecture" (and related terms) pointed

Virtual Worlds as Emerging Cyber-Hybrids   23

in the direction of a phenomenon called "wikitecture," and a community of Second Life residents who sometimes meet online to discuss or experiment with architecture. Wikitecture has been called "a visual analog to how people might write and edit an entry on the popular reference Web site Wikipedia"[2] and is a showcase of how Second Life might be used in real life building projects. In the Second Life community, residents have varying interest in real-life construction, but some do navigate the crossover between Virtual Worlds Architecture and physical building projects. The online live debate show in Second Life, Metanomics,[3] hosted two proponents of wikitecture about their use of Second Life for purposes of communicating about architecture, and I conducted interviews with these two proponents. They helped establish links to what they saw as relevant corporations and institutions, as well as interview appointments with other people engaged in projects in which they experimented with architecture in Second Life. As a result, I conducted interviews with ten individuals involved in such projects and did documentary research on blogs and webpages. Material about the projects could be found both in virtual spaces filled with virtual building blocks, and in communication around them, on blogs, discussion forums, and so on. Because how much actual activity there is in such virtual spaces varies a lot, I found the most action in discussions about the projects. And, according to ANT, a methodological principle is to look at where the action is (Latour 2005) or identify traces of what actors do. I did this in actors' accounts of their projects.

In analyzing accounts, discursive patterns become more obvious analytical entities than, for instance, technical elements, and actors' accounts were full of reflections on the problem of selling the idea of using existing technologies for new purposes. In blogs, on webpages, and in interviews, the most pertinent pattern seemed to be articulations of visions relating to the use of Second Life, as well as entrepreneurs' accounts of resistance from real life users. These patterns became an object of analysis, and based on the analysis, I would argue that the articulation of visions is an important actant in the establishment of Virtual Worlds Architecture as a socio-technical network. The term *actant* may be used to describe symbolic resources that are collectively established over time (Horst 2008), if they make a difference for a network. From my analysis of interviews and documents, I could see that many types of activities and choices were related to this actant. I chose to investigate the articulation of visions more, and could see that proponents of Virtual Worlds Architecture created visions which could roughly be grouped into three sets of arguments: (1) Virtual Worlds Architecture is a cutting-edge way of addressing the needs and wants of a technology-savvy audience which is supposedly already "out there," expecting state of the state-of-the-art information and communication technology; (2) Virtual Worlds Architecture allows for creative individuals to contribute to collaborative learning; and (3) Virtual Worlds Architecture is a catalyst for democratizing architecture (Plesner and Horst 2010b).

The analytical take, at this point in the research process, was to construct an object—through naming a fluid, hard-to-grasp phenomenon Virtual Worlds Architecture—and to identify patterns in available discursive material that indicated constitutive elements of this phenomenon. At this point, then, the research was following discursive traces of actors' attempts to bridge the inside and the outside of Virtual Worlds by constructing arguments though discussions outside of Second Life, on blogs, webpages, and other sites, which link to demonstrations and visualizations inside Second Life. In specific experimental projects, building blocks within Second Life were no longer just that, but became expressions of ideas and a mirroring of actual buildings.

The research could have continued exploring how this transgression of boundaries between Virtual Worlds building blocks and realized buildings took place in practice and evolved over time, but, as described earlier, the analysis had pointed to a great deal of resistance to the arguments for using Second Life, and I constructed resistance as an object to be followed. Again, this choice was prompted by the many linkages made by actors between vision and resistance. Accounts of the former rarely came without accounts of the latter. In the empirical material described earlier, I found that discursive resistance could be organized in three sets of arguments, countering the previously described three arguments for engaging in Virtual Worlds Architecture. According to my interviewees, when they tried to introduce Virtual Worlds Architecture to new kinds of audiences, they would meet resistance from actors in the following ways: the cutting-edge argument met resistance from accounts of technical difficulties and of emerging, more sophisticated, communication platforms; the argument about user involvement ran into accounts of users who would not spend time and energy on learning new communication tools; the argument about democratic communication came with accounts of disappointed voices lamenting the low impact of Virtual Worlds Architecture experiments. Reflecting more on these discursive resistances and exploring which elements they might be connected to led me to a new research site.

Tracing Resistance: Technical Standards . . .

Research site 2: To better understand what resistance might be linked to, I turned to a group of actors we may think of as nonadopters of Virtual Worlds Architecture: architects working with a range of information and communication technologies that are more established in the profession. Of course, it is slightly inaccurate to call these architects nonadopters, because there is no settled technology to adopt and because they have not been approached by proponents of Virtual Worlds Architecture. In fact, you could argue that this is precisely the problem: that Virtual Worlds Architecture does not exist, except from in some rare instances where it is assembled in visions, accounts, or demonstrations. However, the phenomenon I had conceived of as Virtual

Worlds Architecture seemed to consist of a range of technical, communicative, and social elements that were widely acknowledged as important for architects to take into consideration, also outside a community such as the one in Second Life. At least some architects shared the vision of developing more advanced 3D spaces for communicating about architecture, believed that this was an inevitable technological development, and saw how the young generation of architects was much more likely to skip pencil drawings and work with idea generation in 3D spaces, being familiar with computer game environments. My interviews were meant to provide an understanding of why these observations were not linked to an interest in Virtual Worlds.

Throughout the interviews, I saw that when the topic was "architectural communication and ICT," discussions would tend to glide between two domains that I constructed as "immersion" and "information." Whereas the **immersion** component of 3D Virtual Worlds environments was seen as a means to achieve better spatial understanding (especially for nonarchitects), **information** was constructed as a much more important component of architectural communication in this research site. The focus on this dichotomy was established in relation to the concept of Building Information Modeling (BIM) that kept resurfacing in both interviews and documents, thus showing tight connections to architectural communication. I decided to follow this actor and investigate it more.

The first architect I spoke to kept talking about Building Information Modeling as the central element in architectural communication. Given that he had specialized in helping architectural companies adopt BIM, this was not surprising. In fact, he could be seen as a representative of the information camp, arguing for more precision in technical information and hence less economic loss in the building sector. When I began to follow what seemed to be a more successful method to handle information and communication in the building industry, it appeared that BIM was an almost equally contested entity as Virtual Worlds platforms although it drew some strength from its connection to a variety of other elements. BIMs can be defined as digital models intended to integrate a lot of different information about a given construction project—for example, geometrical, visual, functional, production-related, and product-related properties. From the different people I interviewed, and from the academic literature dealing with BIM, it turned out that BIM had been hard to implement in the building industry. Actually, some of the resistance to BIM looked relatively similar to the resistance I had identified in relation to the use of Virtual Worlds in architecture. However, BIM had been successfully linked to global open-source standards and political visions for cost reduction and had resulted in the rethinking of organizational structures. It was linked to a new kind of format—the IFC format—created by the global open-source forum Building Smart Alliance. IFC is "an open, neutral format which you can export to. From there, you can export into the various proprietary formats." [4] BIM had been advocated by politicians. For instance, in 2001, the Danish government proposed its adoption throughout the industry and took the lead by demanding that large public construction projects be handed in digitally. Because of that political demand, some organizations had to rethink their way of working, employing "BIM consultants" and planning work differently. As one BIM consultant put it,

> *[o]ur experience shows amongst others that with BIM, as much as 70 percent of decisions have to be made earlier than is the case with traditional projecting. This changes the traditional workflow and division of labor and challenges the entire way of thinking in phases in relation to construction.[5]*

In this phase of the research project, I came to consider BIMs as actants that challenged the identity of Virtual Worlds Architecture and that were important entities in the network of resistance toward Virtual Worlds as a platform for professional communication. Because BIM was relatively better linked to political imperatives and successful standards, their existence implied that Virtual Worlds could only be seen as lacking in precision and information detail. My analytical take at this stage was to construct a political and economic outside to Virtual Worlds, but this did not imply that BIM was constructed as a macro-actor in the analysis or as a device representing macro actors: Instead, BIM was considered an actant composed of particular technical elements that were relevant for the future of the inside of Virtual Worlds. This resonated with a study that looked at BIM as an element in a larger network also consisting of architects, contractors, clients, consultants and regulating bodies (Linderoth 2010). The development of Virtual Worlds Architecture was seen by many as crucially dependent on the possibility of "mashups" (i.e., importing real-life data from sources outside the virtual world). To understand how the phenomenon of Virtual Worlds Architecture and BIM were, at one and the same time, connected and disconnected, I found it useful to categorize them as belonging to two different trends—what I called an information trend and an immersion trend. Both could be seen as drivers of innovation in ICTs in relation to the building sector, but both could also be traced to very different roots in, respectively, the field of construction/engineering and the entertainment industry.

Tracing Industry Developments: Gaming, Avatars and Economic Models

Research site 3: To open up the categories of information and immersion that I had constructed, I decided to move to an industry level to look at the developments in ICT more broadly and to be able to reflect on the development and the possible convergence of these two strands. This was partly inspired by an encounter with a technologist who argued insistently that BIM, Second Life, and game engines such as Unity were only tiny, separate steps toward a comprehensive platform that would be the solution to all the building industry's information and communication problems. I began to look into the technological solutions offered by the company he worked for, and saw how the company integrated technologies addressing information problems with technologies offering immersive experiences. My emerging interest in integrated communication platforms and convergence was further spurred by contacts from a semester-long research stay at Stanford University in Silicon Valley, the infamous site of development in new ICTs. I found that although some development takes place online in open forums where people collaborate on shared software code, geographic location was also an important factor in the development of integrated communication platforms. The west coast of the United States seemed to be a particularly productive environment for this work, mostly due to the amount of investment capital flowing there. To explore this, I conducted interviews with a range of entrepreneurs in the area of Virtual Worlds based in Silicon Valley.

This new research site led to a reformulation of the research questions of the project and a rethinking of the object of study. The research question now revolved around processes of convergence, and I asked about the linkages being made between various companies and academic sites and their consequences for "state of the art ICT" that might be used to communicate about space. The object was now less Virtual Worlds Architecture than it was integrated communication platforms and the different elements they were made from. One such element was a game engine, developed by the company Unity. This game engine has found numerous applications. Whereas Unity was once a small Danish company selling technology for computer game development, it is now operating out of Silicon Valley and is also being used to create virtual environments in the medical industry, in industrial production, and in the building industry. Because of the many connections created between the gaming industry and entrepreneurs in various industries, I focused on elements of the gaming industry as actants influencing professional communication. In my ethnographic research, I looked at innovation processes in a small company using the Unity game engine and focused on the relationship between game elements and professional communication. Experience from the gaming industry had led the company owner, a young Danish architect, to develop a platform for architectural communication based on the Unity engine. He had experienced how his architectural drawings (plans and sections) made much less sense to other professionals than did the 3D spaces he could quickly set up based on the game engine.[6] The game industry is not only outside specific Virtual Worlds platforms communicating about architecture; its elements and aesthetics are, of course, very much inside. For instance, avatars are obvious entities to integrate in architectural communication because they can be used to create a sense of proportion, at least if they are created true to scale. In that sense, they are not just linked to participatory ideals, allowing different actors to enter a virtual reality and become active participants in the shaping of given projects. As a particular type of game object, avatars acquire an importance that reaches way beyond their representing a user—they are a promise of how physical beings will relate to a built environment and thus point outside of the virtual world they operate in. However, the avatar is also an actant that influences the identity of the communication platform as a whole, creating expectations among investors in relation to both functionality and value. When developers talk about introducing an avatar in a gamelike environment aimed at communicating about buildings or cityscapes, they find that the visualizations have to "not look like a game" because they are to speak to real-world decisions. On the other hand, games have shaped expectations, and clients are not satisfied with not being able to navigate freely, as the comment of a dissatisfied user demonstrates: "If I say turn left you can't turn left?"[7] The game aesthetics and functionalities are not only becoming part of the inside of such platforms but also reaching beyond their borders, with repercussions for the funding of their development and the business models of companies trying to sell a Virtual Worlds–based ICT solution. Customers have to be brought to understand the value it can add to the construction process, and the resemblance with game technologies makes this difficult. This is a developer's account of such negotiations:

"He said, 'Well yes, I can see the value of it, but that looks like one of my kids' games, so I probably pay you what I pay for one of my kids' games.' And I was like '50 dollars?' And he said 'Yes, that's about right.' And I said, 'You know those games take about 3 million to make?' 'That's not what I pay in the store, so that's what I'll pay for that.' OK, interesting, so then we saw that . . . of course none of the big developers wants to do that, this is something we found in the building industry, they aren't going to pay someone to develop an application for them specifically."[8]

So gamelike aesthetics becomes an actant influencing the creation of viable business models, a new object of analysis that I chose to follow but which I do not discuss in the present chapter.

The analytical take in this phase of the project was to construct an outside to Virtual Worlds platforms, but then to immediately dissolve this outside by highlighting some of the specific elements it consists of, and thus trace how elements of this outside (the game industry) traverse the boundaries of Virtual Worlds platforms with elements like avatars or gaming aesthetics. In a sense, the outcomes of my analyses at this point closed the circle of my research path, now with a broader understanding of the simultaneous development of Virtual Worlds for use in different kinds of professional communication, developments that condition the future of the kinds of Virtual Worlds usage I set out to study.

TO SUM UP

The aim of the preceding analysis has been to capture the development of a research process as I moved from site to site and adjusted research questions in the light of an evolving understanding of a fluid object of study.

The examples of empirical findings in each site were meant as illustrations of how different kinds of elements were included in the study and were allowed to make an impact on its direction. Of course, changes in research sites and research questions are not just consequences of a new and better understanding of the object of study but also actively change the object of study. Naming and categorizing are crucial parts of understanding a fluid phenomenon and, when carried out as described above, they underscore fluidity—that the empirical object of study is hard to define in all its newness, and thus requires renaming. In the preceding examples, the coining of the term *Virtual Worlds Architecture* indicates that there is such an object to study, just as the choice to abandon this term and write about two distinct trends, information, and immersion, indicates that the uses of Virtual Worlds in architectural communication can only be understood in relation to an industry's demand for accurate information. Again, the choice of leaving this dichotomous understanding and recasting the issue as one of convergence (of ideals, technologies, and formerly separate industries) turns Virtual Worlds Architecture into a phenomenon heavily dependent on other technologies and impossible to study as separate from them.

Obviously, the renaming is an expression of a gradually refined understanding of the object of study, and thus, the preceding description may resemble an account of a pilot study. But even if the production of the empirical material discussed here has resemblances with a pilot study, I prefer to conceive of it as an ongoing multimodal, multi-sited research process directed by the strategy of following the actors. The idea of the pilot study implies that a better understanding can be acquired and that this can create a more solid foundation for doing a "real," focused study. By contrast, the previously described research process is likely to proceed in just as unpredictable ways as described here, but maybe with a gradual change in analytical vocabulary.

The analytical vocabulary used here has pointed tentatively to some elements (or actants) in attempts to create socio-technical networks. I have found it helpful to use the concepts of elements and actants to indicate that the elements I am describing are potentially or temporarily part of larger socio-technical networks, but I have not made repeated references to such networks—essentially because the interest here has not been to describe established, solid realities, that is, existing socio-technical networks.

The preceding analysis is not packed with analytical or theoretical concepts. Symmetry is a *principle* lying behind the inclusion of elements such as avatars, hardware, ideals, and a multitude of other elements alongside one another as actants in the analysis. To follow the actors is a *research strategy* that lies behind the jump from research site to research site and the linkage of elements to one another. I have talked about research sites in order to indicate that the production of knowledge is linked to locality and to explicitly account for how and where I followed the actors.

CONCLUSION

The first part of the analysis identified Virtual Worlds Architecture as an object of study, identified actors in and around Second Life who experimented with "wikitecture," and highlighted elements such as visions as central to the work of these actors. The focus on visions raised my interest in the resistance these visions met when actors attempted to connect Second Life architecture projects with real life clients, that is, when actors tried to create building projects with both a Virtual Worlds dimension and a physical realization. The second part of the analysis moved on to investigate resistance in more detail, and found that it could be linked to technical standards, political demands, and a powerful status of accurate information (which again is linked to cost reduction throughout an industry). BIM stood out as a particularly powerful actant that had negative impact on the identity of Virtual Worlds Architecture. This led to an analytical focus on two identifiable concerns in relation to architectural communication and new ICTs—a concern with technologies promising accurate information and a concern with technologies allowing for immersion. It was not only the information trend that had political support: in what are still relatively few cases, politicians have also demanded new kinds of immersive 3D digital communication from architects, for instance, in relation to competitions that involve the changing of cityscapes in a way that is of high public interest (Sunesson et al. 2008) or in order to enroll citizens or nonexperts in city planning (Hudson-Smith 2003). This is just one indication of how the information and immersion distinction may not be tenable, at least not in the future. The last part of the analysis investigated how construction and/or engineering technologies and gaming technologies are brought to interact. Elements such as Computer Aided Design, Computer Aided Manufacturing, and immersive 3D technologies need not be separate elements but are currently hard to package together, among other things, because of the aesthetics and functionalities linked to the game industry. Here, avatars stood out as entities with a lot of promise in relation to representing users and assessing scale, but also as problematic because of the connotations they carry.

As the study has progressed through these phases, the object of study, in my mind, can no longer be the use of Virtual Worlds in architectural communication. Instead, future research has to integrate how software code is written collectively, how entrepreneurs raise money through demonstrations, how the Internet is evolving from being text-based to allowing for 3D content to be transmitted in the same way as text has been until now, how people and knowledge travel via career moves and open online forums, and how the noncommercial work of universities and research and development labs advance the uses of Virtual Worlds, among others. These are the elements of convergence, and as Virtual Worlds technologies become increasingly convergent with other ICTs, this raises entirely new questions about the relationship between architecture and ICT, where Virtual Worlds will neither be a promise, an add on, or an innovation to resist, but will be a part of a toolbox of ICTs.

To produce empirical material, to analyze it, and to arrive at these conclusions, I have drawn on socio-technical approaches (Callon 1986; Latour 2005; Law 2004) to social inquiry in general and innovation processes in particular. The analysis has thus added to the emerging literature on Virtual Worlds inspired by Actor-Network-Theory (Cypher and Richardson 2006; Gonçalves and Figueiredo 2009; Lepa and Tatnall 2006; Wise 1998), with a particular focus on understanding attempts to innovate in relation to the uses of Virtual Worlds for professional communication. I see this emerging literature as one type of reply to the Virtual World literature's call for a dissolution of the in-world/out-world distinctions (Lehdonvirta 2010; Taylor 2006) that has marked Virtual Worlds research.

Methodological Strategies

This approach to the study of Virtual Worlds has demonstrated how a strategy of following the actors and thinking symmetrically about the elements of analysis can render the researcher sensitive to complex, emerging phenomena, and has offered strategies to dissolve the divide between an inside and an outside of these worlds. It has dealt with innovation in and around Virtual Worlds, relating to the communication of architecture, but its methodological approach can be applied in any study of Virtual Worlds aiming to emphasize the heterogeneous elements they are made up from, or their cyber-hybridity. The main principles of the methodology are to

1. Follow the actors as they crisscross the domains of the technical, political, aesthetic, and so on.
2. Think symmetrically about which types of elements to include in the analysis.
3. Create process accounts by accounting for how elements are linked by actors and the researcher, respectively.

As indicated earlier, the methodological advantage of such an approach is its empiricist, symmetrical orientation to the empirical material, whereas the weakness is its inability to produce authoritative, general accounts of what larger phenomena, such as Virtual Worlds, are. So rather than coming closer to defining what virtual worlds are, and, accordingly, how we may study them, the outcome of an ANT-inspired analysis is an understanding of linkages among elements of their use, elements of their technical platforms, and elements of the situations they exist in. If any larger picture is created, it will be of dispersed elements pointing to a vast hinterland (Law 2004) of our object of study.

ACKNOWLEDGEMENT

The study presented in this chapter was carried out as part of the collective research project, "Sense-Making Strategies and User-Driven Innovation in Virtual Worlds: New Market Dynamics, Social and Cultural Innovation, and Knowledge Construction" (2008–12), Roskilde University and Copenhagen Business School. I would like to thank the Danish Strategic Research Council (KINO committee) for funding the project (grant no. 09–063261).

REFERENCES

Bainbridge, William Sims. 2007. The scientific research potential of virtual worlds. *Science* 317 (5837): 472–76.

Bijker, Wiebe E., and John Law, eds. 1992. *Shaping technology/building society—studies in sociotechnical change.* eds. Wiebe E. Bijker, W. Bernard Carlson, and Trevor Pinch, Cambridge, MA: MIT Press.

Callon, Michel. 1986. Some elements of a sociology of translation: Domestication of the scallops and the fishermen of St Brieuc Bay. In *Power, action and belief—A new sociology of knowledge?* ed. John Law, 196–223. London: Routledge and Kegan.

Chase, Scott, Ryan Schultz, and Jon Brouchoud. 2008. Gather 'round the wiki-tree: Virtual worlds as an open platform for architectural collaboration. Paper presented at ARCHITECTURE 'in computro': Integrating methods and techniques, Proceedings of the 26th Conference on Education in Computer Aided Architectural Design in Europe, Antwerp.

Christiansson, Per, Kjeld Svidt, Kristian B. Pedersen, and Ulrik Dybro. 2011. User participation in the building process. *Electronic Journal of Information Technology in Construction* 16:309–34.

Costa, Christina Chuva, and Paulo Rupino Da Cunha. 2009. Business model design from an ANT perspective: Contributions and insights of an open and living theory. Paper presented at AMCIS 2009 Proceedings, San Francisco, CA.

Cypher, Mark, and Ingrid Richardson. 2006. An actor-network approach to games and virtual environments. Paper presented at proceedings of the 2006 international conference on game research and development, Murdoch University, Western Australia.

Czarniawska, Barbara, and Tor Hernes. 2005. Constructing macro actors according to ANT. In *Actor-network theory and organizing*, eds. Barbara Czarniawska and Tor Hernes, 7–13. Malmö: Liber; and Copenhagen Business School Press.

Fruchter, Renate. 1999. "A/E/C teamwork: A collaborative design and learning space." *Journal of Computing in Civil Engineering* 13 (4): 261–70.

Giddings, Seth. 2007. "Playing with non-humans: Digital games as techno-cultural form." In *Worlds in play: International perspectives on digital games research,* ed. Suzanne De Castells and Jennifer Jenson, 115–29. New York: Peter Lang.

Gonçalves, Fernando A., and Jose Figueiredo. 2009. Organising competences: Actor-network theory in virtual settings. *International Journal of Networking and Virtual Organisations* 6 (1): 22–35.

Horst, Maja. 2008. The laboratory of public debate: Understanding the acceptability of stem cell research. *Science and Public Policy* 35 (3): 197–205.

Hudson-Smith, Andrew. 2003. *Digitally distributed urban environments: The prospects for online planning.* London: University of London.

Jenson, Jennifer, and Suzanne De Castell. 2008. "Get up and play!" from simulation to imitation in digital games. *Education Canada* 48 (2): 40–44.

Latour, Bruno. 1987. *Science in action—how to follow scientists and engineers through society.* Cambridge, MA: Harvard University Press.

Latour, Bruno. 1991. Technology is society made durable. In *A sociology of monsters. Essays on power, technology and domination.*, ed. John Law, 103–31. London: Routledge.

Latour, Bruno. 1999. Give me a laboratory and I will raise the world. In *The science studies reader,* ed. Mario Biagioli, 258–75. New York: Routledge.

Latour, Bruno. 2005. *Reassembling the social—an introduction to actor-network-theory.* Clarendon lectures in management studies. Oxford, UK: Oxford University Press.

Law, John, ed. 1991. Introduction: Monsters, machines and sociotechnical relations. In *A sociology of monsters: Essays on power, technology and domination,* vol. 38, 1–23. London: Routledge.

Law, John. 1999. After ANT: Complexity, naming and typology. In *Actor network theory and after,* ed. John Law and John Hassard, 1–14. Oxford, UK: Blackwell Publishers.

Law, John. 2004. *After method—mess in social science research.* London: Routledge.

Leander, Kevin M., and Jason F. Lovvorn. 2006. Literacy networks: Following the circulation of texts, bodies, and objects in the schooling and online gaming of one youth. *Cognition & Instruction* 24 (3) (): 291–340.

Lehdonvirta, Vili. 2010. Virtual worlds don't exist: Questioning the dichotomous approach in MMO studies. *Game Studies* 10 (1). Accessed April 6, 2013. http://gamestudies.org/1001/articles/lehdonvirta.

Lepa, Jerzy, and Arthur Tatnall. 2006. Using actor-network theory to understanding virtual community networks of older people using the Internet. *Journal of Business Systems Governance and Ethics* 1 (4): 1–14.

Linderoth, Henrik C. J. 2010. Understanding adoption and use of BIM as the creation of actor networks. *Automation in Construction* 19 (1): 66–72.

Plesner, Ursula. 2012. "Building networks with vague intentions: A vocabulary of enrolment and negotiations in collaborative research practice." In *Knowledge and power in collaborative research: A reflexive approach,* ed. Louise Phillips, Marianne Kristiansen, Marja Vehviläinen and Ewa Gunnarsson, 236–56. New York: Routledge.

Plesner, Ursula, and Maja Horst. 2012a. Before stabilization: Communication and non-standardization of 3D models in the building industry. *Information, communication and society,* 1–24. Accessed April 6, 2013. http://www.tandfonline.com/doi/abs/10.1080/1369118X.2012.695387.

Plesner, Ursula, and Maja Horst. 2012b. Selling the selling point: How innovation communication creates users of virtual worlds architecture. *Convergence: The International Journal of Research into New Media Technologies* 18 (1): 49–70.

Shaffer, D. W., and K. A. Clinton. 2006. Toolforthoughts: Reexamining thinking in the digital age. *Mind, Culture, and Activity* 13 (4): 283–300.

Sunesson, Kaj, Carl Martin Allwood, Dan Paulin, Ilona Heldal, Mattias Roupé, Mikael Johansson, and Börje Westerdahl. 2008. Virtual reality as a new tool in the city planning process. *Tsinghua Science & Technology* 13 (Suppl. 1): 255–60.

Taylor, T. L. 2006. *Play between worlds: Exploring online game culture.* Cambridge, MA: MIT Press.

Wise, J. Macgregor. 1998. Intelligent agency. *Cultural Studies* 12 (3): 410–28.

3 Presence in Virtual Worlds

Mediating a Distributed, Assembled and Emergent Object of Study

Dixi Louise Strand

This chapter presents the author's entry into a virtual world, Second Life, to conduct a case study on presence in virtual worlds. The object of study is not the IT platform that might provide opportunities for presence, nor the human actors that might experience presence, but what happens when they come together to create an event of presence. The chapter relates how this object of study was approached and produced through a theoretical framework and methodology based on post-actor-network theory (Law 2002; Mol 2003; Latour 2005). Methods such as participant observation, interviews, and reading blogs and web texts are understood as mediations. The chapter traces how these mediations create and gather specific visibilities and how they may lead to interest, surprise, and new insights into virtual worlds as an emergent, distributed phenomenon. The concepts of assemblage (Deleuze and Guattari 1987) and imaginaries (Flichy 2007) are applied to view the notion of presence in virtual worlds in a novel way.

First, an outline of Second Life, the virtual world under study, is presented. Then I discuss how my own initial experiences in and with presence sparked a curiosity that shaped the study. Following this, the chapter outlines the concept of presence in the research literature, focusing on three main approaches: presence and immediacy, presence as sociality, and presence as fantasy. The next section of the chapter discusses the case-study approach and the empirical methods applied in the study. Research results are presented in two sections: (1) how presence *appears* in interviews with virtual world creators and users and (2) how presence *appears* in a virtual world concert event. The analytical concepts of imaginaires and assemblage are applied to highlight how presence as a virtual world phenomenon can be found not as an a priori characteristic of inherent feature of virtual worlds but rather as a set of dreams and expectations and as a very practical accomplishment. This view of presence sheds light on the emergent nature of virtual worlds and complements existing literature that tends to position presence as inherent to the technology, the social life and community, or the imaginations of individuals. In conclusion, the chapter proposes a set of analytical strategies that may improve our understanding of how virtual worlds and their related characteristics continually emerge through a range of differing sites, practices, and concerns.

ABOUT SECOND LIFE, A VIRTUAL WORLD

Second Life was launched by the company Linden Lab in 2003 as an open Internet platform that provides a set of tools and three-dimensional spaces in which users can develop their own avatars, objects, and surroundings. The official Linden Lab site, maps.secondlife.com, provides Cartesian overviews of Second Life as a place built around land, sky, ocean, day and night, and gravity. In order to create an account and enter this world as a user, one must represent oneself as an avatar. Avatars can be designed by users and may take any shape or form and may be encoded with a range of characteristics. Creating one's avatar as well as other objects in Second Life is done through the purchase of features from other users or through the use of a three-dimensional modeling tool that allows a resident to build virtual objects. This can be combined with a Linden Scripting Language to add functionality to objects (Edwards 2006; Boellstorff 2008).

Unlike many other virtual worlds, Second Life is not a game. All activities in Second Life are facilitated and maintained by users, and no concrete rules exist on how people should behave. Users' main objectives can differ and shift. Regular users of Second Life, for example, engage in various social activities: education, design and/or coding, artistic performance, political practice, commercial interests, religion, role-play, and sexual practices. Due to the range of possible activities, Second Life is made up of many heterogeneous micro communities. In-world activity spills out into a range of other media formats, such as an abundance of weblogs connected to specific Second Life communities, topics, and commercial activities. Additionally, movies filmed in Second Life proliferate on YouTube, and more recently, Second Life seem to be gaining the attention of professional cinema production (Frølunde 2013). These various user activities are carried out by "a user" through an avatar in virtual space: the virtual home, a workspace or, for example, a nightclub in Second Life. And simultaneously, these activities unfold in front of (or through) a computer screen in the user's home or workplace.

PRESENCE

The interest in presence grew out of my initial surprise in meeting with the field of virtual worlds. At first glance, virtual worlds might be characterized by distance between human actors linked by technology and Internet protocols. Most often, the people involved as users of virtual worlds are distributed geographically as well as across time zones. They are often working in front of a screen alone at home or at work. People are physically distant from one another. Yet presence, the opposite of distance, seems to reappear as a central theme when speaking to both the users and the creators of virtual worlds and when tracing the concepts used by academics to describe and analyze virtual worlds. Virtual worlds such as Second Life are often described in terms of a place and space in which the individual user has a sense of presence (Schroeder 2006). And this apparent paradox sparked my interest as I initiated research in Second Life. As a beginner, I struggled with the interface and the navigations, and a sense of presence was not the first emotion I would refer to when describing my in-world experience.

To explore this theme of paradox and to subsequently challenge the assumption that presence is inherent to virtual worlds, I outline how the concept of presence has been developed in the research literature to describe the essence of experiences in virtual environments.[1] I have divided the literature into three approaches to presence: presence as immediacy, presence as sociality, and presence as fantasy.

The next section also serves to exemplify how both my own initial interest in presence as phenomenon *and* the research literature led to the choice of presence as a viable starting point of analysis in carrying out research on virtual worlds.

Presence as Immediacy

Much scientific and practitioner-oriented research is concerned with defining and measuring presence as well as optimizing technologies and designs that can create user experiences that are more natural, immediate, direct, and real. Gumbrecht (2004) describes presence as a spatial relationship to the world and its objects—the present is what is tangible to bodies. This is a material, corporeal process, and Gumbrecht (2004) discusses the possibilities for creating presence through new media special effects. Linked to developments in virtual reality, an array of studies also approach presence as a "mental state making users feel, act, and react as they would in a real-world setting" (Whitton 2003, 46), thus making presence the personal, psychological response to sensory immersion due to technological advances in graphical realism, sound, smell, data-gloves, head-mounted display, helmet, motion trackers, and other extended possibilities for interaction (ibid.). Observations of presence as immediacy seek to measure how present a user feels in a virtual environment. Physiological responses (e.g., stress, relation, heart rate, and skin reactions) have, for example, been studied as measurable indicators of presence. This notion relies on a one-way transmission approach and presence becomes an effect of technology where the user is the somewhat passive perceiver or receiver. Solomon describes this as a realism-based conception of presence (Solomon 2002).

Presence as Sociality

Another strand of literature based in anthropology and sociology moves away from evaluating the immersion capabilities of different technological designs and towards the notion of presence as sociality, sociability, or social engagement. Part of the success of virtual worlds is ascribed to this social engagement. The very concept of sociability (Simmel and Hughes 2007) has, for example, been applied to improve our understanding of virtual worlds (Ducheneaut, Moore, and Nickell, 2007). Likewise, Taylor (2009) emphasizes the shared experience, the collaborative nature of most virtual world activities, and the reward of being socialized into a community, acquiring a position and a reputation. In this literature, the avatar has been explored as an important way of seeing oneself, as well as of being seen, thus adding to the personal and social experience of presence (Boellstorff 2008; Pearce and Artemesia 2011). This literature is much less concerned with how the sense of presence may be created though technological refinements that render the user experience as "realistic" as possible; rather, it proposes that the shared experience of being there is mobilized through sociality.

Presence as Fantasy and Imagination

The third strand of literature I highlight has grown out of the science fiction genre and literature studies. Here the imagination of the reader/user, the ability to engage in a personal or shared fantasy, is what transports the user into the sense of being there (Jacobson 2001; Schneider 2004). Seegert (2009, 25), for example, explores how presence is generated in interactive fiction through both verbal signifiers and the user's own actions. In this sense, presence is performed through the user's engagement and actions: "[A] reader (of interactive fiction) can, through imagination, conjure up worlds potentially as vivid and as body-affecting as the visual and aural effects presented through a multimedia entertainment system." This approach again shifts the notion of presence from something produced through graphic realism, sound, and sensory effects to something that can be created and enhanced through the imagination of the individual. The links are close between this body of literature and the literature concerned with sociality because fantasy can be inhabited by a group, as a "consensual hallucination" as coined by Gibson (Gibson 1984; see also Pearce and Artemesia 2011).

The following table summarizes the three approaches to presence in the research literature

Approach to presence	Focus and characteristics	Realm
Immediacy	"I am there, see, feel, sense it"	Technical/material/bodily
Sociality	"Community, sharing, being seen"	Social
Fantasy	"My imagination transports me there"	Individual/personal

In these three approaches, presence is constituted in the technical/material realm (immediacy), the social realm (sociality) or the individual/personal realm (fantasy). To do the literature justice, it is important to note that approaches also cut across these realms in various ways. Niches of research, for example, explore virtual worlds as socio-technical assemblages (Taylor 2009), embodied game play (Bayliss 2007), or presence as "material imagination" (Doyle 2011), where the materiality and the physicality of the act of imagining are emphasized. As a whole, this literature provides a number of possible paths pointing to how presence can be studied, found, and understood.

Existing research takes part, methodologically, in constituting presence as an interesting and viable object of study. The object of study has also been shaped by my own initial experiences in discovery of virtual worlds and by my own fascination with the underlying complex technical infrastructure and the set of highly laborious and distributed practices that maintain it. My earlier research on, and interest in, technical infrastructures and distributed development practices also took part in shaping the subsequent steps of the study. The following section illustrates these steps in my study of presence in which I put together a case study and selected relevant theoretical and methodological tools.

Constructing a Case Study of Presence in Virtual Worlds

The case study approach is in line with Flyvbjerg's (2006) view of knowledge as always historically located and context-dependent. Flyvbjerg (2006, 223) argues for an understanding of good research in terms of a learning process involving concrete experiences, a sustained proximity to the studied reality and feedback from those under study. But what is a case study and how can it serve to establish new knowledge about presence in virtual worlds? Flyvberg asserts that concrete, context-dependent knowledge is more valuable than a search for universals. He suggests that generalization is overvalued as a source of scientific development, whereas "the force of example" is underestimated. Flyvbjerg states that

> *It is correct that summarizing case studies is often difficult, especially as concerns case process. It is less correct as regards case outcomes. The problems in summarizing case studies, however, are due more often to the properties of the reality studied than to the case study as a research method.* (241)

This quotation seems highly relevant to the empirical study of virtual world practices. How can the researcher access a distributed virtual/real phenomenon empirically? How can the researcher summarize a set of complex practices unfolding both online—in a virtual space—and in a set of globally distributed homes and offices in a neat, coherent scientific text?

When investigating the design and the use of emergent and distributed technologies in networked organizations, locating and delineating exactly where the case study begins and where it stops is not a simple matter. The social and technological practices in question are emergent, designed, and used across distributed locations. As such, they pose challenges when it comes to pinpointing exactly what and where the good case or object of research is to be found. Presence in virtual worlds such as Second Life seems to "happen" as simultaneous occurrences in a broad range of sites for design and use that may be more or less connected.

Such challenges have been approached as issues that require the development of new and better research tools such as log file analysis (Williams 2005). Challenges of distribution are viewed from this perspective as technical difficulties that may be tackled by refining the methods and techniques of data production. Other options involve using video cameras in-world and out-world (Jensen, this book), perhaps combined with screen-tracking and screen-capture technologies that allow the researcher to record mouse movements on many screens at once (Murray et al. 2009). However, in such strategies, it seems that one kind of complexity is substituted for another. With one problem "solved," a new one arises, such as how to sort and visualize the mounds of unmanageable data produced by way of such methods. Drawing on science and technology studies (STS), this chapter suggests that all methods can be understood as creating translations—that is, particular (and perhaps technologically mediated) ways of seeing and analyzing the subject matter. Particular methods mediate the object of study, rendering it visible for science in particular ways (Latour 2005).

The theoretical and methodological approach of the study presented in this chapter builds on post-actor-network-theory (ANT) and its methodological strategy that takes relationships and networks as its focus of inquiry (Law 2002; Mol 2003; Latour 2005). Post-ANT belongs to a wide body of STS research that is theoretically concerned with shifting social science away from dealing only with social structures, communicative layers, symbols, and meaning and with moving sociological theorizing into the physical realm of material objects, nature, and bodies. These concerns entail new ways of thinking about relations of the social and the material as mutually constituted and as not belonging to different ontological domains.

Rather than providing a total overview or mapping of general patterns, a juxtaposition of sites and situations dives into selected moments and explores in detail the specific arrangements and situations in which presence appears and unfolds. Such a strategy can bring out differences, connections, and disconnections between the practices and thereby produces data material for thinking about presence in novel ways. Using Flyvbjerg's (2006) term, the "force of example" is the source of scientific development and insight. In my case study, I have used the mundane methods of interviewing, participant observation, and document analysis.

POP ART LAB

The next section presents the case in question, a Second Life media center, Pop Art Lab (PAL). The media center opened in September 2008, with the mission of "exploring how to present and promote new music in 3D environments," according to the PAL website (www.popartlab.com). Since then PAL has developed into a virtual "lab" comprising the following: four listening booths for previewing newly released music recordings while socializing with other listeners, a central dance floor hosting parties and events, a lower clubbing level, and a stage set where musicians are interviewed and conduct live-music performances. PAL was founded by a devoted Second Lifer, Claus Uriza, and was developed by his team of about ten people. The notion of presence immediately appeared to me as researcher as pivotal to PAL as its visitors share listening spaces and concert experiences with other visitors in real time. The concept and design are built around the idea that people are present there and hear music while they see, share, and experience it with others. This single case was thus selected based on an expectation that it was an exemplary site where presence might "appear" and thus be accessible for the researcher to analyze and relate to existing literature.

The empirical study was conducted from October 2009 to June 2010. Methods included participant observation ("hanging out" and event participation), real-life observations, semistructured interviews conducted offline and online, and analysis of related weblogs. Interviews were carried out by the author and by fellow researcher Ates Gürsimsek.

Analysis was conducted continually throughout the research process. The data material was coded openly (Emerson, Fretz, and Shaw 1995). This coding consisted of writing themes, notes, and memos of interest in the margin of interviews (on paper and in Word) as well as keeping notes in separate documents. The coding drew on both theoretical concepts and concepts from the field, continually shifting between the empirical material, literature, and discussions with fellow researchers. During coding, the concepts of desire, imaginaire, practicalities, and assemblage, for example, emerged as themes. Based on the open coding, themes and storylines were developed around material when the concept of presence appeared or emerged. The method of analysis has thus been an oscillation between condensing the data material through writing summaries, listing themes, and finding "story lines," on one hand, and expanding the material through an interpretive analysis of selected excerpts in relation to one or more particular themes of interest, on the other hand (Emerson, Fretz, and Shaw 1995). Drafts of the ongoing analysis have, along the way, been shared with the main informants from PAL and with fellow researchers in the research project in order to discuss and further develop analytical themes and ideas.

Again, these various practical steps are understood as mediating steps that bring presence into view for scientific inquiry. The methods for both data production and analysis create particular appearances of presence. Presenting the material as appearances of presence is thus proposed as an "analytical trick" that foregrounds empirically the very practices, events, and situations in which the object of inquiry is handled, made, and remade.

In the following, examples from the case study are presented in two sections. In the first section, selected interview and conversation excerpts illustrate the ways in which notions of presence circulate and how they are taken up and used among some of the actors involved in PAL. The second section applies a different level of analysis, that of the situation. The focus here is on a concert event and on how presence in this situation is a collective socio-material achievement. The two sections thus exemplify two slightly different methodological approaches and the results they can produce.

INTERVIEW APPEARANCES OF PRESENCE IN PAL

In a semistructured interview with Claus, the founder of PAL, he describes the early days and his first visions for PAL. The founder's work outside Second Life consists of cataloging and creating metadata on new music releases for a Danish national cross-library institution. His employers supported the establishment of PAL by allowing access to the music and by providing economic support for the initial purchase of the Second Life space in which the music environment was to be built. The initial design was conducted collaboratively by a team of friends and volunteers, and PAL opened in September 2008. In an interview, he explains:

> *The PAL concept was to take the best albums, CDs released, to try to find a way to present all this music in a 3D, virtual environment, instead of just normal text material, so people can experience it differently . . . We subdivided the land into four rooms you can enter, each playing a different CD and genre. The rooms have couches and sitting animations where people can hang out and chat with each other.*

The founder emphasizes the aim of creating a different experience than that of, for example, Internet radio and music websites, music accompanied by text, or still images. This new music experience is organized in virtual space through the design of four virtual rooms the visitor can enter and move between with their avatar. Furthermore, people can hang out together, sit, or dance with the various animations built into the rooms while communicating through the Second Life chat facility or using "voice" (real-time conversations using a headset speaker and microphone). As presented by Claus, it seems that the very vision and design were organized around notions of presence similar to those I had found in the literature. For Claus, the compelling aspect of presenting music in a three-dimensional space is the capability to listen while being there, immersed in a space shared with others. The founder's vision thus mobilizes both the immediacy and the sociality approach to presence. It seems the same ideas about presence found in the research literature also circulate among those living and acting in Second Life. Ideas about presence seem to be applied as a resource for retrospectively explaining and making sense of the Second Life project the user Claus has been involved in.

During the spring of 2010 the PAL virtual location was redesigned entirely to create a new look, new spaces, and new possibilities for the music lab. The head designer, Emily, explains this work and the idea behind the design:

> *We are three designers and Claus—and the overall idea behind this design is that people could come here, bring friends, listen to music while chatting, that they could come again and again for new music. You need to have seats because a vast majority of people like to sit, you need to give them many opportunities to dance, sit, stand, walk, fly, teleport, they can watch the sea, visit the place, discover the artwork, find new places within the sim, go to the club, etc.*

The designer explains that people like to sit or do something while hanging out at PAL and that this has shaped the design of the space and animations. She finds it important to give people opportunities to do something while in PAL. In this space, the music listeners and the concert audience must also be able to perform themselves in relation to each other, to stage themselves through their avatars and the things their avatars are able to do, and to be recognized as doing so at the show. This resonates with the sociality approach to presence. In PAL, people can explore and share experiences of beautiful ocean scenes, virtual artworks, listening to music, and dancing together. This draws on the sociality approach to presence, and interestingly, this notion of presence actually *guides* the designers' coordinated choices and actions in redesigning and refining the lab in 2010.

The last excerpt is a blog post from a visitor and blogger of virtual worlds, Cyberloom. This visitor sees PAL as a glimpse of the future in which one is immersed in sound and listening that transforms into something with which one can interact through, for example, movement in space:

> *Pop Art Lab can be described as an immersive, 3D radio station. You can see which dome plays what, go in and find out the name of the artist and the title of the track. PAL provides a glimpse of the future for listening to music on the Internet; we will immerse ourselves in the sound and listening will potentially become a more interactive visually immersive experience. Our avatars will walk around inside internet radios, changing the music streams by where they choose to walk just as we can in PAL.*

Cyberloom draws a parallel to walking around inside an Internet radio. Being immersed in sound and interacting through movements resonates with the immediacy elements of presence as well as aspects of fantasy because the very experience of PAL is characterized as a glimpse of the future that one can step into together with other avatars.

These examples foreground presence as an important element in how the PAL team (the founder, the designers, and the visitors) envision a virtual music lab. In these interview events, presence can be understood as a shared vision that had joined actors together and enabled their cooperation. It appeared as a resource for initiating the PAL project, for visiting and returning to the lab, and for redesigning it in specific ways. In this PAL case study, ideas about presence express various justifications and expectations related to acting, designing, and traveling in Second Life.

Presence as a Technical Imaginaire

With this analysis, new visibilities and new questions about the object of study are created. Perhaps presence should not only be understood as a characteristic of virtual worlds (what it is), but also as a shared dream about the future (what it might become)?

In the book *The Internet Imaginaire*, Flichy (2007) puts forth an analytical approach to understanding utopias, ideologies, and representational frames as integral parts of the development of any technical system. Flichy stresses how specific "imaginaires" of new technologies enable users and designers to coordinate their actions. According to Flichy, all technological activity is situated in one or more imaginaires. The actors involved in a technological project mobilize a particular framing that enables them to perceive and understand the phenomenon they witness and to organize their own actions accordingly. Similar to Star and Griesemer's (1989) boundary object, a technical imaginaire has to be rigid enough to maintain some coherence between actors as well as being flexible enough to take into account specific projects of the various actors. Imaginaires are thus understood as produced and used by the actors engaged in daily activities and as the resources that actors mobilize when necessary (Flichy 2007).

In PAL, the actors' own framing of PAL through presence both justifies and orients their actions. The vision and expectations of presence seem to be one of the elements on which the voluntary team project is based. It enables those involved in PAL to construct an identity around what they are doing and serves as a framework for coordinating actions and directions. Different forms of presence are mobilized in turn (immediacy, sociality, and fantasy), yet the overall vision of presence cuts across and is shared by the founder, the visitor, and the designer.[2] This first analysis of the PAL thus enables a new view of presence as a discursive imaginaire (Flichy 2007), produced and used by the various actors involved in the PAL project. This view complements existing literature reviewed earlier in this chapter in proposing that presence need not only be analyzed as a characteristic of virtual worlds but might also be understood as something that productively participates in the creation of virtual worlds. In the appearances presented and connected here, my object of study seems to be productive and can perhaps be ascribed agency.

APPEARANCE OF PRESENCE IN THE PAL CONCERT EVENT

Let us return to the situations in which presence can be experienced in a more bodily or material way. As mentioned earlier, my own initial experiences were devoid of any sensation of presence during my first visits to Second Life. Yet presence seemed pivotal to the literature and to virtual worlds developers such as Linden Lab's own presentation of their product. To explore this paradox and how and when presence can be experienced, the following section illustrates another way is which presence appears, not only in the justifications and expectations attached to the PAL project but also in a very practical and material sense. The second empirical section of this chapter analyzes the concert event, a second event in which I investigated how and where presence appears. The material presented is based on participant observation and informal conversations at the PAL location in Second Life.

The concert event usually starts with an interview with the performing artist conducted by two members of the PAL team. Meanwhile, the audience is seated around the stage in a TV-studio-type setup. Thereafter, the musicians move to the stage, the music begins, and the dance floor opens for the audience. The musician MommaLuv SkyTower is on stage performing, backed by her band and dancers, and below on the dance floor, a couple move back and forth to the music. A regular at the PAL concerts explains:

> I love hearing a good artist, dancing and you're maybe 30 people chatting together. When you are there you are sharing the experience with others, like you really are hanging out together. You get a lot more sensory input than if you are only looking at a little text box while listening. Someone will do some clapping animations, they can shout things out while dancing or ask the artist to play a specific song, perhaps something weird will fly across the room and every one laughs. You are spread across the globe and have this shared experience of being there together. It's just really powerful. (Visitor Pete)

Here again, presence is part of the experience of this person participating as part of the audience in the concert. The concert can be seen as a concentrated and orchestrated moment of presence, and it is productive to look into the highly distributed set-up behind this experience. Presence is not necessarily experienced when entering Second Life at random. For example, my own first visits seemed fraught with frustrations over how to orient myself, buy hair, turn off dancing avatar animations once off the dance floor, or conduct conversation in Second Life lingo, rather than being characterized by an experience of presence in any of its three senses, immediacy, sociality, or fantasy. Presence is thus not available for anyone, anywhere. It apparently does not always emerge in its full scale. The following looks further into the complex of elements that are assembled, aligned, and "working" in sync to create a moment of live performance, audience participation and presence for a PAL visitor such as Pete.

The first characteristic I highlight here is the nature of PAL performance as both live and recorded. This creates a trace and an archive that one can go back to and view afterward—where presence can be said to linger and, over time, add to the establishment of a community and a history. Pete knows many of the other people/avatars at the PAL concert, and the experience of presence is underscored by a set of previous concerts and events. Claus explains the shift from a media center to making music TV:

> *Shortly after opening the music lab, I [the founder Claus] was contacted by the producer of Treet.tv, one of the biggest tv stations in SL [Second Life], asking if I wanted to make music TV in Second Life. This started the Pop Vox music series featured as a regular show in Treet.tv's selection and web-archive. The concerts are live, based on the real time performances of musicians with the audience and they are at the same time recorded by Treet.tv, streamed live to screens at other locations in Second Life and to Treet.tv's web-site.*

The fact that the concerts are both streamed externally and recorded for future viewing expands the scope of participants and stages the event in a broader setting of distant and future viewer-participants. The recording also provides the possibility of creating a trace, a historical archive of shows one can view retrospectively. According to Claus, the fact that the music performances have been filmed and distributed has been an important factor in the development and popularity of PAL—and consequently for actualizing events in which presence can appear.

Presence, it seems, is emergent and distributed in both time and across media. The fact that these reoccurring events are filmed and leave popular traces on the web perhaps strengthen their potential for presence. Their recognizability becomes an opportunity for presence. Next we will see how presence is also distributed geographically and across people and technologies.

Assembling Presence—Keeping It Together, Making It Happen

Through interviews and observations, how a lot of work goes into preparing and executing these shows, and the technologies involved are numerous became visible. Extensive advertising for the shows goes out beforehand from the Second Life TV station and the PAL website as well as from Facebook, Twitter, and affiliated blogs. In planning a show, a set of globally based individuals are brought together in real time—the founder's house in Copenhagen, the Treet.tv filming and editing studio in Melbourne, a music studio in Boston, and a global audience, most of whom are situated in their own home settings. At these locations, the screens flick between Second Life, the chat space, and sound-regulating pop-up screens. All the participants engaged in interviewing, performing, hosting, or helping are connected through chat sites and one single Skype conference connection streamed back into Second Life and to the Web from the Treet.tv site in Australia. From here the recording from within Second Life and real-time editing also take place. Often coordination may be done on parallel instant messaging in Second Life, additional Skype lines, email, and phone text messaging. Work has often gone into preparing the stage, the props, and the avatar's outfits and animations beforehand. And during the show, one or more persons will also be controlling more-advanced animation through specifically developed software (also known as avateering).

The fact that these concerts actually do occur and can be experienced as "powerful," as noted in the earlier audience member's quotation, can be seen as a distributed and collective socio-technical achievement. The moment of presence, the experience of the audience, is carefully prepared, arranged, and tinkered into sync in order to be available for experience. The founder himself invokes a theatre metaphor to describe the set-up:

> *It's like the local drama club and doing theatre. And I can do that kind of thing, here, from my comfy couch with people from all over the world. This screen is my little aquarium from which it all opens up.* (Founder Claus)

Unpacking some of the preparations, complications, and efforts involved illustrates how presence is not only about the user being present, but also about how the team behind PAL put extensive work into *actualizing* presence. They not only mobilize presence in their descriptions, vision and expectations for PAL, but they realize it through extensive efforts.

All of these people are usually online thirty to sixty minutes before the show starts to check the equipment and sound connections, to show content, and to troubleshoot any difficulties that might arise. Often new people are involved which makes it difficult to establish fixed routines. The shifting staff includes both volunteers for whom this work is leisure and others who are paid to perform this work, that is, semiprofessionals attempting to make a living through their Second Life activities. The level of commitment thus varies greatly. Claus explains that, on the one hand, the need for experience makes it difficult to depend on volunteers, while at the same time it is their participation, enthusiasm, and the shared sense of responsibility that also drive the project and events forward.

The founder Claus describes this situation of uncertainties in the following way: "It is always really stressful up till a show starts because something always goes wrong." People do not show up and meet as planned and technicalities create continual unforeseen obstacles. The many technologies—and people—involved in this set-up do not work in and of themselves but depend on adjustments, adaptations, and continuous tinkering (Mol, Moser, and Pols 2010). The preparation and execution of a show is characterized by troubleshooting, breakdowns, and work-arounds. Sometimes the Internet connection of an important location/avatar goes down, Skype might "act up," and contacts do not show up as they should; sometimes applications or entire laptops freeze and block a person's participation and, perhaps crucial, contribution. The Second Life application itself, because of the maintenance work performed on the Linden Lab servers, also frequently gives uneven and abbreviated experiences of not being able to see other avatars and objects, of animations gaining their own life, or of not being able to teleport or move to a desired location. In spite of the continuous flow of hurdles, "there are always possibilities to fall back on," as Claus explains. Only one show has actually been canceled in the history of PAL. Lastly, the geographical distribution and time differences add to this setup of shifting, yet continuous flow of complications. For example, a person involved may not be able to be contacted at the time agreed, and those waiting on the other end are in the dark as to whether this person has slept through the alarm (it might be still be the middle of the night in Australia) or whether there is a technical issue with the person's connection.

In sum, these practices—practices that create presence—can be characterized by heterogeneity and very few routines. There is very little explanation of "how we usually do it" and much more ad hoc, here-and-now coordinating and problem-solving. Everything shifts between a range of coordinating mechanisms (Schmidt and Simone 1996) such as email, Skype, and a central chat site. A range of very diverse technologies, people and locations are thus in play. Lastly, there seems to be no center or overall control. Even decision making about "what to do next" in a critical situation is negotiated ad hoc between the people available.

Presence as Fluctuating Assemblage

Here, based on the post-ANT theoretical framework, I draw on the concept of assemblage to analyze the coming together of various technological features, applications, platforms, infrastructures, people and competencies, routines and experience, visions, and desires—traced during the empirical case study. Derrida (1978) applies the term *assemblage* to understanding the production of meaning as a never-ending combination of elements and practices that are continually reshuffled together to produce new effects. The term *assemblage* in post-ANT refers to an endless weaving together, an interlacing of many different elements (of texts, but also of people, objects, and resources) that form different temporary collage constellations of meaning. The notion of assemblage has also been used analytically in exploring the relationship between technology and practice, as in the work of Suchman, Blomberg, and Trigg (2002). These authors explore how a new digital work system (for an engineering bridge project work) is designed through ongoing practices of assembly, demonstration, and performance. Assembly refers to the continual linking up of a technological prototype to contingent local circumstances. "Like any technology, the prototype does not work on its own, but as part of a dynamic assemblage of interests, fantasies and practical actions, out of which new socio-material arrangements evolve" (Suchman, Blomberg, and Trigg 2002, 175). Lastly, the concept is often used in studies inspired by actor-network-theory as a conception that better designates the continual flow of translations than do networks (Deleuze and Guattari 1987; Law 2002; Latour 2005). The concept conveys the impossibility of making a clear distinction between signs and objects, the discursive and the material. Assemblage is a way of looking at socio-technical phenomena such as virtual worlds as a collage collection, a jumbling together of technological parts and pieces, artifacts, people, competencies, ideas, visions, and so forth. The concept works to describe how the bringing together of such heterogeneous elements produces particular effects. This chapter argues that it may provide new views to analyze presence as effect.

The concept of assemblage helps us to understand some of the flux and transience of presence. The PAL practices in which presence is envisioned also involve painstaking efforts to create it. Through extensive and time-consuming technological preparations and tinkering, presence is made available for the concert audience to experience. Likewise, the audience must be conditioned into place and have a certain amount of experience with both the technology and the community in order to "take on" presence. Presence is tinkered into place through the alignment of an extensive assemblage of people and technologies. Parts of this assemblage are only loosely connected and aligned. The assemblage is also in flux as elements can be added and substituted when necessary.

This view complements existing literature in proposing that presence not only can be analyzed as a characteristic of virtual worlds, but might also be understood as something that is assembled in practice, in specific moments and places. It cannot be attributed to the technology (immediacy), to the social realm (sociability), nor to the individual experience (fantasy), but it seems to require the coming together of elements from all of these realms.

CONCLUSION

Other studies of virtual worlds such as EverQuest (Taylor 2009) and Habbo Hotel (Johnson et al. 2010) have similarly pointed towards understanding virtual worlds in terms of emergence. Taylor (2009) describes the artifact Everquest as continually changing and evolving through the practices of designers, legal and marketing departments—that is, a wide range of differing players as well as the materialities involved. Johnson, Hyysalo, and Tamminen (2010) likewise present a longitudinal and multi-sited approach to the study of the virtual world Habbo Hotel. This work focuses on how many different actors mingle in continually constructing and constituting the virtual world and its infrastructure. Their work also stresses the need for studying both development and use practices, being on "both ends" of the complex user–producer relationship (Johnson, Hyysalo, and Tamminen 2010, 47). In a study of Second Life, Malaby and Burke (2009) also high-light the need for understanding process, contingency, and open-endedness when studying emergent phenomena such as virtual worlds.

Following these authors, this chapter has looked at the emergence of one aspect of virtual worlds, presence, and how it comes into being both through the material/digital, through the social, and through the imaginative. The object of study is not the IT platform that might provide opportunities for presence, nor the human actors that might experience presence, but what happens when they come together to create events of presence. Following Giddings and post-actor-network-theory, the event is a coming together of a media-cultural practice, human subjects, and a set of technologies (Giddings 2009, 149). In this way, the chapter suggests that the very object of study is best understood as an event.

The chapter has analyzed, first, the appearances of presence in interviews and, second, the appearance of presence in a concert situation. As mentioned, such appearances are made visible through the mediations of the various research moves and methods as well as the academic literature. The analyses have also been informed by the researcher's experience of presence as lacking, as not *there* to be experienced in my initial meetings with Second Life technologies as researcher. As brought forth through analysis, moments of presence emerged over time, through the researcher's own involvement and personal engagement in events. This personal experience forms an important part of the case study methodology and exemplifies a way in which the researcher can access a distributed virtual/real phenomenon empirically. In this case, the researcher's proximity and engagement over time have served as a foundation for creating new insights into presence, including insights into how history and experience form a necessary part of the situations in which presence appears.

The concepts of event, imaginary, and assemblage provide a new per-spective from which the ongoing process through which presence comes into being can be comprehended. The concepts are proposed in this chap-ter as descriptive tools and sensitizing mechanisms in contrast to definitive concepts (Blumer 1954). A sensitizing concept does not have a precise speci-fication and does not allow us to move directly to and from an instance and its relevant content. Blumer (1954, 7) proposes that sensitizing concepts provide us with a general sense of reference and guidance in approaching empirical situations: "Whereas definitive concepts provide prescriptions of what to see, sensitizing concepts merely suggest directions along which to look . . . they rest on a general sense of what is relevant."

The first concept of imaginaire seeks to sensitize the task of understanding presence as an object closely linked to an imaginary and desirable future— "what is" is inseparable from the dream of "what will be" (Plesner and Horst 2012). The second concept of assemblage seeks to sensitize the task of understanding presence as an emergent effect. The assemblage of elements from various realms creates presence, as an effect that appears in one situation and may disappear in the next.

Sensitizing Research to Emergence, Process, and Flux

In conclusion, this chapter puts forth a set of analytical strategies inspired by post-actor-network-theory. The principles are proposed as an analytical resource for sensitizing research to the situated practices and events of which virtual worlds are part and parcel. The approach suggested refrains from starting with a fixed definition of the object of study (e.g., presence in virtual worlds), but instead starts with practices, situations, and events in which the object of study appears, asking openly what occurs and what emerges. Here, the research literature can be thought of as a site or a practice in which the object also appears.

This implies the following analytical strategies:

• Always understanding emergent phenomena through the specific settings, situations, and relations in which phenomena such as virtual worlds or presence are made to work and are brought into being
• Applying and developing analytical concepts that may sensitize research to the imaginary and the future (and the past) as part of the present
• Applying and developing concepts that may sensitize research to the distributed and assembled
• Paying special attention to materiality and continual redistributions of agencies

It is suggested that these analytical strategies are particularly fruitful when studying an emergent phenomenon such as virtual worlds. The strategies highlight the way in which presence, as well as virtual worlds as phenomena, continually comes into being as an emergent effect of practices and events.

ACKNOWLEDGMENTS

I would like to acknowledge that the research presented in this chapter was part of the collective research project, "Sense-Making Strategies and User-Driven Innovation in Virtual Worlds: New Market Dynamics, Social and Cultural Innovation, and Knowledge Construction" (2008–12), Roskilde

University and Copenhagen Business School, funded by the Danish Strategic Research Council, KINO committee (grant no. 09–063261).

REFERENCES

Bayliss, Peter. 2007. "Notes toward a Sense of Embodied Gameplay." In *Situated Play, Proceedings of DiGRA 2007 Conference*, 96–102. Tokyo: Digital Games Research Association.

Blumer, Herbert. 1954. "What Is Wrong with Social Theory?" *American Sociological Review* 18:3–10.

Boellstorff, Tom. 2008. *Coming of Age in Second Life: An Anthropologist Explores the Virtually Human*. Princeton, NJ: Princeton University Press.

Bracken, Cheryl C., and Paul Skalski, eds. 2009. *Immersed in Media: Telepresence in Everyday Life*. New York: Routledge.

Deleuze, Gilles, and Felix Guattari. 1987. *A Thousand Plateaus. Capitalism and Schizophrenia*. Minneapolis: University of Minnesota Press.

Derrida, Jacques. 1978. *Writing and Difference*. Chicago: University of Chicago Press.

Doyle, Denise. 2011. "The Body of the Avatar: Constructing Human Presence in Virtual Worlds." In *Creating Second Lives: Community, Identity and Spatiality as Constructions of the Virtual*, edited by A. Enslinn and E. Muse, 110–123. Oxford, UK, and New York: Routledge.

Ducheneaut, Nicolas, Robert. J. Moore, and Eric Nickell. 2007. "Virtual 'Third Places': A Case Study of Sociability in Massively Multiplayer Games." *Computer Supported Cooperative Work (CSCW)* 16 (1–2): 129–66.

Edwards, Chris. 2006. "Another World [3D Virtual World]." *Engineering & Technology* 1 (9): 28–32.

Emerson, Robert M., Rachel I. Fretz, and Linda L. Shaw. 1995. *Writing Ethnographic Fieldnotes*. Chicago: University Of Chicago Press.

Flichy, Pierre. 2007. *The Internet Imaginaire*. Cambridge, MA: MIT Press.

Flyvbjerg, Bent. 2006. "Five Misunderstandings about Case-Study Research." *Qualitative Inquiry* 12 (2): 219–45.

Frølunde, Lisbeth. 2013. "Facing the Audience: The Hybrid Film." In *Understanding Machinima*, edited by J. Ng and J. Barrett,. London and New York: Continuum International Publishing Group Ltd.

Gibson, William. 1984. *Neuromancer*. New York: Ace Books.

Giddings, Seth. 2009. "Events and Collusions: A Glossary for the Microethnography of Video Game Play." *Games and Culture* 4 (2): 144–57.

Gumbrecht, Hans U. 2004. *Production of Presence: What Meaning Cannot Convey*. Palo Alto, CA: Stanford University Press.

Jacobson, David. 2001. "Presence Revisited: Imagination, Competence, and Activity in Text-Based Virtual Worlds." *Cyberpsychology and Behavior* 4(6): 653–73.

Johnson, Mikael., Sampsa Hyysalo, and Sakari Tamminen. 2010. "The Virtuality of Virtual Worlds, or What We Can Learn from Playacting Horse Girls and Marginalized Developers." *Symbolic Interaction* 33 (4): 603–33.

Latour, Bruno. 2005. *Reassembling the Social: An Introduction to Actor-Network-Theory*. Oxford, UK: Oxford University Press.

Law, John. 2002. *Aircraft Stories: Decentering the Object in Technoscience*. Durham, NC: Duke University Press.

Malaby, Thomas, and Timothy Burke. 2009. "The Short and Happy Life of Interdisciplinarity in Game Studies." *Games and Culture* 4 (4): 323–30.

Mol, Annemarie. 2003. *The Body Multiple: Ontology in Medical Practice*. Durham, NC: Duke University Press.

Mol, Annemarie, Ingun Moser, and Jeanette Pols, eds. 2010. *Care in Practice—On Tinkering in Clinics, Homes and Farms*. New Rockford, North Dakota: Transcript Publisher.

Murray, Norman, Dave Roberts, Anthony Steed, Paul Sharkey, Paul Dickerson, John Rae, and Robin Wolff. 2009. "Eye Gaze in Virtual Environments: Evaluating the Need and Initial Work on Implementation." *Concurrency and Computation: Practice and Experience* 21 (11): 1437–49.

Pearce, Celia, and Artemesia. 2011. *Communities of Play: Emergent Cultures in Multiplayer Games and Virtual Worlds*. Cambridge MA: MIT Press.

Plesner, Ursula, and Maja Horst. 2012. Selling the selling point: How innovation communication creates users of virtual worlds architecture. *Convergence: The International Journal of Research into New Media Technologies* 18 (1): 49–70.

Schmidt, Keld, and Carla Simone. 1996. "Coordination Mechanisms: Towards a Conceptual Foundation of CSCW Systems Design." *Computer Supported Cooperative Work* 5 (2–3): 155–200.

Schneider, Edward F. 2004. "Death with a Story." *Human Communication Research* 30 (3): 361–75.

Schroeder, Ralph. 2006. "Being There Together and the Future of Connected Presence." *Presence: Teleoperators & Virtual Environments* 15 (4): 438–54.

Seegert, Alf. 2009. "'Doing There' vs. 'Being There': Performing Presence in Interactive Fiction." *Journal of Gaming & Virtual Worlds* 1 (1): 23–37.

Simmel, George, and Everett C. Hughes. 2007. "The Sociology of Sociability." *American Journal of Sociology* 55 (3): 254–61.

Solomon, Richard J. 2002. "As If You Were There." *Matching Machine Vision to Human Vision*, April, 1–26.

Star, Susan L., and James Griesemer. 1989. "Institutional Ecology, 'Translations,' and Boundary Objects." *Social Studies of Science* 19 (3): 387–420.

Suchman, Lucy, Jeanette Blomberg, and Randy Trigg. 2002. "Working Artefacts: Ethnomethods of the Prototype." *British Journal of Sociology* 53 (2): 163–79.

Taylor, T. L. 2009. *Play between Worlds: Exploring Online Game Culture*. Cambridge MA: MIT Press.

Whitton, Mary C. 2003. "Making Virtual Environments Compelling." *Communications of the ACM* 46 (7): 40–47.

Williams, Dmitri. 2005. "Bridging the Methodological Divide in Game Research." *Simulation & Gaming* 36 (4): 447–63.

4 Understanding Cyborgism
Using Photo-Diary Interviews to Study Performative Identity in Second Life[1]

Ulrike Schultze

In contemporary organizational settings marked by globalization, virtual work and the use of social media, individuals are increasingly experiencing their lives in a liminal space that combines virtual and actual reality (Madge and O'Connor 2005). Using technological platforms such as Facebook, Twitter, YouTube, and virtual worlds, more and more people rely on digital material (e.g., profiles, images, and videos) to present themselves in multiple settings. Although these digital objects are intangible, they nevertheless have materiality, both in the sense that *they materialize* or instantiate an activity (e.g., gesture), an idea (e.g., an imaginary place) or a physical thing (e.g., an avatar body) and in the sense that *they matter*, that is, they have significance (Leonardi 2010).

That we rely increasingly on digital bodies (Boyd 2006) to interact with the world implies that our identities (i.e., who we are) are increasingly hybrid, simultaneously performed in physical and in digital spaces. We are cyborgs,[2] that is, human beings whose bodies are extended through technology (Borer 2002) and whose identities are entangled with technology (Introna 2007; Nyberg 2009). As such, we find ourselves having to construct and manage who we are in a space where distinctions between the "real" and the virtual are increasingly blurred (Hardey 2002).

Despite the increasing recognition that the actual[3] and the virtual are inextricably intertwined and mutually constitutive of everyday reality, the virtual is frequently seen as an inherently separate space (Slater 2002). Not only is the virtual often conflated with the nonmaterial and the digital in computer-mediated environments (Van Doorn 2011), but it is also defined as the opposite of the "real" (Shields 2003). Thus conceptualizing digitally mediated spaces as disembedded and disembodied is prevalent in research about the virtual (Hardey 2002). Much of this research theorizes the user's body as the source of identity, such that online performances are understood as more or less faithful re-presentations of a "real," corporeal self (Donath 1999; Galanxhi and Nah 2007).

The problem with this *representational* view of online identity (Gregson and Rose 2000), is that it perpetuates an on- and off-line dualism that is out of sync with the entanglement that contemporary users experience in virtual settings:

> The Internet to us is not something external to reality but a part of it: an invisible yet constantly present layer intertwined with the physical environment. We do not use the Internet, we live on the Internet and along it. ("We, the web kids" manifesto by Piotr Czerski, YouTube)

Because it assumes a physically embodied self that preexists online actions, representationalism cannot fully grasp this entanglement of people and technology and the intertwining of actual and virtual identities. *Performativity*, in contrast, offers a theoretical lens capable of conceptualizing the cyborgism people experience in a world increasingly enabled by social media (Schultze and Orlikowski 2010) in which it is difficult to distinguish between the technology (the material) and the person with whom we interact by means of this technology (the social/discursive) (Contractor, Monge, and Leonardi 2011). Performativity invites us to view the world as constituted through practices in which social and material elements are inherently intertwined (Orlikowski 2010).

Applied to identity performance in an increasingly technology-infused world, a performative lens sees the actions people take, whether in physically and virtually embodied form, as constitutive of identity. It does not make a priori distinctions between physical and digital materiality but explores the practices through which boundaries between the virtual and the "real" are situationally enacted (Barad 2003). As such, a performative perspective starts from a position of entanglement and seeks to understand the practices by which distinctions between on- and off-line identities and actual and virtual reality are produced and stabilized. In other words, it treats virtuality as an accomplishment rather than an inherent property of Internet technology (Slater 2002).

This chapter illustrates and discusses how the theoretical lens of performativity can be used in research on virtual worlds. The empirical illustration derives from a study of how Second Life (SL) users interacted with and through their avatars. The empirical focus is on how, as cyborgs, people perform identities in virtual settings. The aim of the data analysis is to identify the practices SL users rely on to enact situationally drawn distinctions between their physical and virtual bodies, their online and offline identities, and actual and virtual realities.

First, the chapter gives an overview of the identity performance literature in which representational and performative notions of identity are contrasted, which is followed by a brief discussion of identity research in virtual worlds. Then, the photo-diary interview method is described and its suitability for gaining insight into not only discursive but also material practices in the performative constitution of identity is discussed. Following this, the methods of data collection and analysis used in the empirical illustration are presented.

The empirical illustration focuses on identifying the material-discursive practices used by SL users to make distinctions between actual and virtual reality, physical and digital embodiment, and human and nonhuman agency. The chapter concludes by identifying three characteristics of performing cyborgian identity in virtual worlds. In addition to suggesting directions for future research, the conclusion also considers limitations of the theoretical lens of performativity and the photo-diary method.

IDENTITY PERFORMANCE AND IDENTITY RESEARCH IN VIRTUAL WORLDS

While identity is typically seen as the answer to such questions as "Who am I?" and "What am I like?" (Chatman et al. 2005), there are different theoretical perspectives on what identity is. Broadly speaking, identity is either conceptualized as a more or less stable object (i.e., a self) that is carefully performed for others in an act of impression management (Goffman 1963), or as an ongoing process of identification in which an individual is performed by (and subjected to) the discourses that are operating in a given social space (Butler 1990). Adopting Barad's (2003) language, these perspectives are respectively labeled *representational* and *performative* identities (Brickell 2005).

Underlying representational identity is an assumption of intentionality and a conscious, agential self (an "I") directing the performance (Blumer 1969). The performer has shaped in his or her mind the kind of person he/she wants to portray. This suggests that during a performance, the self is divided into two aspects: the *performer* who fabricates the impressions and the *character* who emerges out of the ongoing performance (Goffman 1959). In other words, there is a doer behind the deed (Gregson and Rose 2000), a core, essential self that is perceived as the source of an individual's identity and the origin of his or her thoughts and actions (Hickey-Moody and Wood 2008).

Representational identity creates the impression that we can grasp the self's nature, its very essence (Mouritsen 2006). This essentialist view of the self implies that identity is composed of elements and properties that exist prior to social interaction. Research on identities in computer-mediated settings (Bessiere et al. 2007; McKenna 2007; Jin 2009), which categorizes the self into different types—for example, a true, an ought-to-be, and an idealized self—is emblematic of this perspective. Virtual identities are also characterized by their correspondence to the actual self with lesser or greater degrees of mystification in which aspects of the "real" self are hidden when creating an online front (Vaast 2007).

In contrast to the theatrical metaphor underlying representational identity, a performative perspective rests on a linguistic understanding of action. It builds on speech-act theory's insight that not only do words signify or represent things (Mokros and Deetz 1996), but that they can also enact them. Performatives *do* things; they are actions that produce what they name (Butler 1993).

Instead of seeing performances as conscious, willed and staged, the theoretical lens of performativity sees identity as the result of being performed by unconsciously deployed discursive and material practices in a stream of repetition (Gregson and Rose 2000). This implies that performative identities are produced through the citation of social norms and practices that ultimately subject the individual to cultural regimes (Strozier 2002). The notion of self is thus replaced with that of subject.

For instance, Butler (1990) maintains that being born biologically female does not make one a woman. Instead, by repeatedly engaging in normative behaviors such as wearing dresses, shaving one's legs, and putting on makeup, one enacts femininity and thereby becomes a woman. By performing femininity, the female body is materialized (Butler 1993); it becomes gendered and thus intelligible in a discourse of heteronormativity. Gender, as an identity marker, is thus a verb rather than a noun; it is a *doing*—a process of materialization (Barad 2003). Performative identities are thus the effect of people's unconscious repetition of material and discursive practices rather than the source of their intentional presentation of self (Hickey-Moody and Wood 2008).

Performative identity represents a post-structural understanding of identity as an ongoing accomplishment that is distinct from other constructivist views of identity, specifically Giddens's (1991) notion of the self-identity as a reflexive project. Here, identity is not regarded as a set of traits (e.g., gender, race, and age) or observable behaviors (e.g., performances for others), but a person's reflexive understanding of his or her own biography. In other words, identity is the "capacity to keep a particular narrative going," which entails "continually integrat[ing] events which occur in the external world, and sort[ing] them into the ongoing 'story' about the self" (Giddens 1991, 54). Thus, the identity project generates a coherent account of a unified, continuous self.

Giddens (1991) maintains that this form of self-reflexive identity work is amplified in modernity, an era characterized by increasing space-time distantiation. With new forms of mediated experiences facilitated by electronic communication and globalization, distant happenings are increasingly accessible to, and have an impact on, individuals. This heightened awareness and the increased interconnection between individuals and global events contribute to a self that is continuously explored, constructed, and revised. For instance, technological change has implications for people's sense of security, while also providing opportunities to chart new career paths (Barrett, Sahay, and Walsham 2001), both of which entail the self as a reflexive project.

However, many argue that the technological landscape of global social networking in which individuals find themselves today, is more characteristic of postmodernity than of modernity (Kreps 2010), thus raising questions about the appropriateness of Gidden's (1991) identity theory. Whereas modernism is frequently associated with universality, generalization, wholeness, rationality, and homogeneity, postmodernism is described in terms of localities, partialities, positionalities, contradictions, and heterogeneity (Clarke 2003). Consequently, the self is not perceived as a coherent entity but conceived of in antisystematic, piecemeal, and tentative terms (Kreps 2010).

Instead of assuming a "true" self behind the social media profiles, users rely on to write themselves into being (thus rendering the online profile a copy of the original), a poststructuralist notion of identity acknowledges that the digital body, and the co-constructed, networked identity that is created when for instance, friends write on one's Facebook wall, have a life of their own (Boyd and Heer 2006). These virtual bodies are not entirely under the user's control. Furthermore, as Facebook profiles bring together multiple images or masks—for example, the mask of professionalism, family, school friend, or college acquaintance—a "soup" of occasionally clashing and contradictory masks (Kreps 2010, 112) is presented, replacing the image of a seamless and coherent identity.

These examples of social media use highlight that neither representational nor self-reflexive, narrative notions of identity are adequate for theorizing identity in an era of postmodernity. Instead, a poststructural conceptualization of identity that can accommodate the de-centered, fragmented, and contradictory nature of identity performance evident in a world infused by social media is called for (Kreps 2010). Performativity provides such a theoretical lens.

Bardzell and Bardzell (2008) maintain that most of the research on identities in the context of virtual worlds builds on a representational ontology. For illustration purposes, this ontology is summarized diagrammatically in Figure 4.1a. Here, virtual bodies are conceptualized as passive, disembodied signifiers that refer to—and are separated from—the "real" thing, namely, the user's physically embodied identity (Bardzell and Bardzell 2008). For instance, Vasalou et al. (2008) found that people used avatars (1) to accurately reflect their offline selves by displaying stable self-attributes, (2) to construct a playful representation of the self, and (3) to send an avatar-embodied message. This suggests a unidirectional relationship between the user and the avatar, with the user directing and controlling the virtual re-presentation of self.

Turkle's (1995) early research on MUDs, that is, text-based virtual worlds, is indicative of the representational lens. It demonstrated how MUDers used different windows to role-play multiple online personae simultaneously. Even though this research challenged the notion of a unitary self by presenting identity as fragmented and distributed performances in different windows, it nevertheless emphasized the user's mind as the driving force

1a) Representational Identity   **1a) Performative Identity**

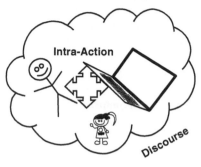

- Physically   - Virtual body
  embodied user   - Avatar (or words)
- "Real" identity;   - "Virtual" identity;
  original; source   copy
- Referent;   - Disembodied
  "thing" to be   representation
  re-presented

- Cyborg is sociomaterial assemblage
  whose components are entangled
  (i.e., intra-acting)
- Distinctions between components are
  enacted through material-discursive
  practices

Figure 4.1   Identity performance in virtual worlds

behind these multiple selves that were consciously constructed through the choice of words.

Critiquing the disembodied notion of online identity associated with representationalism, Whitley (1997, 148) points out that people's "choice of words is the result of a process of socialization associated with a particular identity," thus making online identity performance not merely a matter of mind (the discursive) but also of body (the material). Similarly, O'Brien (1999) maintains that people's imaginations—and thus the identities they are able to perform online—are limited by their corporeality. This is illustrated by Bassett's (1997) research, which found that online users tended to describe themselves in hypermasculine and hyperfeminine terms even when they were offered a wide choice of genders.

Another limitation of the representational perspective is that not all aspects of a three-dimensional (3D) avatar's performance are under the user's control. Because both avatars and the objects they interact with are scripted, avatars are frequently perceived as acting almost autonomously (Bailenson and Segovia 2010; Schultze and Leahy 2009), suggesting that the bodies and selves users create have some rooting in a social world outside of the user.

For instance, virtual worlds users are frequently confronted by hypersexed avatars that are difficult or impossible to change (Taylor 2006). These virtual bodies can be seen as the materialization of the heteronormative discourse—that is, a materially grounded field of possibility from which statements, subjects and identity performances can emerge (Barad 2003)—which is iteratively and unconsciously re-cited through the social practices that constitute the doing of gender (Butler 1993).

To address the limitations of the disembedded and disembodied view of online identity performance, a performative perspective is put forward that regards the physically and digitally embodied user as part of the socio-material assemblage that is the cyborg (see Figure 4.1b). Importantly, the bodies in this entanglement "are not objects with inherent boundaries and properties; they are material-discursive phenomena" (Barad 2003, 823). As such, they are always in the making and their boundaries are neither given nor stable. This implies that the components that constitute the cyborgian assemblage intra-act, rather than interact which would imply the objectification and independence of the components involved.

In spite of the socio-material entanglement that is the cyborg, situated distinctions between the components are enacted and their boundaries are stabilized through material-discursive practice (Barad 2003). To illustrate this boundary drawing within socio-material assemblages, Nyberg (2009) relies on a call center example. To a customer, the components that form part of the service delivery (i.e., the telephone system, the computer systems, the customer service representative, etc.) are experienced as an entangled whole until customer service representatives distance themselves from the (failing) technology with such utterances as "the computer has a mind of its own" or "it is not happy." By means of such performative utterances, identities, properties, and agency are materialized. In other words, this discursive practice produces the computers that it names (Butler 1993).

Thus understanding cyborgian identity from a performative perspective entails a study of the material and discursive practices of drawing situated boundaries between actual and virtual reality, physical and digital embodiment, as well as human and non-human agency. The next section reflects upon how such an investigation might be conducted.

METHOD: PHOTO-DIARY INTERVIEWS

The Diary Method

Diaries that are solicited for research purposes are not so much intimate journals as contemporaneous, personal records kept by individual research participants themselves (Alaszewski 2006). Diarists take on an adjunct-ethnographer role, observing and recording their own performances and well as those of the people around them at or close to the time that events unfold (Zimmerman and Wieder 1977). Diaries provide researchers with insights into the everyday public and private events that are significant to the diarist, as well as into how he or she makes sense of them (Kenten 2010).

Like observational research, diary methods adhere to the tenets of studying individuals and communities in their natural setting with minimal intrusion (Alaszewski 2006). However, they are particularly useful in situations in which first-hand observations are not possible (Czarniawska 2007), for example, in computer-mediated environments in which participants are simultaneously physically sitting in front of the computer and are present in a virtual space.

Diary methods also address some of the shortcomings of interview research. Retrospective interviews are subject to the vagaries of memory and thus frequently generate abstracted biographical narratives, idealized accounts, and general opinions (Alaszewski 2006). Because diaries are kept contemporaneously, diary-based research is better able to capture the complexity of events and the specificity of decisions made and actions taken by individuals. Thus, like ethnographic research, diaries are well suited to studying practices.

Diaries are frequently the method of choice when the phenomenon of interest is of a highly personal, sensitive or even shameful nature. For instance, Kenten (2010) used diaries to explore gays' and lesbians' daily experience of their sexuality, Elliott (1997) studied illness episodes among patients with ongoing musculoskeletal problems, and Coxon (1996) undertook a diary study of sexual behavior among gay men in an era of AIDS.

Diaries' usefulness in research of a highly personal nature can, in part, be attributed to the fact that journaling entails a conversation with oneself (Alaszewski 2006), even in a context of solicited diaries where diarists acknowledge the researcher as their audience (Elliott 1997). Diaries thus tend to be seen as relatively safe, nonjudgmental spaces for articulating, externalizing, and reflecting on incidents, and the diarist's thoughts and feelings about them. Also, because of the reflexive distance between events and their textual reconstruction, diaries tend to make visible experiences that are often hidden, thus producing more complete and honest accounts than do other methods (Kenten 2010).

Although diaries solicited for research purposes may be seen primarily as a surrogate ethnographic data collection strategy, they are also occasions for diarists to construct their own identity in support of a particular account of social reality (Alaszewski 2006). By recording everyday incidents in their diaries, participants raise their consciousness about the things that happen, their surroundings, and their interactions with others. Making sense of these events frequently entails the kind of self-reflexive identity work Giddens (1991) describes, as diarists narrativize what they did and why in an effort to construct an authentic, coherent self (Riessman 2008).

As such, diaries can be seen not only as a contemporaneous record of events but also as a storied construction of the diarist and the social reality around him/her (Alaszewski 2006). They provide insights into the linguistic, cultural, and material resources on which diarists draw in their narrativization, thus making diaries suited to studying identity performance and discourse (Riessman 2008).

The diary method is frequently coupled with direct researcher–participant interaction (Alaszewski 2006). Most researchers who use diaries rely not only on a face-to-face meeting (e.g., an interview or a focus group) with diarists at the beginning of the process in order to motivate the study and explain to participants how to keep diaries but also on in-depth debriefing interviews after participants have submitted their completed diaries. In these follow-up interviews, participants are typically asked to expand on their diary entries and are questioned on the less observable features of the events they recorded such as their meaning, properties, and typicality (Zimmerman and Wieder 1977).

One key advantage of a diary-based approach to interviewing is that the research process is rendered more collaborative and egalitarian as researcher–participant interaction is grounded in the participant's language and terms of reference rather than the researcher's (Elliott 1997). Also, by virtue of writing the diary, the participant is as prepared for the interview as the researcher.

Photo-Diary Interview Method

The "photo-diary: diary interview" method (Latham 2003)—referred to here simply as the photo-diary interview method—combines visual representations (photos), diaries (written text), and interviews (verbal interactions). As such, this method leverages multiple modes of communication in an effort to elicit the diversity of the diarists' experiences (Elliott 1997). By incorporating snapshots of the physical and social context in which events took place, the material conditions of incidents that are frequently left out of textual diary descriptions (e.g., the configuration of the space, what postures people held and how they were positioned vis-à-vis objects and others, what people were wearing) become part of the record. In this way, the role of (digital) material resources and material practices, that is, how (digital) artifacts were used and what meaning they were given in the performance of identities, can be explored more readily.

EMPIRICAL ILLUSTRATION

Data Collection Method

In order to illustrate the study of cyborgian identity performance, this chapter relies on data from a single case drawn from a population of thirty-five participants who took part in a study of the avatar-self relationship in SL. The reasons for choosing this virtual world include (1) its large membership (about eighteen million accounts in January 2010); (2) the customizability and hence diversity of activities (including gaming, education, and commerce), landscapes, as well as avatar appearance and the behavioral characteristics it supports; and (3) its ownership policies and economic openness that encourage residents to develop their own virtual objects and businesses. The latter two features imply that SL residents have to define and enact their in-world identities, activities, and interests with little guidance, thus making it a particularly suitable setting for exploring cyborgian identity performance.

The participants were interviewed between July 2008 and March 2010. Each participant lived in the southwestern United States, within driving distance of the author, and spent at least ten hours a week in-world. The data collection method was intended to gain maximal insight into the participants' own understanding of their identity performance in-world and how they made sense of them. It proceeded in two phases:

- *Initial two-hour, face-to-face interview:* This initial interview was held in a wi-fi-equipped bookstore so that the interviewee could log into SL during the interview. A key objective of the face-to-face meeting was to acknowledge the role of physical embodiment in cyborgian identity. Furthermore, this face-to-face encounter was deemed important to establish rapport and trust between the researcher and each participant (Orgad 2005). This was critical for sustaining the more longitudinal photo-diary phase of the research. Furthermore, given the highly personal and frequently intimate nature of people's in-world activities, it was important to erase any doubts that participants might have about the researcher's "real" identity and her sincere interest in, and nonjudgmental stance toward, their SL experiences (Sanders 2005).
- *Weekly photo diaries (for three weeks), which provided the basis for interviews:* These photo-diary interviews (Latham 2003) were conducted by phone and took about one hour each. Participants were asked to proceed with their SL activities as they normally would, but to take at least five snapshots a week of incidents that were in some way meaningful, significant, or important to them. These snapshots were then pasted into a researcher-supplied photo-diary template, which outlined the annotation questions—that is, the when, what, why, who, and how of the incident. The incidents documented in the photo-diary were then used as the basis for intensive interviewing.

Participants were recruited via SL groups that had some association with the targeted geographic area. In recognition of the considerable time commitment required by this research (i.e., approximately eight hours over a four-week period), participants were paid $150. With the participants' permission, all interviews were audio-recorded.

Data Analysis: Dialogic Narrative Analysis

Alaszewski (2006) highlights that solicited diaries can be viewed either as a reflection of a social reality external to the text (i.e., a representation), or as a product of the self-reflexive practice of journaling situated in a given social and material context (i.e., a performance). Because a performative orientation is adopted in the research presented in this chapter, the reflective metaphor of the diary as a mirror on reality (Barad 2007) is rejected. Instead, the diary is regarded as the outcome of specific social practices that reiterate normative discourses surrounding, for instance, journal writing and research interviews.

Indeed, like the localist conceptualization of interviewing (Alvesson 2003), a performative framing of this data collection method creates skepticism about the interview as a window on social reality, that is, an occasion where individuals report on internal experiences or external events. Instead, it is regarded as a local accomplishment within a given interview scene in which situated and morally adequate accounts are produced. Nevertheless, these accounts are unlikely to be uniquely conceived for the researcher; instead, they will be part of the well-rehearsed narratives that have been legitimated by the teller's social world (Czarniawska 2004). As such, these accounts provide us with insights into the discourses that are operating in a given social setting.

In line with a view of the interview as a dialogue in which narratives that construct and revise the teller's local, situated, and morally adequate sense of self are co-constructed by the investigator and the research participant, *dialogic narrative analysis* was selected. Dialogic narrative analysis focuses not purely on the content and structure of the text (i.e., "what" was said and "how"), but also on "to whom" it was said and "why" (Riessman 2008). Answering these questions requires repeated interpretive readings of the text and consideration of the context in which the narratives were produced. Contextual considerations include the interviewer–participant interaction, as well as things said in other interviews or in other parts of the same interview.

Case Selection: Rene/Angela

The case chosen for this chapter was selected for its richness of insight regarding the performance of cyborgian identity. The participant, Rene[4], had considerable experience in virtual worlds, having spent a number of years in MUDs and ten months in SL at the time of the interviews. She was also very self-reflexive and articulate. Moreover, she used her avatar, Angela, for highly personal and deeply introspective identity work.

Rene was in her early thirties, single, and a racial minority (part-African American). She had attended a highly competitive school for the talented and gifted and subsequently had earned an undergraduate degree in systems engineering as well as an MBA. At the time of the interview, she was working in a small insurance office, where she dealt with accounts payables, receivables, newsletters, and client relations.

Originally, Rene had entered SL to learn more about Gorean role-play, which enacts unconventional master–slave relationships (Bardzell and Odom 2008). Finding the abusive relationships played out in Gorean communities distasteful (she referred to some of their members as "riff-raff"[5] who "perverted the real nature of Gor" by treating slaves like "cattle"), Rene endeavored to build her own community of "family" and friends, with whom she could hang out and role-play BDMS[6] relationships in the way she understood them. In particular, she saw "dominants" as being responsible for their "submissives'" well-being: "[I]t is the dominant's responsibility to take care of the submissive, help them explore whatever it is they need to explore about themselves and their interests in a safe way."

Her SL "family" consisted of three male submissives (or "subs"), whom she referred to as her "boys" and who called her "Mistress," as well as her master with whom she was also "partnered" (i.e., married) in SL. Playing both dominant and submissive roles meant that Angela was "pretty much taken care of" because her submissives followed her commands and her master made her feel "safe, protected and cherished." As part of her endeavor to create a feeling of family rather than maintaining multiple individual relationships, Rene had built a home in SL, which she had called "Committed Love Forever." She wanted this to serve as the primary place for their time in-world.

For Rene, SL represented a fantasy and escape from her real life (RL), which she felt was "out of control." Her role-play in SL gave her "something or someone to control." Ultimately, she yearned for a committed romantic relationship in RL, a hope she expressed in the name of her SL home. She thus saw SL relationships as somewhat inferior to RL ones: "I would hope that if I was married, I wouldn't even need Second Life . . . for communication and understanding and comfort and intimacy." She pointed out that despite being engaged in multiple intimate relationships in SL, she was "monogamous" in actual reality.

She did not tell her RL friends about her SL presence and the life she had created there, keeping it her "private secret world" instead. In part, this was because she believed that her RL friends would not understand SL and, worse, would make her feel like a "loser" for escaping actual reality. Additionally, she believed that she had a more meaningful social life online than offline. She attributed this partly to virtual others judging her on her actions ("how I behave in public, how I speak, how well I type and it's kind of more of an intellectual, creative level") rather than on such "shallow" criteria as her physical appearance. Her SL friends also regarded her as "really special and gifted and talented," whereas in her actual life she felt "really unappreciated, especially at work."

EMPIRICAL INSIGHTS: PRACTICES OF CYBORGIAN IDENTITY PERFORMANCE

In this section, one of Rene's photo-diary entries (Figure 4.2) together with the relevant interview excerpts are analyzed to gain insight into the material-discursive practices employed to enact boundaries or cuts among the

When:
- **Date: Friday, July 11, 2008**
- **Start and end time** [*of your visit, event or encounter*]: 7:30pm – 10:00pm

Where: [*name of place where event or encounter happened and snapshot was taken*]
Committed Love Forever, my home

Why: [*why did you visit the place or participate in the event or encounter*] I was being low-key because I was feeling under the weather in rl. So, both of my boys were on and they pampered me to make me feel better.

Who: [*names or short description of other people in place or at event or in encounter; something about your relationship to them*] Red, Andreas, and myself

What: [*what happened and what was interesting, important or significant to you*] The boys can segregate themselves. Tonight was special because 1) they were both actively talking and interacting with me instead of trying to speak with me just one on one in IMs; and, 2) it felt like we were a family instead of having separate relationships.

How: [*how did you feel before, during and after the visit/event*] I felt relaxed and content in SL but very tired in rl.

Notes: [*any additional thoughts, observations or information, e.g., copied chat or IM conversations, regarding what happened that was interesting, important or significant to you*] None

Figure 4.2 Photo-diary entry[9]—Angela getting a foot massage

intra-acting components that constitute the cyborg, specifically the embodied user and the avatar. To this end, an incident was chosen in which Rene drew unprompted distinctions between her experience in RL and in SL in her photo-diary annotation. This selection strategy was based on the assumption that the segregation between the components that constitute cyborgian identity was key to making sense of the incident being described. Analyzing such an incident was expected to maximize the likelihood of yielding insights into the material-discursive practices of boundary drawing.

Interview excerpts that illuminated the how, when and why of boundary drawing were identified and analyzed. Consistent with the tenets of dialogic narrative analysis, most of the interviewer's utterances are included in the interview transcript (Figure 4.3) to acknowledge the co-constructed and performative nature of this data generation method.

The interviewer's utterances, identified by the author's initials, also provide insights into the narrative interviewing strategies employed. Instead of asking for discrete bits of information (e.g., "When did X happen?"), prompts such as "Tell me what happened" were explicitly or implicitly used in order to encourage storytelling (Riessman 2008), especially in the initial stages of each photo's discussion. The transcript further highlights the investigator openly speculating about the meaning of the participant's narratives particularly with respect to performing cyborgian identity.

The photo-diary entry (Figure 4.2) shows Angela sitting on a throne-like chair in what looks like a big hall with wrought-iron curtain walls and a marble floor. This hall is part of the home she had recently completed. She is wearing a black-and-silver bodice, a short organza skirt, long gloves, and thigh-length stockings. Her two submissives, Red and Andreas, are kneeling at her feet. Both are wearing cuffs around their wrists and arms, as well as collars around their necks by which they can be chained to their mistress. In fact, elements of their respective chains are visible in the image. Angela's chair also has rings to which she could chain her "boys."

This photograph provides us considerable insight into the material-discursive practices on which Angela relied in order to perform her identity as a dominant. She is reclined in a relaxed pose on a big, throne-like chair while her submissives are kneeling at her feet in supplicative, head-bowed poses. While she is wearing a flashy, expensive outfit, her "boys" are dressed in "silks" (i.e., a loincloth and a "houseboy" outfit, respectively). Furthermore, her subs are chained to her. These material elements of her identity performance are all imbued with meaning, making them inherently social. Indeed, Angela's performance as a "mistress" in this scene relies on the shared, discursive meanings entangled with the digital materials that were visible to and deployed by both her and her subs in this instance.

The photo's annotation[7] highlights the distinction Rene made between actual and virtual reality based on embodiment. In RL, Rene was "under the weather" and felt "tired." However, in SL she was "relaxed and content" because her boys were rallying around her to cheer her up. This distinction presents RL feelings as more embodied (i.e., feeling tired) while associating SL feelings more with mind (i.e., feeling content)[8]. Thus, the cut enacted here re-cites the Cartesian mind–body dualism that is evident in much prior research on online identity (Slater 2002).

In the interview excerpt (Figure 4.3) we can identity another set of boundary-drawing practices. For instance, Rene jumped from referring to her boys as "cute" and "sweet" as they pampered her as part of their sub–dom role-play to commenting on how "weird" it was that "people you've never met before can care so much."

U.S.: Okay, so then the last picture, which we haven't talked about yet, is where you're feeling really lousy and you're getting a nice foot massage--

Rene: (Laughs), yeah, (Laughs).

U.S.: So, you were certainly dressed to the nines that day.

Rene: I think it was a new outfit I had picked up somewhere and I just put it on. I just change clothes randomly (Laughs). And yes, so it was nice and it was nice to have them both there like kind of forgetting their concerns about each other and just talking to me and making me feel better and pampering me in a sense. Uhm — they're so cute! (Laughs). They're so sweet. But it's weird to think that people that you've never met before can care so much and they sincerely do. I mean, you can tell that they do.

[...]

U.S.: So when you see yourself in this picture, you know, really decked out as a dominant, how did that make you feel seeing Angela like that on a day when you were feeling quite the opposite of a dominant? (Laughs)

Rene: (Sighs heavily)—Looking at the picture. (Laughs).

[...]

I felt dominant because of the position and the clothing, but even in this picture, I felt the like sadness. I was still feeling sad, so I mean, my real life emotions also have an effect on how my avatar is feeling and sometimes I fake it, but on that day, I was like — "Oh!" and it's weird, you know what I've observed, when I'm tired or whatever, I want to sit my avatar down. I don't want to stand up. I look around and I'm like, "Where's a chair? She needs to sit down." And it's the most absurd thing in the world. (Laughs). I'm thinking, "Oh my God! I'm tired, I'm weary, I need to sit down. I wanna sit her down." It doesn't matter that I'm sitting down in real life. ...

And that's pretty much the instance in this. I sat down on my chair, I leaned back and I was like, "I'm exhausted." And so, it's kind of like an inter-relationship there. Because when I'm not feeling good, she's not feeling good.

[...]

I mean, what I feel there I feel in real life and vice versa.

Figure 4.3 Excerpt from photo-diary interview

Since she was spending hours each week with each of these men on SL, her assertion that she had never met them before—other than in avatar form—indicates her making a distinction between their actual and virtual identities. By bringing the actual people behind the role-playing avatars into this story, she effectively signaled that the relationships being enacted in this scene were "real": The men behind Red and Andreas "sincerely" cared about her, Rene. This suggested that her SL family was "real" and that, despite SL being a game environment, she had people who were committed to her beyond role-play in a virtual world.

It is also interesting to note that—in an attempt to counter-balance the "weirdness" of this observation—she shifted from a first-person ("I") to a third-person ("you" as a surrogate for "one") account. Furthermore, this comment was articulated in the present tense, compared to the past tense of the story accompanying the picture. This signals an attempt to move to a position of third-person omniscience and eternal presence in order to gain control and authority over the claim made. Presenting a claim to universality—"being able to tell that people you've never met before care so sincerely about you"—she turns an intimate, personal experience into a shared, "everyman" one. Thus she adds weight to her claim, making it more credible to herself and others. She relied on this discursive practice to materialize her SL family as "real" and thus realize one of her objectives.

A further distinction between Rene and her avatar was introduced by the interviewer/researcher when she asked what the interviewee was feeling when she "saw herself in the picture," looking at her avatar "decked out as a dominant" on a day when she herself was feeling "quite the opposite." Until that point in the interview, all online activities were ambiguously attributed to the interviewee, for example, "You're getting a nice foot massage" and "You were certainly dressed to the nines."

This cut between the player and the avatar reflects the distinction between the digital and the physical materiality of bodies in virtual worlds. For instance, the avatar is a technological artifact that is identified by a name and an appearance that is typically quite distinct from the user's. Furthermore, the physically embodied user who sits at the computer is looking at his or her avatar performing on a computer screen. The photo-diary entries in effect re-create these material conditions of performing identity in virtual worlds, as both the interviewer and the interviewee see in the snapshot the separation between the user's physical and virtual embodiment.

The investigator's question about the effects of seeing the avatar thus focused attention on the distinction between the physical and digital material that constitutes cyborgian identity performance. It also recognizes that avatar performances are not only directed at others but also at the user. It is this self-directed performance which Powers (2003) labels reflexive performativity, that the investigator is seeking to explore by asking the interviewee to look at her avatar as a distinct entity separate from herself.

That this cut was meaningful if not familiar to Rene was evident in her response about how she perceived the contrast between her embodied emotional state and her avatar's appearance. Pointing to the material elements of this scene, namely, her avatar's outfit, which was new and randomly worn that day, as well as Angela's positioning on the chair that gave her a sense of dominance, she conceded that she was unable to keep the sadness she was feeling in RL out of her SL performance. She also highlighted that she was unwilling to "fake" an alternate emotional state that day.

Once the entanglement of Rene's and Angela's bodies had been disturbed in favor of separate identities, the remainder of the interview revolved around making sense of the relationship between the two. At first, Rene tried to complete Angela's identity by attributing properties such as emotionality to her. Claiming "my real life emotions also have an effect on how my avatar is feeling," and "when I'm not feeling good, she's not feeling good," she cited a discourse of anthropomorphism, constituting her avatar as an independent sentient being.

However, the avatar's independence was somewhat limited. For instance, Angela was not accorded agency. It was Rene, rather than Angela, who decided that the avatar needed to sit down. Also, Rene's assertion that she was able to "fake" her avatar's feelings suggests that she, Angela's owner, was ultimately in control of the avatar's performance. In this sense, Rene constituted herself as the ultimate "mistress": She controlled what Angela did and how she felt, just as she controlled her submissives.

In the light of Rene's conclusion that "what I feel there [in SL] I feel in real life and vice versa," it is unclear how stable the distinction between Rene and Angela is. It seems that Rene reconciles her actual and virtual embodiments by suggesting that there is only one "I" that is doing the feeling in both RL and SL. Thus the spatial distinction between the real and the virtual body is maintained while their embodied responses, for example, emotions or the urge to sit down, are attributed to only the physical body. Rene admits that she finds it difficult to segregate her emotions along actual and virtual lines, despite her earlier claims of being able to "fake it."

It is, however, interesting to note the ambivalence Rene seemed to feel about the fluidity of the SL–RL boundary, especially with respect to embodied responses. For instance, she deemed her urge to sit her avatar down when she was tired in RL "absurd." This suggests that she regarded the continuous flow of some emotions across SL–RL lines more acceptable than others.

DISCUSSION

The objective of this chapter was to explore empirically how people, as cyborgs, perform identities in virtual worlds. Adopting a performative rather than a representational ontology, individuals are viewed as cyborgs, that is, people whose physically embodied senses are extended through technology (Borer 2002). Cyborgs are sociomaterial entanglements which means that the components by which they are constituted do not have inherent boundaries, identities and properties. Instead, they are the result of boundary-drawing practices. Thus a performative study of online identity requires a focus on the situated, material-discursive practices (Barad 2003) by which distinctions between physical and digital embodiment, actual and virtual reality, and user and avatar identities are produced.

As the chapter has shown, the photo-diary interview method is well suited to such an investigation. Not only do diaries provide researchers access to situations that are difficult or impossible for them to observe otherwise (Czarniawska 2007), but they are also devices that encourage diarists to reflect on and narratively construct answers to questions such as "Who am I?" and "What am I like?" Diary interviews thus provide an occasion for constructing a coherent self by telling stories about experienced events captured in the diary. Adding photos to the diary entries not only made for a more complete record but also provided insight into the material aspects of identity performance online.

What has this brief empirical illustration of a single photo-diary interview with a member of Second Life taught us about cyborgian identity performance? The empirical insights can be summarized along the following three lines:

1. *Cyborgian identity assumes the fundamental entanglement of actual and virtual embodiment:* The empirical example highlighted how Rene perceived her feelings as fluid, freely flowing across actual and virtual reality. When she felt sad and tired in RL, she found it difficult to enact a different emotional state in SL. Similarly, when upsetting things happened in SL, they affected her in RL also. This suggests that cyborgian identity should neither be seen in either representational terms where the boundaries between the user's and the avatar's identity are seen as given and stable nor in self-reflexive terms with its assumptions that a unitary, coherent self can be achieved through narration. Rather, cyborgian identity should be regarded in performative terms as fundamentally entangled social and material (both digital and physical) components that intra-act in the production of indeterminate, local, and situated identities.

2. *Material-discursive practice that re-cite extant discourses, draw distinctions among intra-acting components that constitute the cyborgian assemblage:* Despite the entanglement of actual and virtual bodies in online identity performance, distinctions are nevertheless made among the components that constitute the cyborg. The empirical example revealed a number of boundary-drawing practices. For instance, reciting the Cartesian mind-body dualism, Rene describes her RL emotions in more embodied terms (e.g., tiredness) than her SL emotions (e.g., contentment), which were associated more with mind. She also attributed the source of embodied responses (e.g., emotions and the urge to sit down) exclusively to the physical body. Furthermore, the material conditions of SL that rely on technological artifacts such as the avatar whose name and body are generally significantly different from that of the user and whose identity performance is seen by the user from a third-person perspective, serve as the basis for another set of boundary-drawing practices.

Although the empirical example analyzed in this chapter illustrated four material-discursive examples of boundary-drawing, systematic analysis of these boundary-drawing practices and the discourses they cite should identify the resources available to individuals as they attempt to construct their cyborgian identities. Such future research would highlight the kinds of identities that cyborgs can perform.

3. *The enactment of boundaries is situated:* Even though the material-discursive practices used to make cuts between actual and virtual spaces, physical and digital embodiments and off- and online identities are deemed to be somewhat universal and stable in that they re-cite extant discourses, the actual enactment of boundaries is situated and dynamic because discourses are never cited perfectly (Butler 1993). For instance, whereas Rene shied away from according Angela agency in this particular photo-diary interview, at another time she was willing to concede more decision-making power to her virtual other. At other points in the interviews she also maintained that she was able to separate her RL emotions from her performance in SL whereas, in the example analyzed here, she highlighted the continuity of her feelings across the actual and virtual space.

The situatedness of boundary enactment suggests that future research might fruitfully investigate under what conditions certain material-discursive practices are deployed and why. In this way, even more fine-grained insights into cyborgian identity performance could be gained. For instance, Rene used the distinction between her submissives' avatars and the actual men behind them in order to bolster her claim that her SL family was "real." By stressing that the people behind the avatars cared about her, she sought to move the family bonds enacted in SL beyond the realm of role-play virtuality into the realm of actual reality.

CONCLUSION

Thanks to mobile technologies and social media, individuals are increasingly experiencing themselves as entangled with nonhuman actors and digital embodiments of various kinds such as texts, pictures, videos, and avatars. More and more people are extended through technology, continuously making themselves present in multiple spaces at the same time. They are cyborgs and, as such, increasingly confronted with the challenge of performing multiple identities with both digital and material embodiments in the liminal space that combines actual and virtual reality.

This chapter provides insight into the material and discursive practices that users of Second Life engage in to perform cyborgian identity. The photo-diary interview method employed for this study is well-suited for identifying the digital materiality users relied on to enact an identity in Second Life, as well as the discursive meanings associated with the material used. Even though the photo-diary method serves as a valuable alternative to ethnographic research in that it engages the research participants as surrogate ethnographers, one of the shortcomings of this method is that participants select the events they record and report. As such, it is likely that events that put the participant in a bad light (e.g., a failed identity performance), or that in some way are at odds with the reality and self-image he or she wishes to narrate, are unlikely to make it into the photo-diary. In contrast, ethnographic observations of a SL community, for instance, would increase the researcher's access to a broader range of events, meanings, and practices.

In order to explore cyborgian identity performance, this research has adopted a performative lens, which stresses the entangled and indeterminate nature of social and material configurations, as well as the local and situated nature of the cuts people make to distinguish among the elements of a socio-material configuration like the cyborg as they make sense of their identity performance. The situatedness and indeterminacy of socio-material practices and the uniqueness of socio-material assemblages make it difficult to theorize and ultimately identify patterns of how the digital and physical materiality, actual and virtual reality, and human and nonhuman agencies interrelate. Leonardi and Barley (2010) see this lack of conceptual and empirical separation between the social and the material in performative research as limiting researchers' ability to generate insights into the role of information technology in people's lives.

However, this limitation can be addressed by focusing on the discourses that users cite in their identity performances. These discourses are socially shared and relatively stable, thus facilitating the identification of citational practices and the development of more general, theoretical insights; however, they are also imperfectly and variably enacted, thus accommodating contingencies and the specificity of a given situation. Indeed, how closely a discourse is copied depends on how individuals position themselves vis-à-vis a given discourse (e.g., for or against it). Thus to develop theory on the socio-material assemblage that is the cyborg, future research should—in addition to paying attention to the material conditions of a given practice and site—take seriously the discourses operating in a given virtual world and trace individuals' positions toward these discourses. In this way, we will be able to develop more insights into the whats, hows, and whys of cyborgian identity performance.

REFERENCES

Alaszewski, Andy. 2006. *Using Diaries for Social Research*. Thousand Oaks, CA: Sage.

Alvesson, Mats. 2003. "Beyond Neopositivists, Romantics, and Localists: A Reflexive Approach to Interviews in Organizational Research." *Academy of Management Review* 28 (1): 13–33.

Bailenson, Jeremy, and Kathryn Y. Segovia. 2010. "Virtual Doppelgangers: Psychological Effects of Avatars who Ignore their Owners." In *Online Worlds: Convergence of the Real and the Virtual*, edited by W. S. Bainbridge, 175–86. New York: Springer.

Barad, Karen. 2003. "Posthumanist Performativity: Toward an Understanding of How Matter Comes to Matter." *Signs: Journal of Women in Culture* 28 (3): 801–31.

Barad, Karen. 2007. *Meeting the Universe Halfway: Quantum Physics and the Entanglement of Matter and Meaning.* Durham, NC, and London: Duke University Press.

Bardzell, Jeffrey, and Shaowen Bardzell. 2008. "Intimate Interactions: Online Representation and Software of the Self." *Interactions*, September–October, 11–15.

Bardzell, Shaowen, and William Odom. 2008. "The Experience of Embodied Space in Virtual Worlds." *Space and Culture* 11 (3): 239–59.

Barrett, Michael, Sundeep Sahay, and Geoff Walsham. 2001. "Information Technology and Social Transformation: GIS for Forestry Management in India." *The Information Society* 17 (1): 5–20.

Bassett, C. 1997. "Virtually Gendered: Life in an Online World." In *The Subcultures Reader,* edited by K. Gelder and S. Thornton, 537–50. London: Routledge.

Bessiere, Katherine, A. Fleming Seay, and Sara Kiesler. 2007. "The Ideal Elf: Identity Exploration in World of Warcraft." *CyberPsychology & Behavior* 10 (4): 530–35.

Blumer, Herbert. 1969. *Symbolic Interactionism: Perspective and Method.* Englewood Cliffs, NJ: Prentice Hall.

Borer, Michael Ian 2002. "The Cyborgian Self: Toward a Critical Social Theory of Cyberspace." *Reconstruction: Studies in Contemporary Culture* 2 (3): http://reconstruction.eserver.org/023/borer.htm (last accessed 24. March 21, 2013).

Boyd, Danah. 2006. "Identity Production in a Networked Culture: Why Youth Heart MySpace." In *McArthur Foundation Series on Digital Learning—Youth, Identity and Digital Media,* edited by D. Buckingham, 119–42. Cambridge, MA: MIT Press.

Boyd, Danah, and Jeffrey Heer. 2006. "Profiles as Conversation: Networked Identity Performance on Friendster." Paper presented at the Hawai'i International Conference on System Sciences (HICSS), Koloa, Kauai HI.

Brickell, Chris. 2005. "Masculinities, Performativity and Subversion: A Sociological Reappraisal." *Men and Masculinity* 8 (1): 24–43.

Butler, Judith. 1990. *Gender Trouble: Feminism and the Subversion of Identity.* New York: Routledge.

Butler, Judith. 1993. *Bodies that Matter.* London: Routledge.

Chatman, Celina M., Jacquelynne S. Eccles, and Oksana Malanchuk. 2005. "Identity Negotiation in Everyday Settings." In *Navigating the Future: Social Identity, Coping and Life Tasks,* edited by G. Downey, J. S. Eccles, and C. M. Chatman, 116–39. New York: Russell Sage Foundation.

Clarke, Adele E. 2003. "Situational Analyses: Grounded Theory Mapping after the Postmodern Turn." *Symbolic Interaction* 26 (4): 553–76.

Contractor, Noshir, Peter R. Monge, and Paul M. Leonardi. 2011. "Multidimensional Networks and the Dynamics of Sociomateriality: Bringing Technology inside the Network." *International Journal of Communications* 5:682–720.

Coxon, A. P. M. 1996. *Between the Sheets: Sexual Diaries and Gay Men's Sex in the Era of AIDS.* London: Cassell.

Czarniawska, Barbara. 2004. *Narratives in Social Science Research.* London: Sage.

Czarniawska, Barbara. 2007. *Shadowing and Other Techniques for Doing Fieldwork in Modern Society.* Copenhagen: Liber.

Donath, Judith. 1999. "Identity and Deception in the Virtual Community." In *Communities in Cyberspace,* edited by P. Kollock and M. Smith, 27–58. London: Routledge.

Elliott, Heather. 1997. "The Use of Diaries in Sociological Research on Health Experience." *Sociological Research Online* 2 (2). Accessed March 21, 2013. http://www.socresonline.org.uk/2/2/7.html

Galanxhi, Holtjona, and Fiona Fui-Hoon Nah. 2007. "Deception in Cyberspace: A Comparison of Text-Only vs Avatar-Supported Medium." *International Journal of Human-Computer Studies* 65 (9): 770–83.

Giddens, Anthony. 1991. *Modernity and Self-identity: Self and Society in the Late Modern Age*. Cambridge, UK: Polity Press.

Goffman, Erving. 1959. *The Presentation of Self in Everyday Life*. Garden City, NY: Doubleday.

Goffman, Erving. 1963. *Behavior in Public Places: Notes on the Social Organization of Gatherings*. New York: Free Press.

Gregson, Nicky, and Gillian Rose. 2000. "Taking Butler Elsewhere: Performativities, Spatialities and Subjectivities." *Environment and Planning D: Society and Space* 18:433–52.

Hardey, Michael. 2002. "Life beyond the Screen: Embodiment and Identity through the Internet." *The Sociological Review* 50 (4): 570–85.

Hickey-Moody, Anna, and Denise Wood. 2008. "Virtually Sustainable: Deleuze and Desiring Differenciation in Second Life." *Continuum: Journal of Media and Cultural Studies* 22 (6): 805–16.

Introna, Lucas D. 2007. "Towards a Post-Human Intra-Actional Account of Socio-Technical Agency (and Morality)." In *Moral Agency and Technical Artefacts*, Netherlands Institute for Advanced Study in the Humanities and Social Sciences *(NIAS)*.

Jin, Seung-A Annie. 2009. "Avatars Mirroring the Actual Self versus Projecting the Ideal Self: The Effects of Self-Priming on Interactivity and Immersion in an Exergame, Wii Fit." *CyberPsychology & Behavior* 12 (6): 761–65.

Kenten, Charlotte. 2010. "Narrating Oneself: Reflections on the Use of Solicited Diaries with Diary Interviews." *Forum: Qualitative Social Research* 11 (2): Article 16.

Kreps, David. 2010. "My Social Networking Profile: Copy, Resemblance or Simulacrum? A Poststructuralist interpretation of Social Information Systems." *European Journal of Information Systems* 19: 104–15.

Latham, Alan. 2003. "Research, Performance and Doing Human Geography: Some Reflections on the Diary-Photograph, Diary-Interview Method." *Environment and Planning A* 35:1993–2017.

Lee, Kwan Min. 2004. "Presence, Explicated." *Communication Theory* 14 (1): 27–50.

Leonardi, Paul M. 2010. "Digital Materiality? How Artifacts without Matter, Matter." *First Monday* 15 (6–7): http://www.uic.edu/htbin/cgiwrap/bin/ojs/index.php/fm/article/viewArticle/3036/2567, last accessed March, 24 2013.

Leonardi, Paul M., and Stephen R. Barley. 2010. "What's Under Construction Here? Social Action, Materiality, and Power in Constructivist Studies of Technology and Organizing." *The Academy of Management Annals* 4 (1): 1–51.

Madge, Clare, and Hanrietta O'Connor. 2005. "Mothers in the Making? Exploring Liminality in Cyber/Space." *Transactions of the Institute of British Geographers* 30: 83–97.

McKenna, Katelyn Y.A. 2007. "Through the Internet Looking Glass: Expressing and Validating the True Self." In *The Oxford Handbook of Internet Psychology*, edited by A. N. Joinson, K. Y. A. McKenna, T. Postmes, and U.-D. Reips, 205–21. New York: Oxford University Press.

McLuhan, Marshall. 1964. *Understanding Media: The Extensions of Man*. New York: McGraw-Hill.

Mokros, Hartmut B., and Stanley A. Deetz. 1996. "What Counts as Real?: A Constitutive View of Communication and the Disenfranchised in the Context of Health." In *Communication & Disenfranchisement: Social Health Issues and Implications*, edited by E. B. Ray, 29–44. Mahwah, NJ: Lawrence Erlbaum.

Mouritsen, Jan. 2006. "Problematising Intellectual Capital Research: Ostensive versus Performative IC." *Accounting, Auditing & Accountability Journal* 19 (6): 820–41.

Nyberg, Daniel. 2009. "Computers, Customer Service Operatives and Cyborgs: Intra-actions in Call Centres." *Organization Studies* 30 (11): 1181–99.

O'Brien, Jodi. 1999. "Writing in the Body: Gender (Re)Production in Online Inter-actions." In *Communities in Cyberspace,* edited by M. Smith and P. Kollock, 75–106. London: Routledge.

Orgad, Shani. 2005. "From Online to Offline and Back: Moving from Online to Offline Relationships with Research Informants." In *Virtual Methods: Issues in Social Research on the Internet,* edited by C. Hine, 51–65. New York: Berg.

Orlikowski, Wanda J. 2010. "The Sociomateriality of Organizational Life: Consid-ering Technology in Management Research." *Cambridge Journal of Economics* 34:125–41.

Powers, Thomas M. 2003. "Real Wrongs in Virtual Communities." *Ethics and Information Technology* 5 (4): 191–98.

Riessman, Catherine Kohler. 2008. *Narrative Methods for the Human Sciences.* Thousand Oaks, CA: Sage.

Sanders, Teela. 2005. "Researching the Online Sex Work Community." In *Virtual Methods: Issues in Social Research on the Internet,* edited by C. Hine, 67–79. New York: Berg.

Schultze, Ulrike, and Matthew M. Leahy. 2009. "The Avatar-Self Relationship: Enacting Presence in Second Life." Paper presented at the International Confer-ence on Information Systems, Phoenix, AZ.

Schultze, Ulrike, and Wanda Orlikowski. 2010. "Virtual Worlds: A Performative Perspective on Globally-Distributed, Immersive Work." *Information Systems Research* 21 (4): 810–21.

Shields, R. 2003. *The Virtual.* London: Routledge.

Slater, Don. 2002. "Social Relationships and Identity Online and Offline." In *The Handbook of New Media,* edited by L. Lievrouw and S. Livingstone, 533–46. London: Sage.

Strozier, Robert M. 2002. *Foucault, Subjectivity, and Identity: Historical Construc-tion of Subject and Self.* Detroit, MI: Wayne State University Press.

Taylor, T.L. 2006. *Play between Worlds: Exploring Online Game Culture.* Cam-bridge, MA: MIT Press.

Turkle, Sherry 1995. *Life on the Screen: Identity in the Life of the Internet.* New York: Simon & Shuster.

Vaast, Emmauelle. 2007. "Playing with Masks: Fragmentation and Continuity in the Presentation of Self in an Occupational Online Forum." *Information Technology & People* 20 (4): 334–51.

Van Doorn, Niels. 2011. "Digital Spaces, Material Traces: How Matter Comes to Matter in Online Performances of Gender, Sexuality and Embodiment." *Media, Culture & Society* 33 (4): 531–47.

Vasalou, Asimina, Adam Joinson, Tanja Banziger, Peter Goldie, and Jeremy Pitt. 2008. "Avatars in Social Media: Balancing Accuracy, Playfulness and Embodied Messages." *Human-Computer Studies* 66: 801–11.

Whitley, Edgar A. 1997. "In Cyberspace All They See Are Is Your Words: A Review of the Relationship between Body, Behavior and Identity Drawn from the Sociol-ogy of Knowledge." *Information Technology & People* 10 (2): 147–63.

Zimmerman, Don H., and D. Lawrence Wieder. 1977. "The Diary: Diary-Interview Method." *Urban Life* 5 (4): 479–98.

5 Designing Childhoods
Ethnographic Engagements in and around Virtual Worlds

Minna Ruckenstein

With millions of users, virtual worlds are important sites of communication and interaction. Since virtual worlds are fundamentally places (Boellstorff 2008, 216), the methods and findings of classical anthropological studies can fruitfully be extended to research that takes as its object virtual worlds. This means that it is not only possible but also desirable to explore them with the same ethnographic tools used to study human cultures all over the world, as the subfield of "virtual anthropology" proposes (see Boellstorff 2008). In his ethnography *Coming of Age in Second Life* (2008) Tom Boellstorff argues that virtual worlds are cultural locations needing to be studied "in their own terms." He carries out ethnographic research that takes place entirely within Second Life and makes no attempt to learn about users' or residents' offline lives and identities. Although the ethnographic approach introduced in this chapter benefits from Boellstorff's research, it differs by treating virtual worlds as "spatial extensions" in children's lives (Lee 2001; Ruckenstein forthcoming). By focusing on virtual worlds from the perspective of children and teenagers as users, the chapter argues for empirical research that highlights people's everyday doings in and around virtual worlds.

In ethnography, qualitative methods are applied to produce data about what people say and do in particular situations. Typically, the aim is to illuminate broader questions about social practice (e.g., Van Maanen 2006; Wolcott 1999). In the following, I demonstrate how ethnography can be used in the study of broader economic developments that shape the social and spatial affiliations of childhood in relation to virtual worlds. Ethnography refers here not only to an observational technique or to "a researcher's idio-syncratic experience" (Castronova and Falk 2009, 404), but to a research attitude that appreciates the empirical character of virtual worlds and is particularly appropriate to a research methodology that is eclectic and varied. Because ethnography "allows the researcher to become involved in crafting events as they occur" (Boellstorff 2008, 68), it is well suited to virtual worlds research given the emergent, dynamic nature of virtual worlds. Virtual worlds are projects or sets of projects in the making, constantly in a state of active development. Thus it is counterproductive to analyze them as if they operated in temporal and spatial stasis with the aim of producing some kind of synchronic model—a frozen slice of time; rather, it is important to remain open to the complex, emergent character of virtual worlds.

The research methodology presented in this chapter is founded on the idea that a focus on both children and virtual world developers can contribute to the theorizing of the emergent nature of material and digital encounters and capitalist transformations. The discussion builds on my prior research on Habbo Hotel, a virtual world for children and teenagers owned by the Sulake Corporation (Ruckenstein 2011, forthcoming). The study pays attention to research on the social significance of online networking and virtual worlds for children (e.g., Holloway and Valentine 2003; Livingstone 2002; Weber and Dixon 2007), arguing that it makes sense to focus on virtual worlds in the context of children's and young people's everyday aims and doings. Virtual worlds offer children opportunities to expand their worlds and manipulate their spatial surroundings. From this perspective, virtual worlds can be understood as a consequence of adults' spatial control of children's worlds; they meet a need that has arisen from the increasing constriction of children's independent mobility outside the home (e.g., Matthews and Limb 1999; Mikkelsen and Christensen 2009). Ethnographic research can detail ways in which online services are used by children to extend, enlarge, and multiply their spatial territories (Holloway and Valentine 2003) and ways which those spatialities are designed and shaped by commercial agents.

Virtual worlds are often owned by companies and are backed by venture capitalists who expect to make a profit; this also applies to the virtual worlds discussed in this chapter. From the perspective of children, this means that commercial agents and interests define children's spatial realms while children build social relations online. The study presented in this chapter explores the spatial intertwining of commercial, capitalist aims and children's sociality through analysis of the ways in which commercially run virtual worlds both shape and are shaped by children. Thus the study aims to produce a holistic understanding of value creation and the economy that recognizes the impact of the production of various forms of value through virtual worlds, including flows of money and emerging worlds of sociality. This impact would remain unrecognized if important cultural and spatial continuities between online and offline worlds were not recognized and empirically analyzed in research.

In order to outline my approach, I introduce the concepts of prosumption (e.g., Ritzer and Jurgenson 2010) and creationist capitalism (Boellstorff 2008), suggesting that, rather than being an overarching explanatory framework, capitalism resides in, and is circulated by, actors and organizations; transformations take place because people internalize and enact the possibilities that technologies and changes in capitalist processes open for them. Following this, the ethnographic study of Habbo Hotel is introduced with the aim of unpacking processes of prosumption. By focusing on people's everyday talk and actions in and around virtual worlds, my ethnography highlights the nature of prosumer capitalism as perpetually unfinished and highly adaptive. Then I discuss how the methodological lenses offered by a discourse-centered perspective on culture and actor-network-theory can guide the analysis of the ways in which the design of virtual worlds advances and shapes children's material and digital encounters. The aim is to demonstrate that ethnography can produce insight into how sociality between children is inscribed in the companies' business models and how that sociality creates close connections between children and virtual world developers. The chapter ends with a discussion of what the particular value of ethnography might be for research on virtual worlds.

STUDYING EMERGING FORMS OF CAPITALISM

My ethnographic research approach is informed by, and combined with, theories and methods that are alert to forms of capitalism currently being created and promoted in corporate practices and people's doings in and around virtual worlds. Although processes of production and consumption have always been equally important to capitalism, the scholarly attention given to them shifted from an emphasis on production to consumption. Now the consumption era seems to be being superseded by scholarship that suggests a focus on both production and consumption. In research on digital culture, the concept of "prosumption" is applied in order to capture the merging of the spheres of consumption and production (e.g., Boellstorff 2008; Bruns 2008; Jenkins 2006; Ritzer and Jurgenson 2010). Communication scholar Axel Bruns (2008) describes a continuum characteristic to online services that reaches beyond this dichotomy and that of "work or play." He emphasizes that users of digital services are able to move smoothly across such a continuum; they hardly notice or concern themselves with the fact that their participation contributes to the overall corporate process of content creation and profit-making. Individual participation and creativity interweave with commercial aims: production melts into play and leisure activities. For instance, game researcher Celia Pearce (2006, 8) argues for a notion of play as an act of production; in virtual worlds, people pay money to produce their own entertainment and self-fulfillment.

Although prosumption is not unique to the digital media, the Internet is one of its most prevalent locations, particularly the so-called Web 2.0 which is defined by user involvement and user participation. As virtual worlds bring together producers, distributors, and consumers in efficient and innovative ways, they facilitate novel forms of prosumption by promoting new forms of interaction and power relations. There is a tendency in prosumer capitalism to use unpaid rather than paid labor, and processes of control appear to be more subtle, seductive, and indirect (Ritzer and Jurgenson 2010, 22). Tom Boellstorff (2008, 26) investigates this shift or trend by applying the concept of "creationist capitalism" in order to study how capitalism equates people's creativity with labor and feeds off people's self-expression, social aspirations, and problem-solving skills.

A basic assumption of this chapter is that an ethnographic approach to researching capitalist developments in virtual worlds can provide insight into how online economies and communities create and spread understandings of the economy while opening up new patterns of production, distribution, and consumption. Precisely because the Internet is so relevant to current economic processes, researchers should actively avoid reinforcing the idea that "the virtual economy" is somehow qualitatively different and separable from "the economy." According to Boellstorff (2008, 208), creationist capitalism, as practiced in Second Life, is a form of capitalism that is based on a Christian metaphysics at the heart of Western ideology. Instead of predestination, though, people are guided by individualistic self-fulfillment. In Second Life, the resident becomes "a minor god," who participates in the creation of new worlds for human sociality. As Boellstorff (2008, 207) puts it, "[i]n creationist capitalism, selfhood is understood as the customization of the social."

Defining the self as the creator offers a fruitful point of departure for thinking about virtual worlds because it suggests that people's creative input is closely linked to an economic surplus that makes online worlds both possible and profitable. The commercial underpinnings of people's doings online connect the study of capitalist forms in virtual worlds to questions of value. The notion of the prosumer as the new locus of value creation materializes in joint ventures promoted by companies and consultancies. Emerging forms of co-production, co-invention, co-distribution, and co-consumption are in line with the view that "value will have to be jointly created by both the firm and the consumer" (Prahalad and Ramaswamy 2004, 7). Company-created virtual worlds rely on, and take advantage of, user-generated content. "Second Life *depends* on unanticipated uses by its consumers," as Thomas Malaby (2009, 8) puts it. People, including children, can participate online in creative processes much more freely than in the offline world where people typically need some credentials to become part of established creative communities. In virtual worlds, people are judged by their actions. They do not need to prove themselves to be capable beforehand. This does not mean that virtual worlds are free of power relations and hierarchies, but processes of inclusion and exclusion are played out in new ways.

Prosumer capitalism is driven by a belief in the emancipatory and creative potential of technologies for people's actions and allows people to produce what they consume, turning consumption into a form of production. In this understanding, people are not simply selling their labor power and consuming ready-made products, but rather they are actively co-producing the products and services that they consume. The definition of value suggested by anthropologist David Graeber (2001, 254) is useful for thinking about what might inspire children and young people in virtual worlds: he argues that "value is the way actions become meaningful to the actors by being placed in some larger social whole, real or imaginary." This means that one needs to "define things not in terms of what one imagines them to be in a certain abstract moment, outside time, but partly by what they have the potential to become" (Graeber 2001, 254). Following these ideas, ethnographic research can determine through concrete examples that people are, for instance, not motivated purely or even primarily by the acquisition of things in virtual worlds, but rather by the potentialities that these things open up for them. The purchase of clothes, furniture, and property becomes meaningful in a virtual world, if the actions required for obtaining and owning them make sense in a larger social context. Thus, objects can be treated as part of the processes through which virtual worlds emerge and come into being; it is through the objects that users of virtual worlds expand their sphere of influence and activity.

The preceding theoretical understanding of virtual worlds in terms of creationist capitalism and the prosumer leads to methodological choices designed to explore social and spatial connections between children and commercial enterprises as well as between children. Placing these connections at the center of the research process contributes to the study of emerging capitalist forms and value creation from a perspective that has not been sufficiently explored in virtual world research. In the virtual world Habbo Hotel, developers understand the corporate value of children's sociality and take advantage of it (Ruckenstein 2011). Commercially, the most important insight of the Habbo Hotel is its spatial character; the service offers visitors rooms that can be decorated with furniture bought at a low price. This means that it is economically valuable for companies to create platforms for children's social relations as this encourages children and young people to consume the companies' products and services and become hooked on them.

Users of virtual worlds not only participate in the production of virtual worlds but also make them appealing and inviting to others. As Habbo Hotel grew larger, its users became younger. The virtual world appeared to support the aspirations of children and young people who were the most active and most likely to return to the service. Rather than obsessing about keeping their older users, Habbo's founders began to develop the service for children and young people. Significantly, children support virtual worlds through their being there; mere presence is important because it makes the service more appealing for others. The more people that a virtual world gathers, the more likely it is that the service will become economically viable, because more social aspirations, aims, desires, and creations of all kinds will emerge. The more rivalry and self-expression generated, the more users buy digital objects for making and marking social distinctions. In virtual worlds social interactions have a corporate value; not only are people important for populating virtual worlds, but their presence and creative input are also fundamental to economic action (Ruckenstein 2011).

TRACING CONNECTIONS

My ethnographic approach is designed to trace how connections between children and commercial enterprises, and among children, are made and maintained. The approach is combined with various kinds of methods, including a discourse-centered approach to culture (e.g., Sherzer 1987; Urban 1993, 1996, 2001), the basic premise of which is that discourse circulating in a social entity constructs the social and even natural worlds in which the entity is situated or situates itself. In other words, "talk" is the means by which people continually re-construe social worlds in ongoing processes of cultural transmission. In particular, I draw on the discourse-centered approach to culture in order to investigate how prosumer capitalism is discursively created and promoted in a constant effort to create value for both the company and the children as users of virtual worlds. Methodologically, "talk" is an important key to what people are interested in and what drives them; a discourse that excites interest in a certain milieu is one that is being actively transmitted (Urban 2001). Commercial agents that position themselves in the emerging corporate culture promoting prosumption talk enthusiastically about the possibilities of user involvement and user participation. As I demonstrate, the developers of Habbo Hotel aim at promoting a culture of iterative and interactive cooperation and innovation. They see themselves as being part of an emerging corporate culture that promotes prosumption. The everyday talk of corporate agents reflects a practical discourse that pushes forward notions of prosumer capitalism, including notions of children and young people as agents in their own right with power and influence over commercial developments. Not coincidentally, this talk is in line with the marketing discourse focused on children that treats child consumers as sophisticated, demanding, and hard-to-please (Buckingham 2000, 148).

Following a discourse-centered perspective, I have focused on what gets the most engaged attention in the everyday. In the case of children, their talk offers clues to what emotionally ties them to a virtual world. Children talk about furniture in Habbo Hotel and about the successes and losses in their exchange and trade relations, revealing how important and involving they are. When children enthusiastically detail the spatial and material possibilities, their uses and misuses of objects circulating in the online service, they also tell of their social value. Instead of analyzing word by word what people say, I have followed what ongoing discussions point out as particularly engaging and involving for both developers and children.

A discourse-centered perspective offers clues about everyday aims and desires, but it also points toward historical continuities and discontinuities that craft past events in a manner that makes sense in a larger social whole. Stories of the coming into being of virtual worlds provide insight into how virtual worlds are understood by their creators (Malaby 2009). It is typical that important parts of the making of virtual worlds remain discursively invisible and are hardly mentioned in accounts of their history. For instance, the routine and stable repetition, the work of installation, maintenance, and repair do not feature centrally in those historical accounts. The discourse on prosumer capitalism, including virtual worlds, defines privileged sites and privileged topics and by doing so also reminds us of the importance of listening carefully to what is being said and by whom.

Geographer Nigel Thrift (2005, 3) argues that a defining characteristic of capitalism is "its ability to change its practices constantly." A virtual world is an ongoing effort involving a plethora of practices, including advertising, marketing, event planning, user research, and coding. In terms of spatial extensions of childhood, it is methodologically important to highlight how adult-designed virtual worlds practically support and exploit children's mutual relations, open opportunities for these relations, and are aimed at directing their course. This approach resonates with actor-network-theory's insistence on the indivisibility of human and non-human agents and forces (Latour 1992). When people do things, they are not subjects separate from objects, but part of chains "along which competences and actions are distributed" (Latour 1992, 243). Individuals, including children, always engage with other people, objects, and instruments that allow them "to enact each other" (Law and Mol 2008, 58). This also applies to virtual worlds where people, objects, and technical specifications allow each other to expand their sphere of influence and activity. Thus the ethnographic approach presented in this chapter is based on the assumption that objects have generative force or energy that is autonomous from human agency; in virtual worlds, both children and adult-designed play spaces participate in the reproduction and transformation of children's lives and capitalist processes.

VISITING HABBO ROOMS AND SULAKE HEADQUARTERS

My virtual world research did not start out with the intention of studying virtual worlds, but it was my research subjects, the children, that led me there. I was interested in how children use technology, particularly focusing on how children's sociality is shaped by emerging technologies (Ruckenstein 2010a, 2012, forthcoming). During the research process (2008–10), I collected empirical material through participant observation in kindergartens and homes in Helsinki, interviewing children as well as adults. When I became aware of intense relationships between children and commercial enterprises, I started paying more attention to children's talk about Habbo Hotel that appeared to be an important place for children's sociality. This alerted me to the everydayness of virtual worlds and the importance of seeing continuities between virtual and other worlds. Each online service is a world of its own, but from the perspective of children and childhood, they have much in common. They are meeting places for children and young people, platforms for sociality, and a large amount of the interaction between children after the school day can take place through such services. I decided to take this aspect of children's sociality seriously and extend my ethnographic encounters to Habbo Hotel.

At the time of my fieldwork Habbo Hotel operated in thirty-one countries, with local hotels being visited monthly by more than ten million users (Johnson 2009, 178). Similar to Second Life, Habbo Hotel has no established game objectives, and the social openness of Habbo Hotel creates a fascinating platform for children. Designed as a hotel with private and public rooms, Habbo Hotel is a social networking service in which users spend their time in a wide variety of ways, furnishing their private rooms, chatting, and interacting with others.

It has been estimated that a quarter of all ten- to fifteen-year-olds in Finland are active users of Habbo (Johnson 2009, 178). I ended up focusing on eleven- and twelve-year-olds because they appeared to be the most avid users of the service. I met children either at their own or their friends' homes. During the visits I sat by the computer with one to three children, and they showed me how they typically spent time in Habbo. Together, we viewed their private rooms, the public spaces in Habbo Hotel such as restaurants and swimming pools, and their favorite user-generated theme rooms, including hospitals, schools, model agencies, dating rooms, cruise ships, and discos while the children did things they typically do in the service and shared their experiences in lengthy and detailed conversations.

These Habbo visits confirmed findings from earlier research including the imaginative ways in which children represent themselves through their avatars and how they form various kinds of group identities (Johnson 2009; Johnson and Toiskallio 2007). Research has also focused on the consumption of digital objects sold by Sulake, typically furniture that children and young people utilize in decorating and personalizing their private rooms (Lehdonvirta, Wilska, and Johnson 2009). One of the most rewarding aspects of an ethnographic approach is that by listening to people and by following their actions, it is possible to capture the dynamic and emerging nature of virtual worlds. During our joint visits, children demonstrated and often described in great detail their avatars (many had more than one) and the things that they had in their rooms. Sessions were socially active: children met with their friends from school, leisure activities, or their neighborhood, and they talked with complete strangers. They performed makeovers with their avatars, joked at other children's expense, visited each other's rooms, swapped items, and tried to find themselves a girlfriend or boyfriend. They talked about their friends, acquaintances, and Habbo celebrities.

Because my aim was to learn how children's sociality is shaped by emerging technologies, I treated online sessions as an opportunity to understand how social and spatial contexts are organized online. Spending time with children concretizes the fact that online services are platforms of sociality. Children rush home to their computers "to meet" their friends after school and their evening hobbies. The social lives of children and young people online adjust to daily rhythms and the sociality is not very different from that offline; children hang out in virtual worlds just as they do outside them (e.g., Crowe and Bradford 2006). It became apparent during the online sessions that Habbo Hotel extends the interests of children and young people while challenging its users and teaching them new things about themselves and others. In addition, children's activities in Habbo Hotel suggested that, in order to understand emerging forms of capitalism from the perspective of children and young people, the economic underpinnings of virtual worlds need to be taken into account. To gain insight into how Sulake benefits from, and aims to extend the interests and activities of children and young people, I carried out individual and group interviews with key agents of "product and concept development" and "market and user insight" at the Sulake headquarters in Helsinki between October 2009 and January 2010 (Ruckenstein 2011).

In my interviews with the developers in Sulake, I was struck by their familiarity with most of my research findings about children's online lives. This conclusion is instructive in itself because it indicates the importance to virtual world companies such as Sulake of knowing their users and their social worlds. Sulake developers describe Habbo Hotel as an environment created by its users; they emphasize that Habbo Hotel is built by children's desire to be there and participate. Developers in Sulake talked openly about their aim of promoting a culture of iterative and interactive cooperation and innovation. The interviewees rearticulated a basic premise of creationist capitalism: children are indispensable for product and concept development. For children and young people in particular, this kind of corporate approach is seductive because corporate forms that are built around children's activities recognize and support children's social aims and desires.

DOCUMENTING USER RESEARCH

A preliminary way in which I traced the connections between Habbo Hotel as commercial enterprise and children was through study of how Habbo Hotel developers learn how to involve children better by tracking, mapping, and analyzing children's practices and sociality. This appeared important for understanding what kind of a space for Habbo Hotel is for children. Commercially operated virtual worlds that have adopted a strategy similar to Sulake aim to get closer to users and their world of experiences by creating long-term relationships with them. People are not only sold products and services but are also enticed to mix and interact with them. I recorded the methods that Sulake uses for collecting and analyzing both quantitative and qualitative data about Habbo Hotel users. The interviews in Sulake also recalled the history of the company when no such methods were required: the developers were active virtual world users themselves and simply tried to observe what worked and what did not. As the service expanded both geographically and in numbers of users, it became harder and harder to understand what was happening in the virtual world. Virtual worlds can grow quickly with the result that they are social formations no longer directly created, or even foreseen, by the company (Malaby 2009).

In user research conducted by commercial companies, knowledge is not an aim in itself, but rather is perceived as significant in efforts to keep users interested and occupied. It is a means for product and concept developers to better understand how the aims and desires of users could be guided, supported, and exploited (see Cefkin 2009), part of an attempt to shape people's everyday contexts. As in the offline world, user research, and the design and development work based on it, shapes the social and spatial affiliations of childhood (see Gutman and De Coninck-Smith 2008). Virtual worlds offer spatial extensions for children, but they also shape and control children and childhoods by promoting certain kinds of social and spatial ties replicating the prevalent idea of children being different from adults and needing their own spaces where they can play and develop, independent of adult interference (Gutman and De Coninck-Smith 2008, 2).

The spatial character of Habbo Hotel that strongly appeals to children and teenagers has made them the most likely inhabitants of the virtual world, and in order to keep it dynamic and interesting, Sulake invests in knowing its young customers and anticipating their actions by promoting research-based and research-intensive business ventures. Indeed, in terms of virtual world research, it is important to be aware of how one's ethnographic research relates to corporate research efforts and contributes to them. If one's research questions simply replicate the interests of corporate agents in knowing their users and their actions, there is little critical distance between academic and corporate aims.

In my study, I tried to maintain critical distance not only by contextualizing people's everyday talk and aims but also by detailing how online worlds try to manage and circumscribe their users spatially and socially by tracing and recording them through user research. In 2006 Sulake produced an extensive questionnaire that was published outside the company as well. Based on the tens of thousands of responses from various parts of the world to the Global Habbo Youth Survey, a detailed manual was prepared about the hobbies, interests, values, and attitudes of young people spending time online. Based on the responses to the survey, Habbo users were divided into five groups. The purpose of the segmentation model was to help product development to take these groups into account and build the service in a wider-ranging manner. The survey was repeated in 2008, making way for a "persona" project. Personas have become a widely used tool across product design and development for providing concrete representations of the behaviors, characteristics, and needs of customers and users (see Cooper 1999; Flynn 2009; Pruitt and Adlin 2006). The aim of personas is to effectively distill vast amounts of quantitative and qualitative data into consumable and imaginable user representations.

The purpose of these research efforts is to ensure that children and young people continue to use the service and contribute to the overall process of content creation and profit making. They are a means for product and concept developers to better understand how the aims and desires of users could be guided, supported, and exploited. In Sulake the main objective of using personas is to give life to the users' various objectives and aspirations. As archetypes, personas extract what is essential from the research materials and present it in an easily accessible and understandable form. When personas are given a name and a face, they become more like real people. Six teenagers, with names, hobbies, favorite brands, and dreams for the future, were built based on the Habbo Hotel user data. For instance, Anna is a twelve-year-old girl from a middle-class family who has one sibling and a dog and likes swimming. Anna has used Habbo for three months. Tom, in contrast, is a sixteen-year-old Habbo veteran who has a part-time job at McDonalds. He uses Habbo for more than ten hours a week, five days a week. Tom knows Habbo through and through, and his character is a reminder for developers that Habbo should also offer surprises for its loyal users.

Sulake designers recalled how they worked on the stories until they became credible, because they did not want poster people, but reliability and authenticity that would inspire future product development. They explained that the characters developed must support developers in product-related decision making; they need to help guide the design process by providing a constant reminder of the children and teenagers for whom the virtual world is built. One of the designers compared personas to a shared language that clarifies the aims of the design work and makes it easier to understand mutual goals. Thus, user research conducted by companies emphasizes the fact that childhood, virtual worlds, and capitalism become interconnected through research efforts to understand children and make these understandings a cornerstone of design processes. In other words, the user research and the design of virtual worlds become part of the architecture of childhood by framing ideas of children's sociality and participation. In light of the material culture of childhood, Habbo Hotel continues the tradition of demarcating places for children. As with amusement parks, ball pits, and many other commercial play areas, it aims at supporting children's culture and aspirations. What is different is the way virtual worlds spatially expand children's everyday domesticities and aim to tackle their participatory potential, registering their needs and insecurities, and finding their voices. They can draw on deeply rooted cultural divisions between children and adults and on knowledge about children's everyday actions, while presenting new options for children.

RECORDING CHILDREN'S EXCHANGE

I have suggested that virtual worlds extend, enlarge, and multiply spatial territories of children and in order to understand how Sulake aims to create a playground where children and teenagers are "freed from the yoke of adult rules, norms, forms of social propriety and the physical scale of the adult world" (Cook 2007, 45), I needed a thorough understanding of what children do online. My exploration was guided by the notion that virtual worlds allow children and teenagers to explore, manipulate, and interact with other spatialities, people, and objects (Jenkins 1998). For the Habbo world to thrive, it needs to be a place or support some other forms of spatiality. By furnishing their private rooms, children and teenagers build presence and permanence online. In an extract from a conversation during a Habbo visit, Aleksi is showing us around in his room, and we are impressed by the valuable possessions that he has acquired with the skillful exchange of furniture:

M.R: *Is this your room?*

Aleksi: Yes.

Kim: Pretty rich. Those are really rare items.

Aleksi: And here I have chocolate mice.

M.R: *You have a really stylish room. Really stylish.*

Kim: Cool. And you have a grand piano too.

M.R: *And all this you have acquired without money?*

Kim: My room is not as stylish.

Through my ethnographic encounters in Habbo Hotel, I discovered the social value of furnishing and decorating private and public places. Rooms and items are praised and compared; children with rare items are called rich; those without, poor. The importance of furnishing the rooms with desired and rare items, such as the grand piano, intertwines with exchange, one of the core functions that support social aspirations in the service, and highlighted by research as important for children's social relations (e.g., Katriel 1991; Olander 2008; Ruckenstein 2010b). By using various items of exchange, such as money, food, stickers, marbles, or comic books, children create and reinforce their mutual ties, divisions, and hierarchies. Exchange taking place in Habbo Hotel is meaningful from both the social and the economic perspective (see also Cook 2007). Networks of exchange form around digital items, and Sulake attempts to promote these. The business model of Habbo Hotel is largely based on the sale of items within the service such as digital furniture and other goods that can be used at the hotel (Lehdonvirta, Wilska, and Johnson 2009). It is estimated that about 10 percent of users buy Habbo currency that can be used for purchasing goods produced for the service's internal market (Johnson 2009, 189). In addition, items can also be purchased with Pixels which accumulate during Habbo visits.

Significantly, however, Sulake is not in control of what children do with the things acquired. Items also change ownership from one child to another, and furniture can be owned by children who never buy any. Many children emphasize that items that are exchanged for rather than bought are more valuable; anybody can purchase rare items, but only the most skillful Habbo residents pay no money for them. Thus, children have their own ways of distancing the commercial underpinnings of the service by valuing their own actions over those of the company. In terms of Habbo Hotel being a children's place, it is essential that children can exchange items freely without adults interfering, and in fact, exchanges are not restricted but encouraged. The children's exchange economy is important for Sulake as exchanges help to keep rooms and items interesting to children. Sulake supports such relations by constantly producing new, limited batches of items for the Habbo market that are listed in a Habbo catalogue from where they can be purchased. Purchases and exchanges increase the children's commitment to the Habbo world and bring life to the service. Hotel rooms are continuously transformed by goods and their exchange. My ethnographic research provided insight into how, for many children and teenagers, their attraction to Habbo Hotel is linked to the spatiality of the service and related digital objects, particularly furniture, sold by Sulake. Habbo Hotel is spatially attractive, because of its complexity and the possibility of manipulating and controlling it. It meets children's needs by creating a world that can be modified through building new kinds of spatial realities.

EXPLORING THE GENERATIVE FORCE OF DIGITAL OBJECTS

The desire to spend time in Habbo Hotel, and to create content for the service, emerges not only in relations between people but also in relations between people and digital objects. From this perspective, ethnographic encounters highlight the fact that virtual worlds require objects that enable and pin down spatial orientations and social ties, and strengthen and expand them. In the following, Johan and Pessi talk about the acquisition of possessions in Johan's room:

Johan: My first furniture was one of those red lamps. Pessi gave it to me.
Pessi: I started everything.
Johan: All of these I've exchanged. You can purchase virtual pets too. Here is a catalogue, where you can buy everything.

One way to explore further children's fascination with furniture is to focus on what digital things suggest and do to children. Rooms and furniture are important for children in sustaining chains of human and nonhuman action. This means that digital objects have generative force or energy that is autonomous from human agency and that both users and digital objects participate in the reproduction and transformation of virtual worlds. Digital objects in virtual worlds are not merely things, but rather make the emergence of social worlds possible. Observations of children's practices in Habbo Hotel make it obvious that the desire to own, collect, and trade items emerges in social relations and aspirations that are mediated and supported by digital objects. In practice, this means that concept designers in Sulake try to understand how relations between children and objects emerge and expand and how they can advance processes of content creation. There is a huge number of objects circulating in Habbo Hotel; children constantly exchange and trade items with each other. Transactions are typically based on the social value of things; for instance, the age, rarity, previous owner, and how the item was originally acquired all matter. (Lehdonvirta, Wilska, and Johnson 2009, 1069.) Successful exchanges are social events that are remembered and recounted. On the other hand, disappointments in exchanges are also openly discussed and are seen as an important element of individual Habbo histories. One boy recalled how all his Habbo belongings, including his avatar, had been stolen.

Pessi: I was cheated. He promised me eleven pieces of furniture if I did three tasks for him. I had to dance and twirl and tell him my password, and I was so stupid that I told him and then he nicked my man.

M.R: *Oh dear!*

Pessi: I had an awful lot of stuff.

In my interviews, designers stated that they are well aware that they do not fully grasp the complexity of exchange among children, but they do understand that the objects offered to children must promote the dynamics of the game. As one of the designers explained, "The objects must generate new games, fashions, cultures." Various items circulating in Habbo Hotel have inbuilt possibilities of play. For instance, a tree that can be placed in one's room is also treated as a hiding place. If a girl unexpectedly visits a boy's room, he can disappear inside the tree until she leaves. Closets and lockers are teleports that open possibilities for movement within the Habbo world. Taking into account the emergent qualities of human–object relations—how objects establish and maintain chains of interaction and how they encourage the making of social ties and worlds—allows exploration of the social dynamics within virtual worlds. Virtual pets, for instance, not only create life in virtual worlds, but also encourage children to produce content for the service. In Habbo Hotel, children have built vet centers, kennels, hospitals, and day-care centers for their virtual pets. Pet owners can play with their pets, train them, feed them, or race them against other pets.

Designers and concept developers try to find out on a very concrete and practical level what the involvement and the participation of users require; they try to understand and anticipate processes that produce and reproduce the Habbo world. This indicates that successful design and innovation work requires a thorough understanding of virtual worlds as projects or sets of projects in the making. In virtual worlds, people, objects, and technological specifications enact each other. Children and young people are acting and being acted on (Giddings 2009, 151; Law and Mol 2008, 58).

A METHODOLOGY FOR CAPTURING CONTINGENCY: STRENGTHS AND LIMITATIONS

My study suggests that ethnographic research is particularly productive when the objective is to analyze how virtual worlds motivate people to produce value and become part of their everyday communities. I introduced the concepts of prosumption and creationist capitalism with the aim of highlighting the emergent nature of material and digital encounters and capitalist transformations. The methodological choices I have made underline the fluid and adaptive character of capitalism. From the perspective of creationist capitalism, people become users and residents of virtual worlds by participating in processes that generate content for those worlds. The production of economic and social value that is supported through virtual worlds is an inherent part of monetary transactions and emerging worlds of sociality. Online activities are not disconnected from offline practices and social relations; rather they remain reciprocally generated—produced in and through everyday practices (Giddings 2009; Holloway and Valentine 2003). As Thomas Malaby (2009, 11) argues, "technology is more and more directly confronting human sociality, with effects that are not determined by either existing social patterns or the impact of the new." Although technologies increasingly saturate our experiences, engagements in virtual worlds are never entirely separable from physical-world activities.

By paying attention to social and spatial formations, ethnographic research demonstrates how participatory forms of capitalism become naturalized through developments that arrange, extend, and transform everyday actions and aims. At Habbo Hotel, children create and maintain individual orientations and mutual relations by occupying and decorating their rooms and exchanging furniture or other valued items. The fact that children are consuming company offerings and enjoying the participatory potentials of virtual worlds raises questions about the scope and limitations of participation and about the terms on which children are able to contribute and be involved in society (see Gallacher and Gallagher 2008). Ethnographic encounters in virtual worlds offer a poignant reminder that only through a detailed understanding of the ways in which corporate offerings participate in and promote the production of everyday spaces is it possible to address the very complex ways in which they influence and guide us.

The methodological choices I have made in the course of my research highlight the complex nature of virtual worlds and their ability to self-organize in unexpected ways. Ethnographic study typically involves a continuous effort to develop and refine the research approach in the course of a project. As a research approach, ethnography is time-consuming, and it tends to produce uncertainty; research questions are frequently rephrased during the research process. For virtual world research, this is, however, also a strength; ethnography is particularly suited for describing research findings in a manner that reflects the emerging and dynamic nature of virtual world. The original creators of Habbo Hotel did not anticipate the fact that children and teenagers would be the most avid users of their service, but they went along and assisted the ongoing creation of a platform of social interactions for children and teenagers. Likewise, the emergent nature of virtual worlds becomes more tangible through a research approach that is not thoroughly preplanned but appreciates the role that contingency plays in those worlds.

The research on Habbo Hotel suggests that various research methods are useful for highlighting spatial and social formations related to childhood and prosumer capitalism in virtual worlds. A discourse-centered perspective is valuable in exploring what drives people in their everyday actions and aims, whereas the focus on the dynamics of human and nonhuman relations informed by actor-network-theory assists the study of the material underpinnings of virtual worlds. The empirical grounding of both these methods, however, relies on an ethnographic approach that emphasizes the importance of documenting what people say and do in and around virtual worlds. Working closely with people means that one needs to accept the fact that the research process cannot be fully controlled. It is typical in ethnographic research for people, particularly children, to shape the data gathering by acting in unexpected or uncustomary ways. The most revealing insights might emerge when children use the research, or the researcher, for their own purposes (see Gallacher and Gallagher 2008).

Because I have focused on children and young people, parents and educators have not figured centrally in my research. From the perspective of children's everyday lives, this can naturally be seen as a shortcoming. I have deliberately highlighted children's social connections to each other and to commercial aims and agents, because they tell of new ways of designing childhood. As an emergent and open-ended process, prosumer capitalism is difficult to fully grasp, not least in terms of its moral implications. Ethnographic engagements pin down the interplay between companies and their users and demonstrate the synergies, tensions, and contradictions that shape both company practices and children's actions. Although creationist capitalism inevitably exploits and takes advantage of the social dimension, it also contributes to people's aspirations and emotional involvements.

All through my research, I have tried to understand how online worlds discursively and practically promote and accelerate cultural forms and movements. Virtual worlds develop and change in ways that react to a certain situation or circumstance, including technological development, or in more encompassing ways by transforming the nature of what it means to be a child. For example, one of the prominent notions of modern childhood as a non-productive area of leisure is being fundamentally problematized by children's participation in the Habbo world. Meanwhile, children and childhood are providing an expanding field of global commerce in which forms of production, distribution, and consumption are being developed (e.g., Cook 2007; Schor 2004; Wasko 2010). Children are influenced by these developments, but the outcomes remain in many ways uncertain and unpredictable. In relation to virtual worlds, childhood is an emergent condition that consists of open-ended interactions between people, technological specifications, and material objects (Prout 2005). This suggests that virtual worlds can be of key importance in exploring childhood, including ways in which children recognize and take advantage of corporate operations. Regarding creationist capitalism, it is important to tie notions of childhood to Western ideology, which is characterized by a distancing of hierarchy and the endorsement of individuals pursuing an enlightened self-interest as they use technologies for creative expression (Boellstorff 2008; Malaby 2009). Discovering connections, disruptions, and transformations through ethnography offers the potential for a deeper understanding of what inspires and motivates both children and adults in the production of virtual worlds. Ethnographic inquiry can produce cutting-edge research not only on virtual worlds but also on worlds at large.

REFERENCES

Boellstorff, Tom. 2008. *Coming of Age in Second Life: An Anthropologist Explores the Virtually Human.* Princeton, NJ: Princeton University Press.
Bruns, Axel. 2008. *Blogs, Wikipedia, Second Life and Beyond: From Production to Produsage.* New York: Peter Lang.
Buckingham, David. 2000. *After the Death of Childhood: Growing Up in the Age of Electronic Media.* Cambridge, UK: Polity Press.
Castronova, Edward, and Matthew Falk. 2009. "Virtual Worlds: Petri Dishes, Rat Mazes and Supercolliders." *Games and Culture* 4 (4): 396–407.
Cefkin, Melissa. 2009. *Ethnography and the Corporate Encounter: Reflections on Research in and of Corporations.* Oxford, UK: Berghahn Books.
Cook, Daniel. 2007. "The Disempowering Empowerment of Children's Consumer 'Choice': Cultural Discourses of the Child Consumer in North America." *Society and Business Review* 2 (1): 37–52.
Cooper, Alan. 1999. *The Inmates Are Running the Asylum: Why High Tech Products Drive Us Crazy and How to Restore the Sanity.* New York: Macmillan.
Crowe, Nic, and Simon Bradford. 2006. "'Hanging Out in Runescape': Identity, Work and Leisure in the Virtual Playground." *Children's Geographies* 4 (3): 331–46.
Flynn, Donna K. 2009. "'My Customers Are Different!' Identity, Difference, and the Political Economy of Design. In *Ethnography and the Corporate Encounter: Reflections on Research in and of Corporations,* edited by Melissa Cefkin, 41–47. Oxford, UK: Berghahn Books.
Gallacher, Lesley Anne, and Michael Gallagher. 2008. "Methodological Immaturity in Childhood Research? Thinking Through 'Participatory Methods.'" *Childhood* 15 (4): 499–516.

Giddings, Seth. 2009. "Events and Collusions: A Glossary for the Microethnography of Video Game Play." *Games and Culture* 4 (2): 144–57.

Graeber, David. 2001. *Toward an Anthropological Theory of Value: The False Coin of Our Own Dreams.* New York: Palgrave.

Gutman, Marta, and Ning de Coninck-Smith. 2008. "Introduction: Good to Think With—History, Space and Modern Childhood." In *Designing Modern Childhoods: History, Space and the Material Culture of Childhood,* edited by Marta Gutman and Ning de Coninck-Smith, 1–19. New Brunswick, NJ: Rutgers University Press.

Holloway, Sarah, and Gill Valentine. 2003. *Cyberkids: Children in the Information Age.* London: RoutledgeFalmer.

Jenkins, Henry. 1998. "'Complete Freedom of Movement': Video Games as Gendered Play Spaces." In *From Barbie to Mortal Kombat: Gender and Computer Games,* edited by Justine Cassell and Henry Jenkins, 262–97. Cambridge, MA: MIT Press.

Jenkins, Henry. 2006. *Convergence Culture: Where Old and New Media Collide.* New York: New York University Press.

Johnson, Mikael. 2009. "Habbo lasten ja nuorten arjessa" [Habbo in the Everyday Life of Children and Young People]. In *Kulutuksen liikkeet: Kuluttajatutkimuskeskuksen vuosikirja 2009,* edited by Minna Lammi, Mari Niva, and Johanna Varjonen, 177–204. Helsinki: Kuluttajatutkimuskeskus.

Johnson, Mikael, and Kalle Toiskallio. 2007. "Who Are the Users of Habbo Hotel?" In *Mobile Content Communities,* edited by Marko Turpeinen and Kai Kuikkaniemi, 89–107. Helsinki: Helsinki Institute for Information Technology (HITT) Publications.

Katriel, Tamar. 1991. *Communal Webs: Communication and Culture in Contemporary Israel.* New York: State University of New York Press.

Latour, Bruno. 1992. "Where Are the Missing Masses? The Sociology of a Few Mundane Artifacts." In *Shaping Technology/Building Society: Studies in Sociotechnical Change,* edited by Wiebe Bijker and John Law, 225–258. Cambridge, MA: MIT Press.

Law, John, and Annemarie Mol. 2008. "The Actor-Enacted: Cumbrian Sheep in 2001." In *Material Agency: Towards a Non-Anthropocentric Approach,* edited by Carl Knappet and Lambros Malafouris, 57–77. New York: Springer.

Lee, Nick. 2001. "The Extensions of Childhood: Technologies, Children and Independence." In *Children, Technology and Culture: The Impacts of Technologies in Children's Everyday Lives,* edited by Ian Hutchby and Jo Moran-Ellis, 153–69. New York: Routledge.

Lehdonvirta, Vili, Terhi-Anna Wilska, and Mikael Johnson. 2009. "Virtual Consumerism: Case of Habbo Hotel." *Information, Communication and Society* 12 (7): 1059–1079.

Livingstone, Sonia. 2002. *Young People and New Media: Childhood and the Changing Media Environment.* London: Sage.

Malaby, Thomas M. 2009. *Making Virtual Worlds: Linden Lab and Second Life.* Ithaca, NY: Cornell University Press.

Matthews, Hugh, and Melanie Limb. 1999. "Defining an Agenda for the Geography of Children: Review and Prospect." *Progress in Human Geography* 23 (1): 61–90.

Mikkelsen, Romero M., and Pia Christensen. 2009. "Is Children's Independent Mobility Really Independent? A Study of Children's Mobility Combining Ethnography and GPS/Mobile Phone Technologies." *Mobilities* 4 (1): 37–58.

Olander, Anni. 2008. "Darth Vader ja lahjan arvoitus.Vaihdon merkitykset lasten vertaissuhteissa" [Darth Vader and the Enigma of the Gift: The Meaning of Exchange in Children's Peer Relations]. M.A thesis in anthropology, University of Helsinki.

Pearce, Celia. 2006. "Productive Play: Game Culture from the Bottom Up." *Games and Culture* 1 (1): 17–24.

Prahalad, C.K., and Venkat Ramaswamy. 2004. "Co-creation Experiences: The Next Practice in Value Creation." *Journal of Interactive Marketing* 18 (3): 5–14.

Prout, Alan. 2005. *The Future of Childhood*. New York: RoutledgeFalmer.

Pruitt, John, and Tamara Adlin. 2006. *The Persona Lifecycle: Keeping People in Mind throughout Product Design*. Amsterdam: Elsevier.

Ritzer, George, and Nathan Jurgenson. 2010. "Production, Consumption, Prosumption: The Nature of Capitalism in the Age of the Digital 'Prosumer.'" *Journal of Consumer Culture* 10 (1): 13–36.

Ruckenstein, Minna. 2010a. "Toying with the World: Children, Virtual Pets and the Value of Mobility." *Childhood* 11 (4): 501–12.

Ruckenstein, Minna. 2010b. "Time Scales of Consumption: Children, Money and Transactional Orders." *Journal of Consumer Culture* 10 (3): 383–404.

Ruckenstein, Minna. 2011. "Children in Creationist Capitalism: The Corporate Value of Sociality." *Information, Communication and Society* 14, no. 7: 1060–76.

Ruckenstein, Minna. 2012. "Playing Nintendogs: Valued Objects, Desire and the Creative Potential of Human Action." Paper presented at the Nordic Conference on Consumer Research, Gothenburg, Sweden.

Ruckenstein, Minna. Forthcoming. "Spatial Extensions of Childhood: From Toy Worlds to Online Communities." *Children's Geographies*.

Schor, Juliet B. 2004. *Born to Buy: The Commercialized Child and the New Consumer Culture*. New York: Scribner.

Sherzer, Joel. 1987. "A Discourse-Centered Approach to Language and Culture." *American Anthropologist* 89 (2): 295–309.

Thrift, Nigel. 2005. *Knowing Capitalism*. London: Sage.

Urban, Greg. 1993. *A Discourse-Centered Approach to Culture*. Austin: University of Texas Press.

Urban, Greg. 1996. *Metaphysical Community*. Austin: University of Texas Press.

Urban, Greg. 2001. *Metaculture*. Minneapolis: University of Minnesota Press.

Van Maanen, John. 2006. "Ethnography Then and Now." *Qualitative Research in Organization and Management* 1 (1): 13–21.

Wasko, Janet. 2010. "Children's Virtual Worlds: The Latest Commercialization of Children's Culture." In *Childhood and Consumer Culture*, edited by David Buckingham and Vegbjørg Tingstadt, 113–129. Basingstoke, UK: Palgrave Macmillan.

Weber, Sandra, and Shanly Dixon, eds. 2007. *Growing up Online: Young People and Digital Technologies*. New York: Palgrave Macmillan.

Wolcott, Harry. 1999. *Ethnography: A Way of Seeing*. Walnut Creek, CA: AltaMira.

6   A Situated Video Interview Method
Understanding the Interplay between Human Engagement and the Power of Scripted Animations of a Virtual World

Sisse Siggaard Jensen

The world of Second Life is an example of a persistent and immersive multiuser virtual environment (MUVE) that generates a sense of *being inside* the world (Blascovich and Bailenson 2011), hence the embodied experience of *being there together* with other actors and their avatars (Schroeder 2011). In Second Life, the sense of *being there* inside a world results from metaphors of worldliness and from the many scripted animations of the world that are meant to generate the movement and change so characteristic of the experience of living in a world. This worldliness of Second Life is mediated by *visual* and *spatial* metaphors of land and sea, islands and mainland, corners of the world, sunrise and sunset, virtual places and square meters, by the notion of residents and inhabitants and by animated avatars that travel and teleport around and between places and islands. These metaphors and animations organize the conception and perception of the multiuser virtual environment, and they produce a sense of the virtual environment *as if* it were a world.

The animated graphical figures of avatars have important parts to play in this mediation of the sense of *being there together* with other human actors while moving around and acting in the world. The avatars refer to the online presence of human actors, and they do so by semiotic reference and by scripted and animated movements of a body or an object. The many processes of avatar design and redesign undertaken by the human actors and residents of the world create a close relationship and attachment between human actors and nonhuman avatars. This attachment is a well-documented phenomenon in current research on virtual worlds (Jensen 2007, 2010, 2012; Jin and Park 2009; Jin 2010; Magnenat-Thalmann and Thalmann 1999; Schroeder 2002, 2011; Schroeder and Axelsson 2006; L. Taylor 2011; T. Taylor 2006), and it is critical to the immersive experience of *being there* inside the virtual world. In long-term engagement, human actors together with their chosen avatar(s) thus produce a complex in-world and offline personal and social history. A history that can be traced and followed, among others, along the many processes of design and redesign of virtual places, avatar(s) with their outfits, and virtual artifacts and media of the world (Jensen 2012). That is, we can follow the dynamic processes of change that are typical of a virtual world like Second Life which is generated by residents' co-construction of the environment and content. How can we, then, carry out research in which we follow these dynamic processes in order to gain analytical insight into the situated engagement of actors as they co-construct virtual worlds as experienced worlds?

In this chapter, I present methodological reflections on a particular video interview method designed to produce and analyze visual and spatial data that provide insight into how human actors with avatar(s) engage with their virtual being and agency. The data are designed for analyses that focus on the organization and reorganization of the world, and, in particular, the many movements and changes made possible by scripted animations that contribute to the sense of *being there together* in the virtual world.

As presented here, the video interview method presupposes that the experience and the sense of *being there* are constitutive to human engagement with virtual being. This sense, and the actual and situated realization of it, is a phenomenon hard to explore through retrospective methods such as qualitative interviews or to capture in video observational studies of action and interaction, if applied separately. From research on human–computer interaction and interface design, we know that it is difficult to memorize and explain in an interview how we navigate an interface, manipulate an artifact such as an input device, or articulate and express the experience of bodily motor senses when we engage with scripted animations. In video observational studies, in contrast, we can follow some of these actions from an external perspective. However, it is only to some degree that we can gain insight into the many interpretations of such engagement or help the participants of our study to explicate or catalyze their reflections. Video recordings can help us observe, and thus acquire knowledge about, action, emotion, and movement from an external perspective whereas in-depth qualitative interviews provide insight into some of the associated interpretations and reflections. In order to provide both forms of knowledge, the method of video interviews integrates observational video recordings and qualitative in-depth interviews in the study of situated engagement with virtual worlds.

To illustrate the use of the video interview method, I have chosen a situation of engagement from a case study of the Second Life *Literary project* in a public institution. The chosen situation of engagement is a weekly virtual meeting between the project team and some of their professional colleagues, a meeting on a national scale. With images from the recordings of this situation, I analyze and demonstrate how the situation is organized and reorganized by scripted media animations as exemplified by an animated virtual couch.

This chapter does not claim to address all the methodological questions concerning the use of visual data methods. Rather, it aspires to *exemplify* the use of video interviews in the study of virtual worlds and thus to substantiate the argument that the integration of video observational studies and in-depth qualitative interviews in situated video interviews produces valuable knowledge about how scripted animations organize, transform, and reorganize the assemblages of human engagement with the technologies of virtual worlds.

The first part of the chapter presents approaches, methodologies, and concepts that have been drawn on in the development of video analysis methods in general. I concentrate on the ones that I have drawn on as sources of inspiration in developing my video interview method: visual anthropology and ethnography, video interaction analysis, and situational analysis, as well as the concepts of situatedness and assemblages. Second, based on the wider methodology, I raise issues and questions to be dealt with in a video interview. These issues and questions are then exemplified by the case study. Through the example, I demonstrate how to prepare the recordings and produce the situated recordings and how to prepare the analysis and construct and use a storyboard for analytical purposes. Following this, some of the problems and weaknesses of the video interview method are discussed, and finally, the conclusion points to the complexity of analyzing human entanglement with technology in actual use situations.

THEORY AND METHOD

Visual Anthropology and Ethnography

Methods of video interviews have been developed within visual anthropology and ethnography. The question of how to research and communicate embodied experience is a distinctive research issue in the history of visual anthropology. It has been dealt with since the early observational and documentary photographic and cinematic studies of foreign cultures (Mead 1995; Mead and Bateson 2002), but it is also part of contemporary studies based on cultural theory and phenomenological approaches to sensory experience and knowledge (Banks 2001, 2007; Berger 2008; J. Collier and Collier 1967; M. Collier 2001; Grimshaw 2001, 2005; MacDougall 1995, 1998, 2001, 2002; Pink 2001, 2005, 2006, 2009a). The uses of documentary film and photography as research tools and communication media have been seen as a means to communicate sensory experience and the many related knowledge forms. In the course of establishing visual anthropology as an academic discipline, the interest in documentaries gradually decreased as the development of the discipline has turned towards writing. In a recent book, however, the anthropologist and social scientist Sarah Pink (2006) points to the accessibility and ease of use of digital and visual media as one among many developments that influence research methodologies and methods in a digital and networked era. She suggests that future research should consider the use of audio-visual methods, despite her emphasis on the fact that our audio-visual senses only partly mediate embodied sensory experience. To research and communicate sensory experience, Pink therefore suggests that we use the audio-visual medium of video in combination with qualitative interviews, even if this is still a limited representation of an integrated sensorium. In her study of everyday housework and home decoration, she shows how candles, oils, and perfume play a prominent role in the dialogue when interviewees show and describe their homes during video interviews (Pink 2005).¹ In contrast, in his phenomenology of the senses the visual anthropologist and filmmaker, MacDougall (1995, 1998, 2001) suggests that we consider senses as integrated rather than separate modes of perception which means that, by amplifying some senses such as audio and vision, we also evoke the others. Thus, he sees visual experience as a pathway to other senses as it evokes embodied qualities. Watching a film evokes not only audio-visual senses but also touch and kinesthetic as exemplified by the endless car chases in action movies and the battles with horrific monsters in online game play.

In research on virtual worlds and their avatars, the virtual has been seen and constructed as a separate virtual sphere and space in parallel to real space (Bell and Kennedy 2000; Benedikt 1993; Biocca 1997; Boelstorff 2008; Gunkel 2007, 2010; Jones 1994; Levy 1997; Porter 1997; see Chapter 1, this book). This construction of separate spheres and spaces has led some researchers to see avatars as a kind of disembodied representation of the person behind the avatar, a virtual identity that may involve wishful thinking, deceptive expression (Reid 1995), and identity play with no real consequences because it is detached from the real and embodied identity. However, MacDougall's understanding of the integrated sensorium questions this understanding. If we accept MacDougall's emphasis on the integration of senses as mediated by the visual, it makes no sense to separate the two spheres and spaces. Engaging with the avatars of virtual worlds may be seen as just another kind of embodied sensory experience. This is accentuated in the case of virtual worlds and online role-playing games, where the audio-visual and motor senses are evoked by the many scripted animations of, among others, movement, monsters, threats, and achievement.

Emphasizing the importance of embodied, sensory and emotional experience in the analysis of situated engagement with virtual worlds, in the video interview method I draw on knowledge gained from visual and ethnographic studies. These worlds are seen as part of an assemblage and entanglement of embodied and virtual engagement. And, in the example I present and discuss in this chapter, it is shown how the scripted animations evoke visual and motor senses. The scripted animations, among others, make avatars walk, fly, and sit, they open doors and kill monsters—all of this enabled by small scripts attached to virtual objects and actions. The animations are scripted to move and transform these objects and actions and to generate bodily senses and emotional responses. In the video interview method, I strive to make such senses and responses part of the analysis.

Video Interaction Analysis

Video interaction analysis is another source of inspiration for the video interview method. Workplace technology, organization, and practices have been the subjects of anthropologist Brigitte Jordan's and computer scientist Austin

Henderson's research since the mid-1980s. Their article on the foundation and practice of video interaction analysis suggests an ethnomethodological approach to the use of video recordings in ethnographic workplace studies (Jordan and Henderson 1995). In the outline of their approach and practice, they suggest seven foci of observation and analysis: the structure of events, segmentation, temporal and spatial organization of activity, turn taking, participation structures, trouble and repair, and artifacts and documents. The focus of their research is on the organization and reorganization of artifacts, space, and human interaction. They see the reorganization of situations of human interaction as initiated and followed by a reorganization of patterns of spatial and temporal organization. The mapping of how situations of interaction are organized and reorganized is a first step of analysis in Jordan and Henderson's method, but the analytical interest is particularly strong with regard to so-called trouble-and-repair situations, when prevailing patterns break up and undergo significant chances. Usually such situations will reorganize the patterns of organization and interaction (Jensen 2005). In workplace studies, an ethnomethodological method has been practiced with a particular focus on trouble and repair situations and on the reorganization of prevailing patterns of interaction and organization. Similarly, in her research on human–computer interaction and interface design, anthropologist Lucy Suchman has studied the everyday practices of technology design and, in particular, situations of usage. In her research, the analytical focus is on the entanglement of human and machine and in the study of an airline observation room, "Ops Room," observational video recording was applied (Suchman and Trigg 1991). In this, Suchman emphasizes the importance of understanding human practices in particular the *situatedness* of action and interaction.

The video interaction analysis approach has profoundly influenced the video interview method, but there are also important differences. In video interaction analysis, the seven foci of the approach refer to observational video recordings whereas, in the video interview, the approach also embraces in-depth dialogues between the researcher and the participants in the video interview. Also, in the video interview method, the situatedness of human agency is emphasized as it is in video interaction analysis, but a stronger emphasis is placed on the analytical relevance of the bodily and emotional responses of human engagement.

Situation and Situatedness

The concepts of situation and situatedness have been dealt with in theory and practice within several knowledge domains—philosophy, cognitive science, feminist studies, human–computer interaction sciences and in a further development of grounded theory. In the study of language, philosopher Ludwig Wittgenstein stated, "Don't think but look" (Wittgenstein 1953, 66) when he argued for the study of actual language use cases rather than of abstract representations. Wittgenstein's philosophical investigations of language thus initiated a turn from abstract generalizations to descriptions of actual usage. This development from abstract generalization to actual use and practice can also be found in the field of cognitive science. Early thoughts and research on cognitive science were inspired by information processing sciences but gradually theories of situated and embodied cognition emerged. Moreover, feminist studies and research carried out by Donna Haraway (1988), a researcher of the history of consciousness, has also contributed significantly to our understanding of the situatedness of human cognition, arguing for the partiality of knowledge construction.

A similar development took place as digital technology gave rise to computer science and to theories of system development in the 1970s. Critical research on the development of computer systems took concrete and situated practices as a point of departure in order to improve the design of system interfaces. The ideas of design-oriented and situated research on practices was put forward by, among others, Lucy Suchman in her contribution to the very foundation of the science of human–computer interaction and in her contributions to the sociology of science and technology studies (Suchman 1987, 1993, 2000).

In the video interview method, recordings and dialogues in situ and in actual practices are crucial. This is inspired by the different fields of research mentioned earlier: philosophical investigations have shown that meaning making occurs in language use; the situatedness of bodily and tacit knowledge has proved crucial to cognitive processes; the partiality and situatedness of knowledge construction were made apparent by feminist studies; and human–computer interface design showed that situated use is key to the understanding of the use of technology.

Situational Analysis

The notion of situation and situatedness is also pivotal to a recent development of grounded theory method. In her method of situational analysis, sociologist Adele Clarke (2003) proposes three sets of analytical maps—situational, social worlds/arenas, and positional (Clarke and Friese 2007)—as a way to enter into and conduct empirical analyses based on grounded theory. In doing so, she critiques earlier versions of grounded theory with respect to their understanding of context. According to Clarke, there is no such thing as a context that surrounds and conditions the emergent and contingent processes of ongoing actions and negotiations of social worlds; rather, the conditions are *in* the situation. In other words, the actors, human and nonhuman, the many actions, negotiations, and the discourses involved in any situation *constitute* the situation; they are not constituted by it. Situational mapping therefore entails the identification of what is present and/or absent in any given situation. Thus, a careful mapping of the human and nonhuman actors, the ongoing negotiations and discourses, and the ways they interrelate are tools for the analyses of the construction of situations, according to Clarke.

The situational mapping approach has inspired the formulation of questions and the modes of questioning in a video interview analysis; questions and modes that are exemplified in Figure 6.1.

Assemblages

This understanding of situations and situatedness has many things in common with the ideas of assemblages, as also recently mentioned by Clarke (Clarke and Friese 2007, 390). The concept of assemblages was developed in philosophy (DeLanda 2006; Goodchild 1996), and it is crucial to the study of the interrelations of human and technology as dealt with in science and technology studies and actor-network-theory (Bowker and Star 1999, 2000; Latour 1991, 1995, 2005, 2011; Law 2004). From an actor-network theoretical viewpoint, assemblages are seen as constellations and conjunctions of humans and nonhumans that continuously connect and stabilize and disconnect and dissolve because they are made and transformed by actions, negotiations and translations. Unlike the mappings of Clarke's situational analyses, however, an actor-network study of assemblages will, metaphorically speaking, start by grasping the end of threads to follow how they connect, with what and whom they are connected, how the connections emerge, form actor-networks, eventually disconnect, and transform. What connects at one time and instance may disconnect at a later point. To follow how humans and technology connect and to understand the complexity of assemblages as they emerge, become denser and dissolve, involve a methodology that combines long-term, in-depth case studies and situated micro-moment studies of instances and situations of engagement.

In the video interview method, engagement is conceptualized as an assemblage. The assemblages of engagement have a temporal organization, experiential qualities, and affiliated modes of action and interaction. Engagement is emotionally expressed, cognitively processed; it is enacted in some way(s) aimed at some thing(s), it connects and organizes temporal processes, it comes into being and it ends, it is changed and transformed, or it dissolves. My method of video interviews has been designed in order to capture such complexity through its application in long-term case studies and micro-moment analyses.

METHODOLOGICAL FRAMEWORK

The above approaches and concepts have contributed to the methodological framework. The *situated* video interview method enables us to embrace emotional expressions, embodied responses, and physical aspects. A basic assumption about virtuality in the video interview analytical approach is that *being there* in a virtual world is embodied rather than disembodied and that engagement is intertwined with the bodily senses of being in a physical environment.

Analytical Foci and Questions

From the video interaction analysis method, the set of seven analytical foci is borrowed, and, importantly, the method points to the analytical potential of situations involving trouble and repair and the reorganization of prevailing patterns of organization and interaction. In situational analysis, a situation is seen as constitutive rather than contextual; therefore, a careful mapping of a situation is undertaken to observe and ask questions about what is present or absent, different or the same, and what is connected or disconnected. Reorganizations, breaks, changes, and disturbances are analytical foci that are crucial to such observation and analysis. The notion of patterns stems from the video interactional analysis method, but in a video interview method, patterns are seen as only momentarily stable. Therefore, the concept of assemblages is borrowed from actor-network-theory in order to point to the emergent and contingent nature of human connections and our use of nonhuman technologies and artifacts. When seen from this point of view, patterns and networks of connections between human actors and nonhuman technology may be formed and stabilized, as is the case with human actors' attachment to their avatars, but from one moment to the next, this attachment, pattern, and network may be reorganized or dissolve as new networks emerge.

In order to turn these reflections into a methodological framework for video interviews and analysis, I have summarized central questions in Figure 6.1. This summary is not a list to be followed slavishly. In some cases, all of the questions are relevant, in other situations only a few make sense, and additional questions are often needed. The summary therefore only serves to exemplify the systematic line of thought that guides the video interview method.

Qualitative Case Study

In order to illustrate the use of the video interview approach, I now present an analysis of a virtual meeting situation from a case study of the Second Life Literary project. This case study is one among many that I have carried out about human actors and their making sense of their engagement with virtual worlds (Jensen 2007, 2008). In these studies, the qualitative methodology of case studies allowed me to follow the human actors and their engagement with the nonhuman technologies *over time* in long-term processes involving a range of different research methods. The Literary project was chosen as an object of study among a range of possible cases. A central reason for its selection was the project's active participation in the national

	Foci of a video interview	Questions to consider
1.	Relevance	What is the relevance of this method?
		What is the relevance of this situation?
2.	Positioning	How does the researcher position herself
		in the video interview situations?
3.	Emergence	How did the situations come about?
4.	Spatial and temporal organisation	What/who organises the situations? How
		is it organised?
	and patterns of participation	What/who participates in the organisation?
		How do they participate?
5.	Situational analysis	What holds the situation together?
	presence/absence	What/who is present in the situation and
		what/who is absent?
	arrivals/disappearances	What/who moves, who arrives and who
		disappears, what things come in and what
		goes out? How do they arrive/disappear,
		come in/go out?
	differences/samenesses	What/who is different and what/who is the
		same?
	connections/disconnections	What/who are connected and what conn-
		ections dissolve, what/who are disconnected?
		How do they connect and/or disconnect?
6.	Reorganisations of the situations	What leads to a reorganisation?
	changes	What changes are made, and how are
		they made, what is changed?
	break downs	What transformations are made and what
		is transformed?
	transformations	What breaks occur?
	disturbances	What disturbances occur and what disturbs?
7.	Ending	How do the situations of engagement come
		to end? How does the video interview situ-
		ation end?

Figure 6.1   Video interview foci and questions to consider

Danish public debate about virtual worlds as the project was subject to criti- cal debate on blogs and within the profession involved. The approach of the Literary project team can be illustrated by the Second Life phrase "not possible in real life," that emphasizes the differences in this case between professional practices in-world and offline. This approach was a source of extensive criticism and, at times, a very emotional debate. Members of the profession expressed the criticism and debate in-world at meetings, in inter- views and dialogues with members of the project team, and on blogs about virtual worlds. Conversely, with this approach the project also explicitly disputed the endeavor of many Second Life projects to mirror and brand their real-life agency and organization in-world. The project appeared to be a melting pot of emotions, approaches to projects and professional practices and identity, and the meaningfulness or meaninglessness of *being there* in virtual worlds. Because of these qualities, the case was selected during extensive virtual field studies as the object of one of my qualitative case studies of virtual world projects (Jensen 2010, 2012).

The video interview method is only one method among several that I applied to the case study. The other methods include observations at the virtual place, text analysis of blogs and newspaper discussions, participation in debates and interviews, observation at the project team's workplace, meetings and content production in collaboration with the project team members, planning of virtual events, participation in such events and at physical locations, and follow-up talks after the project was closed. Not until late in the case study were the video interviews made with each of the participants in the project team and of the project's weekly meetings. This is to say that it is crucial to carefully select the situations for video interviews because the visual and spatial data produced in situated recordings allow us to do micro-moment studies and the analysis of overwhelmingly dense and diverse data.

For the present example one of the weekly meetings has been selected because (1) the beginnings and endings of the situation are marked; (2) the organization of a session like this is recognizable and well-known, at least from our experience in physical environments; (3) the project team involved usually organizes the meeting sessions together so they are colocated during the session which enables the recording of their dialogues; and (4) over time, these sessions turn out to be the main activity of the project.

VIDEO INTERVIEWS: THE LITERARY PROJECT'S WEEKLY MEETINGS

In this section, I exemplify how the foci and questions that are summarized in Figure 6.1 were used in video interviews with the project team of the Literary project. The examples concentrate on how scripted animations organize and reorganize the project team's situated engagement with the world of Second Life.

The Video Interview Situation Comes into Being

The initial contact and involvement with the project was caused by a scripted animation. During one of the in-world project sessions, my avatar's presence was noticed by one of the project team members and I was invited to join in. My intention, however, was to not interfere with the meeting in a way that was intrusive to the on-going dialogues. But following the join-in invitation, an animated virtual chair was rezzed[2] with a script that caused an instant reorganization of the meeting circle to also include me. The animated chair, and the way it was scripted to bring a new participant into the circle, formed the basis for a follow-up chat with the project team about the design of this chair. The case study was initiated, then, by a welcoming attitude scripted and shaped like a virtual chair with the power to smoothly reorganize a meeting situation and circle. Thus, with respect to questions about what was present in the emergence of the video interview situations, the answer seems to be the animated chairs, but absences should also be addressed. During the initial observations of the animated meeting circle, the absence of a formal meeting structure was conspicuous. There was no meeting table, agenda, or formal turn takings of speech. The meeting was organized by the animated chairs with the rounded off circle and characterized by an informal exchange of ideas. On one hand, this organization resembled an informal meeting in physical space; on the other hand, the animated chairs made possible a virtual organization simultaneously open to newcomers and closed in a circle that generated a sense of closeness. Thus, the "not possible in real life" vision of the project was made quite tangible in virtual terms.

In contrast, setting up the video interview was quite a different process. This situation was prepared in collaboration with the project team at their workplace and realized at the usual weekday of their virtual meetings. I carried out initial video interviews with each of the organizers at their offices. These video interviews were meant to cover questions about their virtual project and the preparations of the virtual meetings. The accounts of preparations revealed some of the many institutional and technological issues with which the project team had to deal in the realization of the project. The virtual meeting, for instance, had to take place in a separate office with computers dedicated to this purpose because of the many security procedures of the institution. Therefore, the virtual engagement was separated from the project team's daily practices at their workplace.

To Record in the Situation

The spatial and temporal organization of the video interview situation that I am about to analyze is organized by an assemblage of three simultaneous situations. They constitute and organize the situation (1) in relationships between the interviewer and the interviewees; (2) by the virtual artifacts, animations, chat, and instant-messaging (IM) dialogues of the virtual meeting situation; and (3) in the physical location and dialogue between the organizers of the virtual meeting. These three situations constitute and organize the video interview.

Entering the Recording Situation

Any observation study raises questions concerning the positioning of the interviewer and observer in relation to the participants in the practices under observation. This is particularly so when the observations entail video recordings integrated with qualitative interviews. In a physical and tangible sense, the choice of place indicates an approach to the participants and to the knowledge produced. In the Literary case study, closeness and collaboration with the participant(s) constitute the video interview. The recordings are made with a handheld camera beside the participants in situ, that is, in the participants' usual surroundings. This positioning indicates that the qualitative video interview is seen and conceived as a collaborative effort involving the co-construction of meaning, sense, and knowledge. By being positioned beside the participant(s), a choice has been made that constitutes the spatial organization of the video interview situation as such.

Being There and Being Here

The sense of being *there* inside a virtual world, as outlined in the introduction of this chapter, is mirrored in a sense of being *here* in front of the computer and screen, hence a movement *from here to there*. The participants in the video interview frequently express this sense of movement, and they do so in spatial terms. According to the participants, what is felt and seen as *here* and *there* continuously shifts between situations. To exemplify this, if, for instance, the participants' attention is focused on the animated movement of their avatar from one in-world place to another when teleporting from island to island, then the movement is conceived and expressed in spatial terms as seen and felt from *inside* the world—from an on-the-screen view in terms of a video interview. In contrast, if the participants' attention is focused on the expression of their avatar changing its looks and design, then the *here* of the sense of presence is expressed from an outside-in view that foregrounds a by-the-screen view. In other words, the participants' focus of attention continuously shifts between several forms of *here* and *there* and in a complexity of felt and experienced situations, as exemplified by *on-the-screen* and *by-the-screen* views of the video interview. The method therefore produces on-the-screen views that are constituted and framed by the computer screen and by-the-screen views defined by the camera(s) and the researcher's focus and angling of the recordings. The snapshots in Figures 6.2 and 6.3 illustrate these two different views.

Zones of foregrounding are a technique that helps us compose the focus of video interview recordings. This is so in virtual as well as physical environments. Depending on the technology and media involved, the spatial and temporal organization will vary; in the present case, computer screens are constitutive to the composition of zones. The zones of foregrounding serve to focus our attention, establish our vantage points, and direct the angling of the video recordings.

Such foregrounding is a construct rather than a quality or property of a foreground, and it always implies that something else is in the background—often, the zones formerly foregrounded. It is important to consider the questions of foregrounding in any kind of observational study, but even more so in video interviews because the camera angle and the scope are much narrower than the vantage points of human perception. In the study of the virtual Second Life meeting session, the zones of foregrounding involve recordings made with two different camera types. Second Life's in-world camera foregrounds the virtual meeting situation, and recordings are made by screen-

Figure 6.2   Different views in the video interview, 1

[Snapshot 1. The avatar Rob wears a white T-shirt and Alice is in a red T-shirt as they participate in a Second Life meeting with colleagues within their profession. This snapshot exemplifies on-the-screen views. The participant's use of the in-world camera and the frame of the computer screen define this view.]

capture software. The data of the recordings with the Second Life camera comprise in-world snapshots and machinima.[3] The machinimas complement the offline video interview recordings. The complexity of this video interview is formed through a data assemblage of two in-world machinima recordings, each made by the participants of the video interview in combination with by-the-screen video recordings that capture dialogues and actions on location.

Whatever the camera setup, however, video interviews are always angled even with the most advanced surveillance technology. In the case of the in-world recordings, as exemplified by the two snapshots from the Literary case in Figures 6.2 and 6.3, the participants of the video interview are in control of the foregrounding by their actions and engagement. The participants control the in-world camera and hence the angling of the virtual meeting situation by actions, in-world chat, and instant messaging. The interviewer, on the other hand, decides the recordings of the video interview situation by the screen.

Questions of what and how to foreground, the decisions to be made about the angling of the recordings and questions about who controls the foregrounding of zones are some of the questions to consider in the preparation of video interviews.

Figure 6.3   Different views in the video interview, 2

[Snapshot 2. The actors Mads and Janne with their avatars Rob and Alice organise the virtual meeting in a separate office at their workplace. This snapshot exemplifies by-the-screen views. This view is defined by the camera and the researcher's focus and angling of the recordings in the physical environment.]

THE VIRTUAL MEETING SITUATION

Preparing the Analysis

The processing of data is systematic. Sequences are not selected without several viewings, and comprehensive descriptions of the recordings are made. Reverse storyboarding and the selection of key frames are some of the systematic procedures that help prepare the data for analysis.

After the in situ recordings, the videos are looked through in different modes, for instance, in a mode with no audio or with some sequences in slow motion. This allows the analyst to defer the interpretation and perception of the recordings. In a view without audio and language, it is easier to focus on the spatial and interactional organization and reorganization of situations and on the nonverbal communication such as facial expression, body language and interactional orientation. These first views are then annotated with text and/or keywords, indicating major reorganizations and nonverbal expressions. As soon as language is included in our analysis, it tends to dominate the interpretations of the situation. Whether or not to fully transcribe the recordings depends on their analytical importance. In the Literary case, the video recordings were fully transcribed. The dialogues of by-the-screen views were transcribed in text, and, similarly, the video recordings were visually transcribed by snapshots generated by analytical software every five hundred milliseconds of the recordings.[4] In addition, annotations were made of the combined video and audio recordings.

The next steps in the process of preparing the data for analysis identify the stepping-stones of the visual analysis. During the processes of annotating the videos, some sequences and snapshots of particular analytical interest are marked as key sequences and key frames that are snapshots of single video frames. Each video frame and snapshot represents a key frame visualizing a scene of significance to the foci of analysis. These key frames are the visual resources of recomposed analytical storyboards as exemplified in the tables of the next section.

Analyzing the Data

Sameness and difference: The virtual meeting situation in focus in this analysis is organized by virtual artifacts. The virtual floor and the carpet outline the meeting place, and throughout the video interview this place is foregrounded by the in-world cameras. Animated chairs and pillows organize the situation. The chairs and pillows which animate the sitting postures of the avatars, and the carpet and the floor are all freebies. The animated chairs of the rounded circle previously mentioned are absent. It appears that the script stopped working, and it could not be repaired. The lack of these chairs means that an important preparation for the meeting is to move the virtual chairs and pillows so that the participating avatars face each other. In Figure 6.4, the pillow with the yellow highlighted line is wrongly positioned, which means that Alice, the avatar of one of the project team organizers, Janne, turns her back to the group. To open the meeting, the organizers therefore have to focus on changing this position to turn around the avatar, Alice.

Mads:	I'll push your chair a bit.
Janne:	Yes, it looks completely silly.
Mads:	Just come; sit behind this, hey!
Janne:	Ihh, my arm. Can't you come to me?
Mads:	Yes, but can you not sort it out yourself, or what?
Janne:	I cannot get to see myself [using the in-world camera].
Mads:	Well, I will help you.
Janne:	Yes, oh, maybe I can manage.
Mads:	I think I have just turned you around.
Janne:	That's it! That's fine, yes!

Figure 6.4   Snapshot 1 from situated video interview

These reorganizations point to the sameness of the situation compared to typical interactional patterns of face-to-face meetings in physical environments. This interactional pattern is not a necessary positioning and orientation among avatars but it appears to be vital to generate the sense of being there together.

Presence and absence: In the background of the meeting situation, quite surprisingly some animated blue bubbles invite visiting avatars to meditate, and we get a glimpse of a red scene which is used for the project's in-world events. These animations contribute to the overall organization of the place, which is divided into the meeting place, the meditation bubbles, and the scene for virtual events. But the bubbles and the scene are absent during the session; they all stay in the background.

The general impression of the outline, and the organization of the place, is a lack of overall design considerations. The design appears to be a bit messy as if generated spontaneously according to actual events and depending on what virtual artifacts can be found in in-world freebie boxes. This absence of an overall design layout points to a lack of economic resources and to the original idea of the project to direct public audiences' attention to virtual world media. The idea was to involve interested users of the public institution to partake in the design of the virtual place. This vision, however, had to be abandoned due to messy and pointless design.

Reorganization of the meeting situation: Figures 6.4 through 6.9 (key frames) form a storyboard that is key to the analysis. The storyboard shows how the virtual meeting situation is organized and reorganized, how trouble and repair situations occur during the meeting, and how scripted animations have a part to play. Quotes from the dialogues by the screen are also included together with my annotations and comments to the quotes.

A Storyboard from the Video Interview

Strong emotions and animated media: Three avatars and a white dog are present in the situation I have chosen to analyze here. The avatar Sils, who sits in the black chair, immediately attracts the attention of the project team. They start discussing who she is because she is not one of the regular participants. Conclusions are drawn from her appearance, outfit, and Second Life profile. In Figure 6.5, Mads points to an artifact lying on the floor. It is an animated record holding a box of music. In the dialogue among the members of the project team, surprise and excitement are emotions strongly expressed in the nonverbal responses to the avatar Sils, her appearance, and her many animated media. The attention of the project team is focused on the avatar Sils.

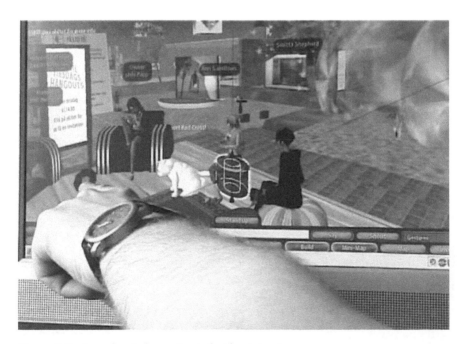

Figure 6.5   Snapshot 2 from situated video interview

Sisse: Do you know her?

Janne: I don't know her. She has been here [in Second Life] for a long
                time, I think. She has expensive hair, and lots of bling, bling.
                She has spent money.

Mads: Maybe she wants to sell something?

Janne: I don't think so

(. . .)

Janne: I've got a fantastic box of music! [from the avatar Sils]

*[Janne is enthusiastic, the box fascinates her, and she almost shouts and
bounces up and down in her chair. Her facial expression shows joy and
surprise. In the chat, capital letters, exclamation marks, and signs express
the excitement.]*

Mads: Yeah, [checking the profile], a member of Denmark and Hip
                Joint [two in-world groups]; she is from Copenhagen Denmark
                [an island in Second Life], I think. Yes, I think so. She says of
                herself: just from Denmark."

*[Janne and Mads focus their attention on the scrutiny of the avatar Sils's
profile]*

Speculations about the avatar Sils and scrutiny of her virtual profile continue during the ongoing meeting session. Figure 6.6 is a zoom-in on Sils,
and it refers to how, again and again, the focus of the project team and their

Figure 6.6   Snapshot 3 from situated video interview

Figure 6.7 Snapshot 4 from situated video interview

dialogue is concerned with Sils, as she continues to rezz and drop animated items and media on the floor.

The meeting situation which is shown in Figure 6.7 shows the general organization of the meeting and the interactional pattern of this. From an external perspective, not much happens. Still, the situation is quite complex. A public chat discussion about the project takes place, simultaneous IM dialogues are exchanged between the project team and some of the participants of the virtual meeting, and there are continuous dialogues between the project team members by the screen. There is a complex of simultaneous dialogues and exchanges of ideas throughout the meeting.

Sisse: What did you find out about her?

Janne: I think she is well educated. There are not many Danes who speak German, Danish, Jutlandish and English! Oh woooow! She has such stylish shoes. She has also got a g-string and everything, sticking up above. She is really modern!

[Janne's excitement about the avatar's shoes evokes a strong bodily response; she almost shouts and gesticulates to emphasize her admiration and surprise. Shoes are Janne's passion. Her attention therefore immediately shifts away from my question to focus on her passion for shoes.]

Mads: I think she is from Korsør [a town in Denmark].

Janne: She has everything, including a huge cat.

Mads: It is a dog.

[Mads' responses are calm; his tone of voice is neutral as he tries to figure out who the avatar Sils is, where she comes from, and why she is present at their meeting.]

Janne: No, that's a cat. I have to find out where she bought her shoes. Her shoes! Noooo! I've got a red dress. Yes! See! I've got a dress for L$ 5. That is sooo cheap. I want to know if she is here for professional reasons. I would like to know if she is joining our meeting, or if she just wants company.

(. . .)

Janne: Have you offered her membership? It is your job! I just got shoes! Oh!! And plates.

[Sils continues to rezz and juggle media, clothes, and objects. Janne and Mads are fascinated as they watch and comment on Sils's show even to the extent that Janne has to remind Mads of his duties as the organiser of the meeting, only to be led astray again when Sils donates a pair of shoes and a red dress.]

The animated couch: Halfway, the avatar Sils suddenly rezzes an animated couch. The scripted animation of the body posture is fairly advanced, inviting, and with sexual connotations as shown in Figure 6.8. This animated couch reorganizes the interaction pattern and the dialogue. Again, it attracts

Figure 6.8   Snapshot 5 from situated video interview

Figure 6.9   Snapshot 6 from situated video interview

the project team's full attention. In Figures 6.8 and 6.9, the avatar Rob therefore stands to face the couch and to try it. Rob stays beside the couch and the avatar Sils throughout the remaining meeting session.

Sisse: Now she stood up from the armchair.

Janne: Well, now she is lying down! What kind of furniture!!? See the posture! It is not ours! [the couch] Where does it come from?

[Sils rezzes an animated couch scripted to posture the female avatar in a challenging way loaded with sexual connotations.]

Mads: Okay, ha, ha [laughing loud], now I would like to invite her into the group, ha, ha.

[Mads is now fascinated; his response is immediate; he laughs and expresses his enjoyment in front of the screen as well as in-world. He moves the avatar Rob to approach Sils and the couch.]

Janne: It is . . . not here! It is forbidden! Up on Mads' long legs!

[Janne reacts to the situation as she tries to stop it from evolving. Mads's attention is now fully focussed on the couch and Sils; he finds the situation amusing and entertaining even if it leads his focus on the meeting astray. He is eager to try the couch and to see the male posture. His calmness has changed into joy and fascination.]

Mads: Yes, I have just invited her.

The situation dissolves: later in the meeting, a new female avatar enters the meeting place. She is also a showcase of advanced, flashy, and funny animations. The project team wonders if the two avatars are friends who travel the world of Second Life together.

The animations appear to take over the control of the remaining part of the meeting.

THE POWER OF SCRIPTED ANIMATIONS

In the storyboard example of the Second Life meeting session among participants from the same profession, I have presented the five analytical steps summarized in Figure 6.1: the emergence of the situation, the spatial and temporal organization of the place and patterns of participation, situational mapping, the reorganizations, and the closing of the session. Through this analysis, I have illustrated how virtual artifacts and scripted animations organize the place to generate a sense of being there together facing each other. These animations prove important to the organization of action and interaction because they demand the participants' attention and evoke emotional and bodily responses. In the meeting situation, on one hand, they organize patterns of interaction that mirror physical face-to-face situations; on the other hand, these situations are different in the sense that the participant's vantage point does not necessarily follow the eyes or the face of the avatar. The in-world camera is the eye of the avatar. It means that the camera can be set to focus quite differently from the orientation of the avatar. In the present case, the organizers of the meeting would have the option to move the in-world camera, for instance, to capture the meeting situation from a bird's-eye perspective, but they choose instead to let the camera follow their avatar. In this way, we find the "sameness" that generate a sense of being inside the world together with other avatars in familiar and recognizable patterns of interaction, as well as the potential otherness of the differences of virtual patterns of interaction.

The video interview storyboard also tells the story of how situations are frequently reorganized as occasioned by scripted animations that attract our attention. Scripted animations such as the sit animation of the avatar Sils in the black chair or her posture on the couch strongly evoke our bodily sense of being inside the world, just as poorly animated walk or sit animations generate a sense of distance.

The video interview shows how the avatar Sils and her juggling with media take over the control of the meeting situation by the means of spectacular animations. The situation is out of the project team's control. The professional meeting session gradually dissolves and disorganizes as the professionals turn into audiences of an avatar performance with animations.

PROBLEMS AND QUESTIONS TO BE CONSIDERED

The strength of the video interview is also a weakness: the situatedness of the mutual dialogue and the concurrent sensory experience of the situation delimit the range and scope of the method. In the case of engagement with virtual worlds, we often deal with a multiplicity of concurrent places and dialogues between human actors located across the globe. It is difficult, if not impossible, to make situated observations and interviews of the multiplicities of such situations unless a team of distributed researchers coordinate their research to conduct video interviews. If this is not an option which is most often the case, a possible analytical path is, first of all, carefully to consider the relevance of doing video interviews, and, if relevant, then to be very critical of which situations to choose. In the case of multisited situations, chat logs of public and private dialogues, and machinima recordings from each of the participants can serve some analytical purposes and complement the in situ video interview. Here, the temporal coordination of the distributed recordings should be meticulously synchronized. Another possible setup would be to introduce simultaneous videoconferencing. In both cases, however, the sensory experience of the mutual dialogues—one of the main points of the video interview method—is lost.

CONCLUSION

In this chapter, it has been shown how video interviews that combine observational video recordings with in-depth and in situ qualitative interviews can be used as a method for generating data for analyzing virtual worlds. To study the assemblages of humans and the technology of virtual worlds involves an analysis of embodied and tacit knowledge, emotional expressions, cognitive effort, actual use situations, and dialogues in and about use situations, to mention some of the important aspects. Applying this method, seemingly simple situations like the example of the virtual Second Life Literary project meeting can be analyzed as a complex assemblage of concurrent situations that are organized and reorganized in a flux of virtual artifacts, connections, contacts, and dialogues. When we follow the simple setup of a virtual meeting, the many movements and changes caused by scripted animations appear to have the powers to organize, reorganize and take over control of the situation. This is valuable knowledge about actual use situations and engagement with virtual worlds and the sense of being there inside the world.

ACKNOWLEDGEMENT

The research presented in this chapter was carried out as part of the collective research project, "Sense-Making Strategies and User-Driven Innovation in Virtual Worlds: New Market Dynamics, Social and Cultural Innovation, and Knowledge Construction" (2008–12), Roskilde University and Copenhagen Business School. I would like to thank the Danish Strategic Research Council (KINO committee) for funding the project (grant no. 09–063261).

REFERENCES

Banks, Marcus. 2001. *Visual Methods in Social Research*. London: Sage.
Banks, Marcus. 2007. *Using Visual Data in Qualitative Research*. London: Sage.
Bell, David, and Barbara M. Kennedy, eds. 2000. *The Cybercultures Reader*. London: Routledge; New York: Taylor & Francis Group.
Benedikt, Michael, ed. 1993. *Cyberspace: First Steps*. Cambridge, MA: MIT Press.
Berger, John. 2008. *Ways of Seeing*. London: British Broadcasting Company/Penguin Books.
Biocca, Frank, and Mark Levy, eds. 1995. *Communication in the Age of Virtual Reality*. Hillsdale, NJ: Lawrence Erlbaum.
Blaschovich, Jim, and Jeremy Bailenson. 2011. *Infinite Reality. Avatars, Eternal Life, New Worlds, and the Dawn of the Virtual Revolution*. London: HarperCollins. PDF e-book.
Boelstorff, Tom. 2008. *Coming of Age in Second Life—An Anthropologist Explores the Virtual Human*. Princeton, NJ, and Oxford, UK: Princeton University Press.
Bowker, Geoffrey, and Susan Leigh Star. 1999. *Sorting Things Out. Classification and its Consequences*. Cambridge, MA: MIT Press.
Bowker, Geoffrey, and Susan Leigh Star. 2000. "Invisible Mediators of Action: Classification and the Ubiquity of Standards." *Mind, Culture & Activity* 7 (1–2): 147–63.
Clarke, Adele. 2003. "Situational Analysis: Grounded Theory Mapping after the Postmodern Turn." *Symbolic Interaction* 26 (4): 553–76.
Clarke, Adele, and Carrie Friese. 2007. "Grounded Theorizing Using Situational Analysis." In *The SAGE Handbook of Grounded Theory*, edited by Anthony Bryant and Kathy Charmaz, 363–98. London: Sage.
Collier, John, and Malcome Collier. 1967. *Visual Anthropology: Photography as a Research Method*. Albuquerque: University of New Mexico Press.
Collier, Malcome. 2001. "Approaches to Analysis in Visual Anthropology." In *Handbook of Visual Analysis*, edited by Theo van Leeuwen and Carey Jewitt, 35–59. London: Sage.
DeLanda, Manuel. 2006. *A New Philosophy of Society. Assemblage Theory and Social Complexity*. London: Continuum.
Goodchild, Philip. 1996. *Deleuze & Guattari. An Introduction to the Politics of Desire*. London: Sage.
Grimshaw, Anna. 2001. *The Ethnographer's Eye: Ways of Seeing in Anthropology*. Cambridge: Cambridge University Press.
Grimshaw, Anna. 2005. "Eyeing the Field: New Horizons for Visual Anthropology." In *Visualizing Anthropology*, edited by Anna Grimshaw and Amanda Ravetz, 17–31. Bristol, UK: New Media Intellect. Gunkel, David J. 2007. *Thinking Otherwise*. West Lafayette, IL: Purdue University Press.
Gunkel, David J. 2010. "The Real Problem: Avatars, Metaphysics and Online Social Interaction." *New Media and Society* 12 (1): 127–141.
Haraway, Donna. 1988. "Situated Knowledges: The Science Question in Feminism and the Privilege of Partial Perspective." *Feminist Studies* 14:575–99.
Jensen, Sisse Siggaard. 2005. "Video Views of Knowing in Action: Analytical Views In Situ in an IT-firm's Development Department." In *Challenges and Issues in Knowledge Management*, edited by A. F. Buono and Flemming Poulfelt, 249–269. Greenwich, CT: Information Age Publishing.

Jensen, Sisse Siggaard. 2007. "Reflective Designing for Actors and Avatars in Virtual Worlds." In *Designing for Networked Communications—Strategies and Development*, edited by Simon Heilesen and Sisse Siggaard Jensen 187–217. Hershey, PA, and London: Idea Group Inc.

Jensen, Sisse Siggaard. 2008. "Acting and Learning with Avatars: Sense-making Strategies of Reflection in the Virtual World of a Massively Multi-User Online Role-Playing Game." In *Informal Learning and Digital Media*, ed. Kirsten Drotner, Hans Siggard Jensen, and Kim Christian Schrøder, 49–70. Newcastle, UK: Cambridge Scholars Publishing.

Jensen, Sisse Siggaard. 2010. "Actors and their Use of Avatars as Personal Mediators: An Empirical Study of Avatar-based Sense-makings and Communication Practices in the Virtual Worlds of EverQuest and Second Life." In "Online worlds as media and communication format," edited by Kjetil Sandvik, Bjarke Liboriussen, Ditte Laursen, Heidi Philipsen, special issue, *Mediekultur* 47:29–44

Jensen, Sisse Siggaard. 2012. "Ways of Virtual World-making: Actors and Avatars." Roskilde, Denmark: Roskilde University Press. PDF e-book.

Jin, Seung-a Annie. 2010. "Parasocial Interaction with an Avatar in Second Life?: A Typology of the Self and an Empirical Test of the Mediating Role of Social Presence." *Technology* 19 (4): 331–40.

Jin, Seung-a Annie, and Namkee Park. 2009. "Parasocial Interaction with My Avatar: Effects of Interdependent Self-construal and the Mediating Role of Self-presence in an Avatar-Based Console Game, Wii." *Cyberpsychology & Behavior?: The Impact of the Internet, Multimedia and Virtual Reality on Behavior and Society* 12 (6): 723–27.

Jones, Steven. 1994. *CyberSociety 2.0: Computer-Mediated Communication and Community.* London: Sage.

Jordan, Brigitte, and Austin Henderson. 1995. "Interaction Analysis: Foundations and Practice." *The Journal of the Learning Sciences* 4 (1): 39–103.

Latour, Bruno. 1991. "Technology Is Society Made Durable." In *A Sociology of Monsters. Essays on Power, Technology and Domination*, Sociological Review Monograph 38, edited by John Law, 103–132. London: Routledge.

Latour, Bruno. 1995. "Pédofilen i Boa Vista: Ett Foto-filosofiskt Montage." In *Artefaktens Återkomst*, edited by Pierre Guillet, Guje Sevon, Barbara Czarniawska, Lars Engwall, Nils Brunsson, Rolf Wolff, and Torbjörn Santérus, 213–269. Göteborg, Sweden: Nerenius & Santérus Förlag.

Latour, Bruno. 2005. *Reassembling the Social. An Introduction to Actor-Network-Theory.* Oxford, UK, and New York: Oxford University Press.

Latour, Bruno. 2011. "Networks, Societies, Spheres?: Reflections of an Actor-Network Theorist." *Journal of Communication* 5:796–810.

Law, John. 2004. *After Method—Mess in Social Science Research.* London: Routledge; New York: Taylor & Francis.

Levy, Pierre. 1997. *Collective Intelligence: Mankind's Emerging World in Cyperspece.* New York: Plenum.

MacDougall, David. 1995. "Beyond Observational Cinema." In *Principles of Visual Anthropology*, 2nd ed., edited by Paul Hockings, 115–133. Berlin and New York: Mouton de Groyter.

MacDougall, David. 1998. *Transcultural Cinema.* Princeton, NJ: Princeton University Press.

MacDougall, David. 2001. "Renewing Ethnographic Film: Is Digital Video Changing the Genre?" *Anthropology Today* 17 (3): 15–21.

MacDougall, David. 2002. "Complicities of Style." In *The Anthropology of Media. A Reader.*, edited by Kelly Askew and Richard Wilk, 148–55. Malden, MS, and Oxford, UK: Blackwell Publishers.

Magnenat-Thalmann, Nadia, and Daniel Thalmann, eds. 2004. *Handbook of Virtual Humans.* Chichester John Wiley and Sons.

Mead, Margaret. 1995. "Visual Anthropology in a Discipline of Words." In *Principles of Visual Anthropology*, edited by P. Hockings, 3–13. The Hague: Mouton de Groyter.

Mead, Margaret, and Gregory Bateson. 2002. "On the Use of the Camera in Anthropology." In *The Anthropology of Media. A Reader*, edited by Kelly Askew and Richard Wilk, 41–47. Malden, MS, and Oxford, UK: Blackwell Publisher.

Pink, Sarah. 2001. *Doing Visual Ethnography*. London: Sage.

Pink, Sarah. 2005. "Dirty Laundry. Everyday Practice, Sensory Engagement and the Constitution of Identity." *Social Anthropology* Vol. 13, issue 03: 275–90.

Pink, Sarah. 2006. *The Future of Visual Anthropology. Engaging the Senses.* New York: Routledge, Taylor & Francis.

Pink, Sarah. 2009a. "Applied Visual Anthropology: Social Intervention and Visual Methodologies." In *Visual Interventions: Applied Visual Anthropology.* Series in Applied Anthropology, edited by Sarah Pink, 3–29. Oxford, UK, and New York: Berghan Books.

Pink, Sarah. 2009b. *Doing Sensory Ethnography*. London: Sage.

Porter, David. 1997. *Internet Culture*. New York: Routledge.

Reid, Elisabeth. 1995. "Virtual Worlds: Culture and Imagination." In *CyberSociety: Computer-Mediated Communication and Community*, edited by Steven Jones, 164–184. Thousand Oaks, CA: Sage.

Schroeder, Ralph, ed. 2002. *The Social Life of Avatars: Presence and Interaction in Shared Virtual Environments.* London: Springer.

Schroeder, Ralph. 2011. *Being There Together. Social Interaction in Virtual Environments.* Oxford, UK, and New York: Oxford University Press.

Schroeder, Ralph, and A.-S. Axelsson, eds. 2006. *Avatars at Work and Play: Collaboration and Interaction in Shared Virtual Environments.* Dordrecht, the Netherlands: Springer.

Suchman, Lucy. 1987. *Plans and Situated Action. The Problem of Human Machine Communication.* Cambridge: Cambridge University Press.

Suchman, Lucy. 1993. "Technologies of Accountability: On Lizards and Aeroplanes." In *Technology in Working Order: Studies in Work, Interaction and Technology*, edited by G. Button, 113–126. London: Routledge.

Suchmann, Lucy. 2000. "Embodied Practices of Engineering Work." *Mind, Culture & Activity* 7 (1–2): 4–18.

Suchmann, Lucy A., and Randal H. Trigg. 1991. "Understanding Practice: Video as a Medium for Reflection and Design." In *Design at Work: Cooperative Design of Computer Systems*, edited by Joan Greenbaum and Morten Kyng, 65–91. Hillsdale, NJ: Laurence Erlbaum.

Taylor, Laramie D. 2011. "Avatars and Emotional Engagement in Asynchronous Online Communication." *Cyberpsychology, Behavior and Social Networking* 14 (4): 207–12.

Taylor, T. L. 2006. *Play between Worlds. Exploring Online Game Culture.* Cambridge, MA, and London: MIT Press.

Wittgenstein, Ludwig. 1953. *Philosophical Investigations*. Oxford, UK: Blackwell.

7 Comparing Novice Users' Sense-Making Processes in Virtual Worlds

An Application of Dervin's Sense-Making Methodology

CarrieLynn D. Reinhard and Brenda Dervin

Any virtual world is a co-construction produced by the actions of producers and users negotiating with the media product's technological, political-economic, and sociocultural structures. Some virtual worlds are structured for gaming, such as Massively Multiplayer Online (MMOs) games and Massively Multiplayer Online Role-Playing Games (MMORPGs) such as World of Warcraft or EverQuest, whereas other worlds are primarily designed to facilitate social interaction, such as Second Life, SpotOn3D, and Habbo Hotel. In order to make comparisons across these two kinds of worlds, the study discussed in this chapter involves one gaming world, City of Heroes, and one social world, Second Life.

The chapter focuses on individual user agency in the negotiation between users' actions and the media product's structures. We adapt our understanding of agency from Anthony Giddens's structuration theory ([1979] 2002). Here, agency is defined as the ability to engage in some activity, be it internal (thoughts, feelings, decisions) or external (observable behavior). Our interest in user agency in co-construction aligns with media studies because it concerns understanding audiences and the use, reception, and effects of media products. For the purposes of this chapter, our users are audience members and our media products are virtual worlds.

In co-constructing a virtual world, agency negotiates with the affordances and constraints of the media product (Griffiths and Light 2008). We assume that to understand agency we need to understand how the user interprets or makes sense of these negotiations. Most methods of studying users' engaging with media products, including virtual worlds, focus on the reception of the product's content and/or technology, or the outcomes of the engaging, such as how the user was affected by or appropriated the content and/or technology. Hence, most methods do not examine explicitly the internal and the external agency of audience members.

For the study reported here, the methods of data collection and analysis were informed by Dervin's Sense-Making Methodology (SMM; Dervin, 2008; Dervin & Foreman-Wernet, 2003). In applying SMM to audience and reception studies, sense-making processes were defined as those internal and external communicating behaviors associated with interpreting and appropriating media products (Reinhard and Dervin 2013). A case study was designed as a qualitative experiment to allow systematic comparison of sense-making processes with different media products. The case study was designed to compare across different users' experiences with virtual worlds and to understand an individual user's experiences with different virtual worlds.

This chapter begins by considering the literature on audience and reception studies of virtual worlds. This review buttresses our claim that the processes of negotiating with a virtual world have rarely received attention in research. We then introduce how we saw SMM as allowing us to study interpretive or sense-making processes in relation to virtual worlds. Next, the case study is detailed, followed by a qualitative analysis that illustrates our use of SMM as a methodology for research on virtual worlds. Our approach was to locate users' multiple forms of sense-makings and to map how such sense-makings intertwined before, during, and after the engaging with the virtual world, thereby influencing the reception of each virtual world.

VIRTUAL WORLD RECEPTION STUDIES

In its origins, media studies assumed media structures could determine reception. This assumption was encapsulated in passive reception models such as the "magic bullet" or "hypodermic needle." By the 1970s, however, a focus on audience agency was inspired by Hall's ([1973] 1993) work with encoding/decoding and Katz, Blumler, and Gurevitch's (1974) work on uses and gratifications. Approaches were developed to counter overly deterministic views of society, culture, media product, and industry by bringing agency into the determination of media reception outcomes. From this foundation, the field of audience and reception studies has proliferated into fan studies, media appropriation studies, and media uses and effects studies. A multiplicity of methods has been deployed to learn how people interpret media products: participant observation, focus groups, surveys, in-depth interviews, surveys, and experiments.

With few exceptions, approaches have continued along the same methodological paths since the turn toward interpretation. However, the changing media environment has recently served as an impetus for innovations in methods for studying reception (Gauntlett 2009). The rapid diffusion of digital communication technologies has generated studies that (re)conceptualize the audience as always active in interactions with these products (Gauntlett 2009; Hermes 2009). In this section, we review research pertaining to virtual worlds, a digital communication technology involving a digital space that is persistently populated by people via their avatars (Bell 2008; Schroeder 2008). Numerous reception studies have concerned related technologies, chiefly virtual environments and virtual reality. Because these technologies do not involve persistent spaces, the studies involving them are not included in this review.

Despite the calls for research to combine qualitative and quantitative methods (Barker 2006; Morley 2006), for the most part, virtual world reception studies have followed separate qualitative and quantitative trajectories. In the qualitative trajectory, ethnographies have been used to study the context of audience engagements with virtual worlds, such as practices of social interaction and identity (Boellstorff 2008), information seeking behaviors (Adams 2009; Ostrander 2008), collaborative problem-solving (Voulgari and Komis 2010), and knowledge creation (Golub 2010). For instance, qualitative interview studies have sought to understand users' interpretations of the morality of inworld actions (Griffiths and Light 2008), learning to play (Oliver and Carr 2009), and basic reactions to playing (Hussain and Griffiths 2009). A qualitative text analysis by Albrechtslund (2010) focused on how stories of experiences contributed to developing collective identities.

In the quantitative trajectory, questionnaires have been used to ascertain how people perceive their avatars (Bessière, Seay, and Kiesler 2007), their social interactions (Cole and Griffiths 2007), and what leads people to use Second Life (Shin 2009). Also common are experiments that compare interpretations of virtual worlds: when engaging with different design aspects (Choi et al. 2007; Jin 2009), when operating in a virtual world compared to the physical world (Fiedler and Haruvy 2009; Friedman, Karniel, and Dinur 2009), and when accessing content via different media technologies (Smyth 2007). Another form of quantitative research—in which large amounts of user data from game servers have been collected—has sought to understand players' interests based on their recorded log-ins and in-world activities (Grabowski and Kruszewka 2007).

Although the use of mixed-method approaches has not been common, it does occur. Prime examples are the Feldon and Kafai (2008) and Fields and Kafai (2008) reports on their comprehensive multimethods approach to understanding how children engaged with Whyville.net. The researchers employed surveys, server logs, interviews, observations, and ethnography, and they explicitly discussed taking this mixed-methods approach in order to offset the weaknesses of each method with the strengths of the others.

In considering how users' reception of these more interactive environments has been studied, we begin to see limitations in relation to the study of interpretation as part of the processes of negotiation that co-construct virtual worlds. One limitation pertains to how situations are defined. There have been primarily two approaches, neither of which conceptualizes the situation as an evolving user-interpreted experience. One approach studies reception in specific instances of engaging, understanding the nature of the situation as a contextual influence on the engaging (e.g., Boellstorff 2008; Fields and Kafai 2008). The second approach asks people to talk about their experiences with virtual worlds in a generalized, aggregated fashion across situations of engagement (e.g., Hussain and Griffiths 2009; Oliver and Carr

2009). Although qualitative studies have focused on grounding data collection in people's experiences, they have usually not been designed to focus systematically on accounting for reception changes across time in one situation or across space in different situations.

Another limitation has been that detailed interpretations have not been elicited from informants; instead, researchers tend to rely on the researchers' own theory-driven explanations (e.g., Adams 2009; Golub 2010). In general, it is fair to say that little attention has been paid to specific sense-making processes occurring within everyday experiences. This challenge can be particularly seen in quantitative approaches that allow less in-depth accounting of sense-making processes in the persons' own words, relying instead on scales to ascertain psychological traits (e.g., Bessière et al. 2007), attitudes (e.g., Shin 2009), and motivations (e.g., Cole and Griffiths 2007). Likewise, experiments have emphasized measurements through scales (e.g., Choi et al. 2007; Friedman, Karniel, and Dinur 2009). Additionally, although experiments, through their artificiality, can allow a focus on specific interpretive processes (Josephs 2000), the resulting constraints necessarily circumscribe sense-making if they do not interface with informants in phenomenologically relevant ways.

As a final limitation, there remains a tendency to focus on the outcomes of, or reasons for, engaging with virtual worlds, concentrating on media effects or uses, instead of on the processes by which a person interpretively engages with and understands virtual worlds. Although this weakness is most often found in quantitative research, it can be seen in qualitative work as well (e.g., Griffiths and Light 2008; Oliver and Carr 2009; Ostrander 2008). In short, there is less rigorous attention to how people come to make their decisions to engage or not engage, to perform this activity or that, or to understand in one way or another.

Overall, there has been relatively little focus on understanding the means by which interpretations come to be, and how these interpretations involve an interplay between what users bring to their engagings and what media structures impose. What is needed is a research approach that can address situationally anchored engaging processes. Barker (2006) and Josephs (2000) issued this as a general call for meaning-making and reception studies. In our review of virtual world reception studies, we found none that pursued this call. The case study presented in this chapter was designed to address this gap.

SENSE-MAKING METHODOLOGY

Dervin's SMM has been applied to user and audience studies in a variety of contexts, for example, media use, information seeking, citizen participation, health communication, knowledge management, and arts audiences (Dervin and Foreman-Wernet 2003). We consider SMM an appropriate methodology for our purposes because SMM accepts the interpretive turn in all manner of reception, audience, and user studies. Further, SMM posits that communication behavior is usefully studied as process, focusing on situationally anchored engagements and the continuing interplays between agency and structures (i.e., technological, societal, and cultural). For these reasons, we see SMM as offering the kind of approach to reception studies called for by Barker (2006) and Joseph (2000).

SMM is one of a number of approaches focusing on a phenomenon labeled sense-making/sensemaking that has emerged since the late 1970s; all these approaches aim to implement the interpretive turn (Dervin and Naumer 2009). Space limitations here allow for only the briefest introduction. Thus, this introductory section on SMM is presented more as preface than full description (for detailed descriptions of the methodology see Dervin [2008] and Dervin and Foreman-Wernet [2003]). What follows is a discussion of the features of SMM especially pertinent to our application: study design, how SMM was used in data collection, and SMM-informed tools for data analysis.

SMM has been designed as a multimethods approach. Methods of data collection have included self-journaling, in-depth interviewing, participant observation, focus groups, surveys, and experiments. Data analysis approaches have included use of frequency displays, statistics, grounded theory, content analysis, and a variety of thematic and narrative tools. For this study, the multimethods included in-depth interviewing, experimental design, narrative reports, and SMM-structured thematic analyses.

SMM mandates the study of communication not as outcome but as a series of micro-practices, what SMM calls "verbings" (Dervin 1993). This methodological move involves a radical paradigm change from a focus on nouns to a focus on processes, both processes that are habitually and are culturally/socially prescribed and those that are inventive and seemingly capricious. For the study presented in this chapter, this application meant redefining reception not merely as outcome but as a series of communicatings. In SMM, communicatings occur internally and/or externally, consciously or unconsciously, innovatively or habitually, as actors move through the time-spaces of their encounters. SMM assumes that the next moment of communicating is never entirely written in advance. Drawing on multiple philosophical sources (Dervin and Foreman-Wernet 2003), SMM encapsulates its assumptions in a metaphor that points theoretically to communicatings of interest but does not predefine the substantive aspects of these communicatings. In the presentation of Figure 7.1, we see an actor moving through a changing time-space, out of the past, in a context, facing the next as yet unbridged time-space, crossing the bridge, and arriving at outcomes.

This metaphor is called a triangle because the situation-gap-bridge-outcome convergence is its core. Sense-making is defined not by particular sides or points of the triangle but by all of them, manifesting a unique

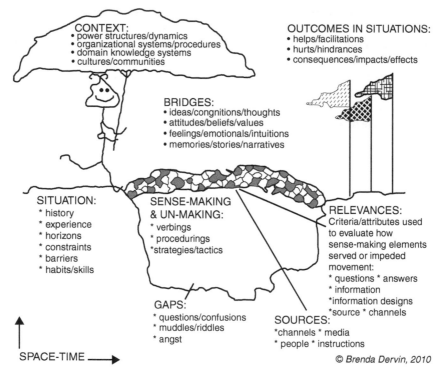

CONTEXT:
• power structures/dynamics
• organizational systems/procedures
• domain knowledge systems
• cultures/communities

OUTCOMES IN SITUATIONS:
• helps/facilitations
• hurts/hindrances
• consequences/impacts/effects

BRIDGES:
• ideas/congnitions/thoughts
• attitudes/beliefs/values
• feelings/emotionals/intuitions
• memories/stories/narratives

SITUATION:
* history
* experience
* horizons
* constraints
* barriers
* habits/skills

SENSE-MAKING
& UN-MAKING:
* verbings
* procedurings
*strategies/tactics

RELEVANCES:
Criteria/attributes used
to evaluate how
sense-making elements
served or impeded
movement:
* questions * answers
* information
*information designs
*source * channels

GAPS:
* questions/confusions
* muddles/riddles
* angst

SOURCES:
*channels * media
* people * instructions

SPACE-TIME ⟶

© Brenda Dervin, 2010

Figure 7.1   Dervin's Sense-Making Methodology Triangle Metaphor

triangular combination for any given time-space. The specific nouns named in the metaphor (e.g., history, experience, cultures, ideas, and emotions) are treated in SMM interviews and analyses as verbings: from the actor's point of view, one may be culture-ing one moment, and not the next, or idea creating one moment, and not the next. One may repeat verbings from the past or implement new ones.

SMM's approach to interviewing is considered by some (e.g., Savolainen 1993) to be its most distinctive characteristic. The reason for this view is that SMM mandates that aside from what is called a critical interviewing entry (e.g., *Tell me what happened when you played this game?*), the interviewer is disciplined to ask questions according to the core SMM questions, as listed in Figure 7.2. These core SMM questions introduce into interviewing practice the aspects of the "triangle" portrayed in the Figure 7.1 metaphor. In its various data collection and analysis tools, each of these query foci (highlighted in bold in Figure 7.2) is called a SMM element.

The distinctive nature of the SMM interview derives from how it interrupts the normative conceptualization of qualitative versus quantitative interviewing. SMM interviewing is, at one and the same time, both highly

> What **questions, muddles, confusions** did you have?
> What **ideas, conclusions, thoughts** did you have?
> What **emotions, feelings** did you have?
> What **learnings** did you have?
> Was anything **helpful** to you? If so, how?
> Was anything **hurtful or hindering** to you? If so, how?
> How did what was happening relate to your **sense of self**?
> How did what was happening relate to your thoughts on **power** and how it operates in the world around you?
> How did what was happening relate to your **past experiences**?
> What **expectations, hopes** did you have?
> If you could wave a **magic wand**, what would you have changed?

Figure 7.2 Core set of SMM interviewing queries

structured and open-ended. It imposes a communicative discipline designed to empower both interviewer and interviewee. The interviewer's task is to use only SMM queries that focus on fundamental aspects of time-space-movement in order to facilitate an articulation opportunity that enables interviewees to name, as they sense them, the entities in their own worlds and the connections between them. The approach deliberately avoids the noun orientations of most interviewing. Thus, in the case study, participants were not asked specifically about game design features or tutorials; rather, they were asked what they encountered and what helped and/or hindered.

Both in interviewing and in analyses, SMM mandates attention to time-space contingencies. The central idea is that one attempts to understand an informant's interpretation, either during the interview or in analysis procedures, by anchoring that interpretation in the center of its own time-space triangle. How this is done in interviewing depends on the specific interviewing approach (see Dervin 2008). The foundational approach calls for an examination of brackets of time-space, such as a single step in a media encounter.

The approach used in this study was the Micro-Element approach. Here, the interviewer asked the core SMM questions as they applied to the encounter as a whole, and informants responded with whatever interpretations were most relevant to them. However, in the actual conduct of the interview, the interviewer considered each SMM element and how it was anchored in time-space. Follow-up interviewing was designed to elucidate these time-space contiguities, with an experienced SMM interviewer digging deeply for thoughts and connections that the informant may not as yet have consciously articulated. Further, as illustrated in the study presented here, a SMM study always focuses on at least several moments in time in one encounter and/or several differing moments across encounters. For this study, the comparison of how participants interpreted their two different virtual world encounters formed the most direct application of this principle.

The SMM core triangle and SMM elements, as tapped in core questions presented in Figure 7.2, form the two primary tools applied systematically in this study, not only during interviewing but also in the analyses. The roster of SMM elements were used as a structured tool for comparing participant interpretations in two ways: for a given participant across two different virtual world encounters and for two participants in terms of how they differed in the same virtual world encounter. The next sections outline the case study with detailed discussion of how SMM informed both the data collection and analysis.

INTRODUCING THE CASE STUDY

Fourteen people, a mix of students and professionals, in Denmark volunteered to be participants in the study. The participants were seven men and seven women who ranged from fifteen to fifty-eight years old. The volunteers indicated differing degrees of experience although overall they had little to no experience with the virtual worlds used in the study.

The project utilized an experimental framework with four sessions in which participants engaged with different media products: watching a film, playing a console video game, engaging with a gaming virtual world, and engaging with a social virtual world. In order to provide similar content across the experiences, the content of the media products reflected the superhero genre (Reinhard 2010). In this chapter, only the sessions involving the two virtual worlds are analyzed. The two virtual world experiences are seen as representing a continuum from individualistic game play involvement to socially interactive collaborative involvement. The execution of the experimental sessions was identical for the two virtual worlds.

For the game-playing session, City of Heroes was used because it was the only superhero MMO in the market at the time. One participant had played the game before, but only briefly several years earlier. Participants completed the sessions individually. The participant sat at a laptop with a video recorder positioned to capture the participant's face and the screen simultaneously, while the senior author, as researcher, sat on the side off-screen. Participants played the game from the start, with their deciding whether to be a superhero or a supervillain, designing their character's appearance and abilities, and deciding whether to walk through the tutorial or go straight into the game.

As the social virtual world, Second Life was used. There were areas in Second Life devoted to superheroes but the senior author wanted more control over the content to make it comparable to the other media products. To this end, a professional designer was hired to construct an area to represent various superhero genre conventions. This area, dubbed "Metrotopia: City of Superheroes," served as the entry point for participants into Second Life. Although one participant had been in Second Life several years earlier, Metrotopia was new to him. Before the session, participants were given instructions on how to set up a Second Life account, including the selection of a basic avatar. On entering Metrotopia, the participants could access in-game tutorial screens, and a printed sheet of instructions was included alongside the laptop. Participants were instructed to dress their avatars in a superhero costume before doing anything else in Second Life.

Qualitative measurements of their sense-making processes occurred at three times: during the sessions, after each session, and after all sessions had been completed. During the sessions, participants were asked to discuss their reactions to the media product via talk aloud protocols informed by SMM. After each session, participants completed a questionnaire consisting of paired numerical-scale and open-ended items in order to assess their evaluations of the engagings. After participants finished the four sessions, they were interviewed on their experiences using the SMM Micro-Element Interview (Dervin 2008). Participants were asked to compare sessions in terms of which were the best/worst and most/least entertaining experiences and what led to each evaluation. After these comparisons, queries focused on delving into the person's experience in each session using the core set of SMM questions displayed in Figure 7.2.

While interviewing each participant, the senior author, as an SMM-trained interviewer, listened to the participant's answers and asked probing questions to follow up on what was said. These probing questions were also SMM-informed as the interviewer asked the participant how what they had just said helped or hindered their experience with the virtual world. Thus, for each participant's virtual world encounter, the interviewer elicited systematically three different situationally anchored SMM surrounds of the participants' experience: (a) comparing that situation to the other three; (b) pursuing in-depth participant recollections of that situation, as informed by the SMM Triangle; and (c) probing participant answers with SMM-informed follow-up queries. Figure 7.3 is an example of these three situationally anchored SMM surrounds that comes from the interview with Jakob, a twenty-four-year-old man, in discussing his experience with City of Heroes.

ANALYSIS OF CASE STUDY

The analysis involved mapping the interview by applying the metatheory that informs SMM. To begin, each interview transcript was mapped using the SMM Triangle Metaphor. The intent of this mapping was to attend to how what each participant said related to the core SMM elements. The example of mapping in Figure 7.4 comes from Jakob's engaging with City of Heroes. His language use was retained as much as possible to demonstrate how answers to specific interview queries mapped onto the SMM Triangle.

EMP3: MMORPG *Let's talk about the City of Heroes role playing game then.* Yup
BEST/WORST: *How does this one rate in terms of being the best, the worst or in the middle?*
It was probably the most interesting one because I've been wondering about what's going on in these multiple, massive multiplayer online games, and actually I thought we were going to sit down and play World of Warcraft, and it took me a while to understand this was actually the genre we were engaged in, and sitting down and playing that game on my own was... well, since I didn't know the conventions for this genre, because I haven't played all these games before, I had a sort of slow start.
QUESTIONS: *Did you have any major questions or confusions during this experience?*
Yeah, first of all, I didn't know what was going to happen when I sat down and created my character. I didn't know what the use of my character would be. But I found that out by continuing and then there was the problem with the tutorial where I didn't know how to accept quests and I could move on in the game and just talk to the next person without accepting it is a quest first and of course the game is structured like that, too. Because I have to follow the rules if I want to engage with this game in a way that makes sense. That what developers had, to be able to use their content, and so...when I found that out it was much easier to go forward.

What would have helped you answer these questions?
Well, you did, when you told me that I had to accept the mission and if I was playing one of these games with my friends, of course, I would ask them all the time, so I would constantly be drawing on them and their experience of the game and their opinions on what skills to choose and which bad guys to visit and beat up, or good guys in this instance, and so... and then the tutorial helped me as well because it...I was faced with these problems and that meant I had to solve them and when I did I could move on.

Figure 7.3   Interview excerpt

To demonstrate how this analytical tool was used to construct narratives, two participants were chosen for their differing overall receptions of the two virtual worlds. Jakob preferred City of Heroes whereas Sofie, a thirty-two-year-old woman, preferred Second Life. Using the coded triangle maps as data sources—repeating Figure 7.4 for both participants in both virtual worlds—narratives were formed to portray how participants saw each encounter before, during, and after engagement. Attempts were made to retain the participant's voice in each narrative. The narratives were designed to communicate the complexity of sense-makings in these encounters in a way that is more accessible than reading coded triangle maps. Additionally, the narratives provide an understanding of the passage of time as experienced by the participants and illustrate the intertwinements of sense-makings.

Using SMM's general emphasis on the search for situational contingencies, the interviews were analyzed for how different SMM elements as described by participants were connected to one another, for example, how they interpreted experiences or expectations as relating to their sense-makings. In the accounts presented in the following, to illustrate these user-interpreted

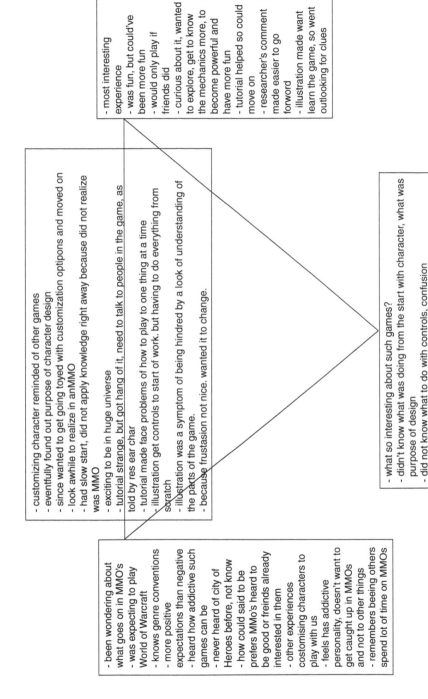

Figure 7.4 Jakob's City of Heroes interview, mapped to SMM Triangle map

connections, the terms that refer to seven categories of SMM elements are incorporated within the narratives in parentheses: "experiences" and "expectations" from before the encounter; "gap-facings," such as questions, confusions and struggles from during the encounter; "bridging" movements such as emotions, ideas, and learnings from during the encounter; "helping" and/or "hindering" from during the encounter; and the "overall reception" and "outcome" of the encounter.

Jakob in City of Heroes reported that, overall, the gaming virtual world session was the most interesting session in the experiment, saying that was fun and could have been more so (overall reception), but that he would only play it again if his friends did (outcome). Before entering this session, he had been wondering about what goes on in MMOs (expectation) and what was so interesting about such games (expectation). He said he did not know the genre conventions for such games (experience), nor had he ever heard of City of Heroes before, so he didn't know how good it was said to be (experience). In fact, he had expected to be playing World of Warcraft (expectation). He had heard how addictive such games can be (experience), and because of his addictive personality (experience), he worried about not wanting to get caught up in MMOs because of how MMOs might interfere with other things (expectation).

The session began with Jacob customizing a character. Jakob said that he had had other experiences customizing characters and that customizing the character reminded him of other games (experience); however, he did not know what he was doing from the start with the character, what the purpose in designing it was (gap-facing), and, since he wanted to get going (bridging), he just toyed with the options and moved on (helping), learning later what the purpose of character design was (bridging). He said it took him a while to realize he was in an MMO (bridging) because of his lack of experience (experience), which meant that for a while, he did not know what to do (gap-facing) and thus got off to a slow start (hindering).

He found himself confused about the controls (gap-facing). He had experience with the controls from other games (experience) but he did not apply it right away (bridging) because he did not realize that it was a MMO (gap-facing). Later, he said knowing the genre did help (helping). At first, he felt frustrated by the controls (bridging) and said that this frustration was a symptom of his being hindered by his lack of understanding of the parts of the game (bridging). However, because he experienced the frustration as not nice (bridging), he wanted to change (bridging), so he worked to learn the controls (bridging) by looking for clues (bridging) and got it to sort of work (helping).

As for the tutorial aspect of the session, he did not know how to accept quests (gap-facing). He thought the tutorial was strange (bridging) but said he got the hang of it (helping). He said the tutorial made him face his problems about how to play (bridging) so that he could move on (helping) and that the tutorial helped with the interface because he had to do one thing at a time (bridging) and learn how the controls worked (helping), rather than having to do everything from scratch.

Jakob went into the session wondering what people find so interesting about these games (gap-facing). He found it exciting to be in such a huge universe (bridging), making him curious (bridging), wanting to explore (bridging) and get to know the gaming mechanics more (bridging) in order to become powerful and have more fun in the game (helping).

Jakob in Second Life found this session to be the least engaging in the experiment (overall reception). He said that he was not going to play it again and that he did not want to spend more time in the world (outcome). He felt that it was a disappointing engagement, but that he expected it to be so, so it was not disappointing ultimately (overall reception). He said that he had a pretty good idea what Second Life was about before the session (expectation). He had expected it to be just people putting on masks and talking to each other (expectation), like his experiences in chat rooms (experience).

As with City of Heroes, the first task was to design an avatar. Jakob said he struggled with how to put clothing on his avatar (gap-facing). He felt that the costume was the silliest part of superheroes (bridging) and again reiterated his experience of designing characters in other games (experience). He felt that it was pointless to put on a silly costume (bridging) and that it was difficult to change the avatar because of the rules (bridging). He was frustrated with not knowing how to redesign the avatar (bridging), which he said was less intuitive than in other games (experience). Because he did not think he would use the avatar again after this session (bridging), he decided to not spend much time on it (helping). Overall, he said he was very confused about, and annoyed with, the interface (gap-facing). The cheat sheet with the instructions provided some help (helping), but he thought it pointless (bridging) because he did not want to engage with the game (bridging).

He wondered why people engage with this world (gap-facing). He felt there were not a lot of people in it (bridging), and the only conversation he had with someone he called halfhearted and pointless (bridging). He wondered what was it all about (gap-facing). He felt that his preconceptions were correct (bridging). It was bigger than he had imagined (bridging), but that didn't matter to him (bridging). He thought that Second Life was a huge, overdone chat room (bridging) and that he didn't need to go there to find people (hindering) because the social tools he had were adequate (bridging). He wanted a game (bridging) and was not interested in the freedoms of just being reduced to "I'm here and I like you and you're here and you like me" (bridging). He said the world was lacking goals to accomplish like other computer games (bridging) to make it interesting to him (hindering). He felt that games were more interesting (bridging) and that this world did not seem to be about anything (bridging). Only his initial curiosity (bridging) about what it was what kept him going as long as he did (helping).

Sofie in City of Heroes differed from Jakob, thinking that this session was the worst experience in the experiment (overall reception). She said that it was the least entertaining and was boring (overall reception) and that she did not think she would play it again (outcome) because it took a long time and was not fun (overall reception). She was disappointed that it did not live up to her expectations (overall reception). Her boyfriend, she said, spent a lot of time online, which amazed her (experience), and she had heard and knew people who spent a lot of time with such games (experience), so she thought this session would be fun (expectation). However, she had tried a game before where she had to build a city, but she stopped after two hours because it was difficult to get into the game (experience).

Sofie complained that there was too much reading and skimming of information (bridging) and she did not understand why she had to read so much information (gap-facing). She said she did not get all of the information she was being given (hindering). She also did not know what she was doing on her first quest in the tutorial (gap-facing). She felt that it took too long (bridging) and that it was annoying how she could not have the map open to see where she was running (bridging). She added that she did not think of herself as a patient person (bridging).

She said she did not know how to do things (gap-facing) like use her powers. She called the fighting element disappointing (bridging) and said that the controls hurt- it was a mouse and old-fashioned keyboard (bridging). Sofie felt that over time she stopped caring for the game (hindering) and did not want to get into how the controls worked in order to play (bridging).

Sofie said she did not grasp the whole scheme of things in the game (gap-facing). She felt like she was wasting her time (bridging), and it was not fun running around doing quests (bridging). For her, the tutorial took too long (bridging), and she never got the feeling of being intrigued by the world (bridging) because it was slow-paced and annoying (bridging). At some point, the game map did help her to see where she was going (helping), but it was not enough (bridging). She felt powerless (bridging) because she was not deciding what to do; she was doing it because the tutorial demanded it. She made the decision that it was stupid and did not make sense (bridging) and, in order not to waste more energy, she stopped (helping), finally deciding it was the worst experience.

Sofie in Second Life said it was a middle experience, perhaps not as good as watching the film or playing the video game (overall reception). However, she indicated being still a little "wow" about what one could do in Second Life (overall reception) and said that maybe she would go do it again (outcome). Sofie had never been in Second Life before (experience) but had been going into chat rooms since 2000 (experience). She also reflected on how, before this session, she had just played two games in the study as a hero (experience).

She indicated that creating the character was confusing (gap-facing) because the inventory was pretty weird (bridging). She also did not understand why she had all this money to buy things (gap-facing). She felt that somehow she had as much money as she wanted (bridging). She said buying and shooting guns was weird (bridging). She was confused about what to do (gap-facing) in the shooting area of Metrotopia and whether or not she was playing a game (gap-facing). Because she did not know if it was a game, she did not know what she was supposed to do (gap-facing).

At one point in the session, she had an encounter with a character encased in a sphere whom she could not contact. She had an idea that she was to save a girl trapped in the cocoon (bridging). She said she had no idea why she thought this as no one said to do so (bridging). On reflection, she thought it perhaps had to do with the other games she had played during this study— that she was still playing the hero (bridging). She thought it was a game and not social, so she was trying to play a game in a social reality (bridging). She felt this hurt her presence and her chance to meet other people (hindering) because she did not know what to do with herself (bridging). She felt happy when people wanted to talk (helping) but rejected and weird when they did not (hindering) because she wanted to get in contact with more people (bridging). She could see herself very much in the world, acting as she would normally to meet people (bridging).

She did meet someone, a "princess person," who led her to a new location. She wondered what was going on with this person (gap-facing). She felt like a newbie just following someone else around (bridging), but this following, she said, helped her learn (helping). She was interested in trying to figure out what was happening (bridging) with this person and the whole world. She wanted to know what it was all about (gap-facing). She felt like it was a social gathering place to meet new people (bridging) or that it was like exploring (bridging). She liked being able to fly to get around fast (bridging), to create landmarks (bridging), and to get unstuck and move away if she was in trouble (helping).

Comparing Sense-Making Processes

The narratives were constructed to provide a cohesive account of participants' recollections in a format that helps readers understand each evolving experience. However, narratives are not inherently conducive to systematic comparison. To explore participants' experiences for overlaps and divergences, particularly for how these may help us understand differing overall reception and outcomes, word tables were constructed based on the core SMM elements analyzed in the narratives.

Two tables compare Jakob and Sofie's sense-makings from engaging with each of the virtual worlds. Producing across-person within-virtual world comparisons, Table 1, shown in Figure 7.5, compares the participants' sense-makings from City of Heroes, and Table 2, shown in Figure 7.6, compares them in Second Life. By looking across these two tables, it is possible to compare each participant's engagings with the virtual worlds. In these word tables, to retain a portrait of the intertwinings among the various sense-makings, the sense-makings are identified as belonging to one of the seven SMM elements labeled in the narratives. The sense-makings are labeled to indicate when certain elements were thematically intertwined. Intertwined

Sense-Makings	Jakob	Sofie
Outcomes/ Overall Receptions	Least engaging in the experiment Disappointing but expected to be so	Middle experience, behind film and Wii A little "wow" about what could do Maybe would go do it again
Experiences	(4)Had experiences in chat rooms (1)Designed characters in other games	Never been in before (g)Had been going into chat rooms (e)Had just played two games as the hero
Expectations	(4)Had pretty good idea what about (4)Thought people put on masks to talk	
Gap-facings	(1)How put on avatar's appearance (2)Confused about interface (3)Why people engage with world (4)What world all about	(a)Creating the character confusing (b)Why had all money to buy things (c)What to do in shooting area (d)Confused if playing game or not (e)What supposed to do (f)What going on with "princess person" (g)What world all about
Bridgings	(1)Costumes silliest part of superheroes (1)Pointless to put on silly costume (1)Difficult to change avatar because rules (1)Avatar design tools less intuitive (1)Didn't think would use avatar again (2)Cheat sheet pointless (2)Not want to engage with game (3)Not a lot of people in world (3)Half-hearted, pointless conversation (4)Felt preconceptions were correct (4)Bigger than imagined (4)Size didn't matter (4)Thought huge, overdone chat room (4)Social tools have are adequate (4)Wanted a game (4)Not interested in freedom of social world (4)Lacking goals to accomplish (4)Games are more interesting (4)This world not about anything (4)Initial curiosity	(a)Inventory weird (b)Felt had as much money as wanted (b,c)Weird buying and shooting guns (d,e)Idea to save girl trapped in "cocoon" (d,e)No idea why thought that (d,e)Thought still play as hero (d,e)Trying to play game in social reality (d,e)Hurt her presence inworld (e)Wanted contact with more people (e)Normally likes to meet people (f)Felt like "newbie" being led around (f)Interested in trying to figure out events (g)Felt was social place to meet people (g)Felt like was exploring (g)Liked being able to fly around (g)Liked being able to create landmarks
Helpings	(1)Not spend much time on avatar design (2)Cheat sheet providing instructions (4)Kept going as long as did	(e)Felt happy when people talked to her (f)Following helped learn (g)Able to get away if get stuck
Hinderings	(4)Doesn't need to find people (4)Goals would make interesting	(d,e)Hurt chance meeting new people (e)Felt rejected, weird when not talk

Figure 7.5   Table 1—Comparing Jakob's and Sofie's sense-makings in City of Heroes

elements from Jakob's transcript are indicated numerically down the column, while for Sofie they are indicated alphabetically.

In Figure 7.5 (Table 1), both Jakob and Sofie were making sense of the controls for and tutorial structure of the gaming virtual world. Both indicated being confused about controls, but Jakob's frustration, which appeared to be connected to having played similar games, served to spur his moving to learn the controls to keep going; Sophie's confusion apparently had the opposite effect, lessening her interest for the game, which had been high going into the encounter. Both struggled with the requirements of the tutorial, such as accepting quests and performing required tasks. Similar to finding the frustration with the controls helping him, Jakob also indicated that the structure

Sense-Makings	Jakob	Sofie
Outcomes/ Overall Receptions	Most interesting session Fun but could've been more so Would play again only with friends	Worst experience in experiment Least entertaining, boring Will not play again Took a long time, not fun
Experiences	(2)Didn't know game conventions (2)Never heard of this MMO Heard MMOs addicting Feels has addicting personality (1)Customized characters for other games (3)Used controls of other games	(d)Boyfriend spends time playing MMOs (d)Heard, knows people spend lot of time (d)Tried game, stopped because difficult
Expectations	(5)Been wondering about MMOs (5)Been wondering what make interesting (2)Expected to be playing different MMO Worried get addicted to MMO	(d)Thought session would be fun
Gap-facings	(1)What purpose in designing character (2)Did not know what to do (3)Confused about controls (4)Didn't know how accept quests (5)What interested about games	(a)Why had to read so much information (b)Not know what doing first quest (c)Not know how to do things (d)Didn't get whole scheme of game
Bridgings	(1)Wanted to get going (1)Learned later purpose of design (2)Took a while realize in an MMO (3)Not apply experience other controls (3)Not realize was playing MMO (3)Realize genre of game later (3)Frustrated by controls (3)Symptom lacked understanding (3)Frustration is not nice (3)Wanted to change frustration (3)Looked for clues about controls (4)Tutorial was strange (4)Tutorial made face problems (4)Had to do one thing at time in tutorial (5)Huge universe exciting (5)Felt curious (5)Wanted to explore (5)Wanted to know game mechanics	(a)Too much reading, skim information (b)Took too long just running (b)Annoying not have map up to see path (b)Not a patient person (c)Fighting element disappointing (c)Controls hurt, old-fashioned (c)Not want to get into how controls work (d)Felt wasting her time (d)Not fun doing quests (d)Tutorial took too long (d)Not felt intrigued by world (d)World slow-paced, annoying (d)Map not enough (d)Felt powerless because of tutorial (d)Game stupid, not make sense
Helpings	(1)Toyed with design and moved on (3)Realizing genre (3)Got controls to sort of work (4)Got hang of tutorial (4)Could move on (4)Learned how controls worked (5)Have more fun	(d)Map did help see where going (d)Decide stop to not waste more energy
Hinderings	(2)Got off to slow start	(a)Didn't get all information given (c)Stopped caring for game

Figure 7.6   Table 2—Comparing Jakob's and Sofie's sense-makings in Second Life

of the tutorial was helpful in guiding him through the game. Sofie only had negative evaluations of her moving through and with the tutorial which seemed linked to a previous experience with a similar type of game.

In Figure 7.6 (Table 2), both participants were making sense of the character creation process and the purpose of the social virtual world. Sofie apparently did not dwell too much on this concern, whereas Jakob, who brought into the process his evaluation of superheroes' costumes, spent time concerned about the interface for this design. His previous experience with character creation interfaces may have led him to expect how this process would occur in Second Life and not having those expectations met, combined with his dismissive idea about superheroes' costumes, led him to give up with the world in order to move on with his day. Jakob's expectations apparently played a role in his evaluation of the world as a whole, calling it a "huge, overdone chat room." Sofie, on the other hand, was confused about whether the world was meant to be another game like City of Heroes. This confusion was met with a desire to be social which appears to have been connected to her evaluations of being interested in figuring out the purpose of the world.

Across his two experiences, as seen in Figures 7.5 and 7.6, Jakob went into City of Heroes with more confusion than when he went into Second Life. For the gaming world, he had a mixture of wonderment about MMOs and confusion about this particular MMO; coming from that perspective, his encounter with City of Heroes appears to have been a mixture of realizing what he was doing while trying to figure out what made what he was doing so interesting. The frustration and curiosity he felt may have alternately, or concurrently, helped to impel his moving through the encounter and his interest in returning to it. However, Jakob appeared to have a less exploratory idea regarding the nature of Second Life of which he gave an overall negative evaluation as a social network that he did not need. He compared the encounter to games that he knew and liked. His negative evaluations and comparisons were perhaps part of his moving through the world just enough to confirm his expectations.

Across her two experiences, as seen in Figures 7.5 and 7.6, Sofie enjoyed the ability to have the freedom to explore Second Life while rejecting the structure of City of Heroes that made her feel powerless. Perhaps Sofie's experience in City of Heroes was predetermined by her recalling a previous experience of stopping in a difficult game after two hours. However, such an explanation does disservice to the nuanced ways in which this particular encounter did not meet the expectation for fun that Sofie had. Her decision to stop playing the game helped her take control of a situation in which she felt powerless because of the requirements placed upon her by the tutorial. In contrast, Sofie's encounter with Second Life appeared to be a similar mix of confusion and curiosity that seemed to have helped Jakob in City of Heroes. Here Sofie's confusion related to an uncertainty about the nature of the encounter, and her curiosity helped her explore more of Second Life and become more intrigued by the social nature of the world.

DISCUSSION

Sofie and Jakob's encounters were chosen for analysis because they reported differing outcomes and overall receptions in how they compared the two virtual worlds. Sofie indicated liking Second Life more whereas Jakob indicated more preference for City of Heroes. In an abstract way, an argument can be made that, for the encounters that each participant evaluated more positively as being more entertaining or a better experience, each reported an amalgam of frustration, confusion, and curiosity that helped them move through those encounters. However, on a less abstract level, the sense-makings in the encounters revealed nuances about how each participant negotiated with the structures of the virtual world in order to have the positive experiences. In City of Heroes, Jakob negotiated with the requirements of the tutorial, linking what was happening during the encounter with his experience with previous games and his expectations, or lack thereof, for this one. In Second Life, Sofie negotiated with the nature of the world, acting for a time as if she were still in a game, but, on finding it to be otherwise, finding the social nature of the world to be just as interesting, if not more so.

What led these two participants to have more of a negative outcome and overall reception evaluation of the two virtual worlds cannot be reduced so easily to an abstraction. Although both had expectations about the worlds going into the encounters, Jakob's expectation was met whereas Sofie's expectation was thwarted. It was only by seeing how they made sense of the worlds, in relation to their expectations, that we could better understand what happened. Jakob's expectation about Second Life being a social network appears to be related to an overall negative evaluation of the world, as he twice referred to the activities in-world as "pointless." Having his expectation met, then, did not appear to be a good thing for Jakob in that encounter. Sofie, on the other hand, had expected City of Heroes to be fun, in part because of how much time she knew people spent in such worlds. However, she found herself feeling increasingly powerless given the requirements for completing tasks and the lack of help. Not having her expectation met by the tutorial appeared to have led her to stop caring, stop playing, and perhaps stop having such expectations.

Although the outcomes of all four encounters could be explained without the focus on the participants' sense-making processes before, during, and after the encounters, it is the analyses of these sense-makings that provided understanding of the nuances of how each participant negotiated the affordances and constraints of each virtual world in order to co-construct an experience that they could evaluate as being good or bad and entertaining or not. In this instance, understanding sense-making processes examined at the micro-level offered a window through which to better understand outcomes and overall receptions.

CONCLUSION

Our purpose has been to illustrate how we used SMM to construct research to compare how people engage with different virtual worlds. In this analysis, SMM data collection and analysis allowed us to see where two participants' encounters with two different kinds of virtual worlds converged and diverged and how their sense-makings related to outcomes and overall receptions.

Moreover, the application of SMM helped us to see how virtual worlds relate to the overall media ecosystem in which users are immersed. We learned from this reception study to see virtual worlds from the perspective of individual users. The participants saw a media product with which they must learn how to engage in order to determine how it will be useful to their lives. This assessment is not meant to downplay the uniqueness of virtual worlds; instead, it is recognition that, as with all other communication technologies, virtual worlds will be engaged with, interpreted, and appropriated in a multitude of ways and that analyzing the user's sense-making processes can help us understand how and why those ways come to be.

How we researched the sense-making process helped us to come to this conclusion. By using SMM as a data collection tool, participants were given space and privilege to co-construct with the interviewer their recollections of the encounters in a way that explored how they interpreted what happened before, during and after the encounters. By providing critical entries and then adhering to the highly structured but open-ended SMM interviewing mandate, the interviewee became a co-theorist in a disciplined form of interviewee–interviewer dialogue. As mandated by SMM's interviewing protocols, the interviewee provided all the specific elements and connections while the interviewer asked questions that facilitated this dialogic dig.

By using the core SMM elements drawn from the SMM Triangle Metaphor, the analysis allowed for an examination of how participants saw themselves as moving through their virtual world encounters. The SMM analytic tools also facilitated systematically examining the complex intertwinings, twists, and turns in each participant's virtual world journey, permitting a focus on both within-person differences across space (i.e., one participant, two virtual world encounters) as well as across-person differences in one space (i.e., two participants, one virtual world encounter).

This study was designed primarily as an intervention in the quantitative media uses and effects tradition and its emphasis in reception studies on outcomes of media engagements. The intention here was to focus not merely on outcomes but on processes of engagings—what people thought and felt while interacting with a virtual world and how these sense-makings related to judgments of the engagement. SMM provided the framework for this data collection. The focus of the interviews was on micro-moments of movement through time-space. This focus is an example of the kind of "slowing down" of research attention that Josephs (2000) called for to better analyze what she called meaning-making processes, and it is similar to the empirical process of "viewing strategies" called for by Barker (2006). Having participants engage in this process after the encounter rather than during as called for by talk aloud protocols, allowed participants to more completely experience the flow of the encounter which could then be co-constructed in a dialogic fashion during the interviewing session.

Additionally, our application of the SMM interviewing approach privileged participants as theorists with capacities to define their worlds and to hypothesize connections between past, present, and future. In SMM, this is considered a disciplined approach to dialogic co-construction. Thus, instead of using scale items or structured questions designed to focus on some particular reason (such as extrinsic motivation), interpretation (such as presence), or outcome (such as trust), the SMM-informed interview focused on movements toward, through, and out of the encounter with the virtual world.

We could have designed an interview or questionnaire to ask about the phenomena we specifically wanted to understand, such as Jakob's curiosity and frustration in City of Heroes or Sofie's social interests in Second Life. But these understandings are strengthened by the powers of hindsight: in designing this study, we did not know that participants would report these particular experiences, and thus would have had no way to prepare a data collection method to account for them. SMM helped the senior author to gain these insights in a structured way through the analysis by removing her own judgments and jargon from the interviews.

However, as with any qualitative approach, there are the issues of self-recall and researcher interpretation to be negotiated. The interview protocol queries, as influenced by SMM, were designed to hopefully not be aggressive or accusatory. By focusing on what SMM calls fundamentals of human sense-making—for example, participant questions, ideas, and emotions—the goal was to empower participants to feel comfortable in co-constructing their recollections. But there could never be a guarantee of this because there was no guarantee that participants remembered all aspects of their encounters. This could mean that some aspects of their encounters that would have been of interest to researchers and/or media designers were not addressed.

Additionally, the senior author struggled with how much of her interpretation of participants' answers to include in analysis—how faithful she should remain to what the participants said—if she wanted to align their recollections to the theoretical underpinnings of SMM which meant deconstructing and reordering their answers into the narratives. This struggle would have been helped by having employed different SMM interview protocols that would have more exactingly asked participants to discuss the intertwinements of their sense-makings. However, employing these would have greatly extended the interview time required of participants.

Aside from these challenges, the reason why SMM has been deliberately designed as a multi-methodology is that, following Gadamer (1975), SMM rests on the assumption that every method both constrains and fails in reaching for understandings of complex human phenomena. By surrounding the phenomena with multiple research projects and approaches that are compared in terms of strengths and limitations, we come closer to comprehending what can never be touched or frozen: the experiences of other human beings and, in this case, how they experience virtual worlds. Our own future plans are to collaborate with those who use different methodologies and also to use SMM in various ways to further elucidate our understanding of how people experience virtual worlds.

ACKNOWLEDGEMENTS

The study presented in this chapter was carried out as part of the collective research project, "Sense-Making Strategies and User-Driven Innovation in Virtual Worlds: New Market Dynamics, Social and Cultural Innovation, and Knowledge Construction" (2008–12), Roskilde University and Copenhagen Business School. We would like to thank the Danish Strategic Research Council (KINO committee) for funding the project (grant no. 09–063261). We would also like to thank Christopher J. Olson for his assistance with data mining and communication theorist Richard F. Carter for his germinal work.

REFERENCES

Adams, Suellen S. 2009. "What Games Have to Offer: Information Behavior and Meaning Making in Virtual Play Spaces." *Library Trends* 57 (4): 676–93.
Albrechtslund, Anne-Mette. 2010. "Gamers Telling Stories: Understanding Narrative Practices in an Online Community." *Convergence: The International Journal of Research into New Media Technologies* 16 (1): 112–24.
Barker, Martin. 2006. "I Have Seen the Future and It Is Not Here Yet . . .; or, On Being Ambitious for Audience Research." *The Communication Review* 9 (2): 123–41.
Bell, Mark. W. 2008. "Toward a Definition of 'Virtual Worlds'." *Journal of Virtual Worlds Research* 1 (1): http://jvwresearch.org.
Bessière, Katherine, A. Fleming Seay, and Sara Kiesler. 2007. "The Ideal Elf: Identity Exploration in World of Warcraft." *Cyberpsychology and Behavior* 10 (4): 530–35.
Boellstorff, Tom. 2008. *Coming of Age in Second Life: An Anthropologist Explores the Virtually Human.* Princeton, NJ: Princeton University Press.
Choi, Boreum, Inseong Lee, Dongseong Choi, and Jinwoo Kim. 2007. "Collaborate and Share: An Experimental Study of the Effects of Task and Reward Interdependencies in Online Games." *Cyberpsychology and Behavior* 10 (4): 591–95.
Cole, Helena, and Mark D Griffiths. 2007. "Social Interactions in Massively Multiplayer Online Role-playing Gamers." *Cyberpsychology and Behavior* 10 (4): 575–83.
Dervin, Brenda. 1993. "Verbing Communication: Mandate for Disciplinary Invention." *Journal of Communication* 43 (3): 45–54.
Dervin, Brenda. 2008. "Interviewing as Dialectical Practice: Sense-Making Methodology as Exemplar." Paper presented at the annual meeting for the International Association for Media and Communication Research, Stockholm.
Dervin, Brenda, and Lois Foreman-Wernet, eds. 2003. *Sense-Making Methodology Reader: Selected Writings of Brenda Dervin.* Cresskill, NJ: Hampton Press.
Dervin, Brenda, and Charles M. Naumer. 2009. "Sense-Making." In *Encyclopedia of Communication Theory*, vol. 2, edited by Stephen W. Littlejohn and Karen A. Foss, 876–80. Thousand Oaks, CA: Sage.

Feldon, David F., and Yasmin B. Kafai. 2008. "Mixed Methods for Mixed Reality: Understanding Users' Avatar Activities in Virtual Worlds." *Educational Technology Research and Development* 56 (5–6): 575–93.

Fiedler, Marina, and Ernan Haruvy. 2009. "The Lab versus the Virtual Lab and Virtual Field—an Experimental Investigation of Trust Games with Communication." *Journal of Economic Behavior and Organization* 72 (2): 716–24.

Fields, Deborah A., and Yasmin B. Kafai. 2008. "A Connective Ethnography of Peer Knowledge, Sharing and Diffusion in a Tween Virtual World. *International Journal of Computer-Supported Collaborative Learning* 4 (1): 47–68.

Friedman, Doron, Yuval Karniel, and Amit Lavie Dinur. 2009. "Comparing Group Discussion in Virtual and Physical Environments." *Presence: Teleoperators and Virtual Environments* 18 (4): 286–93.

Gadamer, Hans-Georg. 1975. *Truth and Method*. Translated by Garrett Barden and John Cummings. New York: Seabury Press.

Gauntlett, David. 2009. "Media Studies 2.0: A Response." *Interactions: Studies in Communication and Culture* 1 (1): 147–57.

Giddens, Anthony. (1979) 2002. "Agency, Structure." In *Contemporary Sociological Theory*, edited by Craig Calhoun, Joseph Gerteis, James Moody, Steven Pfaff, and Indermohan Virk, 232–43. Oxford, UK: Blackwell Publishers.

Golub, Alex. 2010. "Being in the World (of Warcraft): Raiding, Realism, and Knowledge Production in a Massively Multiplayer Online Game." *Anthropological Quarterly* 83 (1): 17–45.

Grabowski, Andrzej, and Natalia Kruszewska. 2007. "Experimental Study of the Structure of a Social network and Human Dynamics in a Virtual Society." *International Journal of Modern Physics* 18 (10): 1527–35.

Griffiths, Marie, and Ben Light. 2008. "Social Networking and Digital Gaming Media Convergence: Classification and its Consequences for Appropriation." *Information Systems Frontiers* 10 (4) (May 28): 447–59.

Hall, Stuart. (1973) 1993. "Encoding, Decoding." In *The Cultural Studies Reader*, edited by Simon During, 90–103. New York: Routledge.

Hermes, Joke. 2009. "Audience Studies 2.0: On the Theory, Politics and Method of Qualitative Audience Research." *Interactions: Studies in Communication and Culture* 1 (1): 111–27.

Hussain, Zaheer, and Mark D. Griffiths. 2009. "The Attitudes, Feelings, and Experiences of Online Gamers: A Qualitative Analysis." *Cyberpsychology and Behavior* 12 (6): 747–753.

Jin, Seung-A A. 2009. "Modality Effects in Second Life: The Mediating Role of Social Presence and the Moderating Role of Product Involvement." *CyberPsychology & Behavior* 12 (6): 717–21.

Josephs, Ingrid E. 2000. "A Psychological Analysis of a Psychological Phenomenon: The Dialogical Construction of Meaning." *Social Science Information* 39: 115–29.

Katz, Elihu, Jay G. Blumler, and Michael Gurevitch. 1974. "Utilization of Mass Communication by the Individual." In *The Uses of Mass Communications: Current Perspectives on Gratifications Research,* edited by Jay G. Blumler and Elihu Katz, 19–34. Beverly Hills, CA: Sage.

Morley, David. 2006. "Unanswered Questions in Audience Research." *The Communication Review* 9 (2): 101–21.

Oliver, Martin, and Diane Carr. 2009. "Learning in Virtual Worlds: Using Communities of Practice to Explain How People Learn from Play." *British Journal of Educational Technology* 40 (3): 444–57.

Ostrander, Margaret. 2008. "Talking, Looking, Flying, Searching: Information Seeking Behaviour in Second Life." *Library High Technology* 26 (4): 512–24.

Reinhard, CarrieLynn D. 2010. "Interviews within Experimental Frameworks: How to Make Sense of Sense-Making in Virtual Worlds." *Journal of Virtual Worlds Research* 3 (1). http://www.jvwresearch.org.

Reinhard, CarrieLynn D., and Brenda Dervin. 2013. "Studying Audiences with Sense-Making Methodology". In *The International Encyclopedia of Media Studies (Vol. IV)*, edited by Angharad Valdivia and Radhika Parameswaran, 81–104. Oxford, UK: Blackwell.

Savolainen, Reijo. 1993. "The Sense-making Theory—Reviewing the Interests of a User-Centered Approach to Information Seeking and Use." *Information Processing and Management* 29 (1): 13–28.

Schroeder, Ralph. 2008. "Virtual Worlds Research: Past, Present & Future." *Journal of Virtual Worlds Research* 1 (1): http://www.jvwresearch.org.

Shin, Dong Hee. 2009. "The Evaluation of User Experience of the Virtual World in Relation to Extrinsic and Intrinsic Motivation." *International Journal of Human-Computer Interaction* 25 (6): 530–53.

Smyth, Joshua M. 2007. "Beyond Self-selection in Video Game Play: An Experimental Examination of the Consequences of Massively Multiplayer Online Role-playing Game Play." *Cyberpsychology and Behavior* 10 (5): 717–21.

Voulgari, Iro, and Vassilis Komis. 2010. "'Elven Elder LVL59 LFP/RB. Please PM Me': Immersion, Collaborative Tasks and Problem-solving in Massively Multiplayer Online Games." *Learning, Media and Technology* 35 (2): 171–202.

8 Exploring Stakeholders of Open-Source Virtual Worlds through a Multimethod Approach

Zeynep Yetis, Robin Teigland, and Paul M. Di Gangi

Recent years have seen a surge of interest by practitioners and academics in the development of open-source software (OSS), computer software that is "made freely available to all" (von Hippel and von Krogh 2003). This interest has also spread to the development of the three-dimensional (3D) immersive Internet or virtual worlds, with OpenSimulator, realXtend, and Hippo Browser representing some of the OSS projects with virtual world applications. For example, the OpenSimulator project is an open-source 3D application server that enables users to develop and customize their own virtual worlds based on their specific technology and use preferences. The OpenSimulator community comprises a very diverse group of actors from across the globe, for example, independent users and hobbyists, freelancers, nonprofit organizations such as universities and research institutes, entrepreneurs and small and large for-profit firms who volunteer their time, effort, and resources for the development of OpenSimulator. The sustainability, or the continuous provision of "benefits for members over the long term" (Butler 2001, 347), of OSS communities such as the OpenSimulator, is dependent on the ability of the community's diverse actors to strike a balance between their often conflicting goals, norms, and values. Furthermore, sustainability may be especially difficult when the community is embedded within an external environment characterized by turbulent change—such as high technological uncertainty.

It seems that OSS virtual world communities continue to increase in number and scope. However, because these communities are a relatively new model for organizing economic activity, we have a limited understanding of how such communities sustain their operations through ensuring benefits and rewards that are attractive to all parties. To improve our understanding of the sustainability of such communities, one approach is to explore the social dynamics among the different sets of community actors or stakeholders and to investigate the structures and resources by which different stakeholder groups share power and resources and self-organize in order to achieve sustainability. This is the approach presented in this chapter. The purpose of the chapter is to address the following methodological question: "How can open source virtual world communities be investigated using the well-established concepts of stakeholders and resources from stakeholder theory?"

To address this question, the chapter discusses the methodological issues we encountered while investigating the OpenSimulator community. We begin by presenting a brief literature review of open-source software and stakeholder theory to familiarize the reader with the relevant theories and concepts. We then present three methods of analysis that we applied in our investigation: stakeholder analysis, content analysis, and social network analysis. We provide brief reviews of previous research using these methods before presenting our reasoning on how we applied them in our study. Thereafter, we present and discuss our case of OpenSimulator before concluding with some reflections and a discussion. Our intention with this chapter is that readers may not only learn how to investigate virtual world communities but also learn about the social dynamics of the emerging phenomenon of virtual world communities.

OPEN-SOURCE SOFTWARE AND STAKEHOLDERS: THEORIES AND CONCEPTS

Open-Source Software Communities

Open-source software (OSS) is computer software created collaboratively through the self-organization of developers voluntarily contributing to developing and maintaining the software's source code due to their shared interest in the software's functionality. The software is available to the public to study, change, improve, and redistribute free of charge. OSS has gained widespread interest in the last decade among scholars and industry, with projects like LINUX (computer operating system), MySQL (relational database management system), Apache (Web server software), and GNOME (desktop environment and graphical user interface) being only a few examples. A growing number of OSS projects and their accompanying communities have led to increased participation by individuals from across the globe and by firms of all sizes looking for ways to leverage the knowledge created in these communities. For example, a study in 2006 revealed that a sample of 158 firms contributing to OSS had a total of 530,000 employees and a total revenue of 231.4 billion (Ghosh 2006; Mehra, Black, and Lee 2010). More recently, several OSS communities have emerged that are developing virtual world technologies such as OpenSimulator, realXtend, and the Hippo Browser. These projects have a 3D aspect that facilitates a strong sense of immersion for both its developers and users, setting them apart from traditional open-source projects in two-dimensional (2D) settings (Figure 8.1).

The ability of an OSS community to sustain itself over time is a challenging task and not always successful. A recent study on SourceForge revealed that although this popular development platform hosts more than 168,000

Figure 8.1 OpenSimulator Core Developer meeting

projects, most of these become inactive soon after registration with the vast majority exhibiting little or no activity after the first year, suggesting abandonment by the project's developers (Chengular–Smith, Sidorova, and Daniel 2010; Madey and Christley 2008; Stewart, Darcy, and Daniel 2006). As a result, firms remain uneasy about expending resources in communities because of the potential for little return on investment which is often attributed to divergent interests among key participants within the community (Gartner 2010). Research has shown that the sustainability of an open source community is dependent upon the ability of the community's different actors to strike a balance between their often-conflicting goals (von Hippel and von Krogh 2003). In contrast to a traditional firm, an open-source community is organized as a network, dependent on contributions, such as time, energy, material, money, and human capital, by a diverse set of individuals and organizations that are loosely affiliated and governed by social relationships (O'Mahony and Ferraro 2007).

Stakeholder Theory

Originally developed for use by firms, the stakeholder approach helps managers understand how they could better manage the firm's various interested parties (Mitchell, Agle, and Wood 1997). Stakeholder refers to any party that has an interest in the outcome of a particular process. Essentially, the stakeholder approach is about "groups and individuals who can affect the organization" (Ramirez 1999, 102). A basic principle of the stakeholder approach is to understand who the stakeholders are and how they influence goal achievement (Freeman 1984).

Stakeholder theory posits that organizations require resources to survive and that these resources are acquired from actors within an organization's environment. Organizational researchers have labeled such actors "stakeholders" (Freeman 1984, 46). Pfeffer and Salancik (1978, 43) have argued that "because organizations are not self-sustained or self-sufficient, the environment must be relied upon to provide support." Similarly to other organizations, an open-source community must also ensure continued access to a pool of resources to sustain itself (Butler 2001; Rice 1982); however, one could expect open source communities to be particularly dependent on the pool of resources brought by their participants due to their more porous and emergent nature compared with traditional organizations.

One of the concerns of the stakeholder perspective is to elicit how a focal organization gains access to resources through its ability to influence stakeholders. Building on Pfeffer (1981), stakeholder theory argues that power accrues to those stakeholders who control resources needed by the focal organization, which may lead to power differentials among stakeholders and between the organization and its stakeholders (Mitchell, Bradley, and Wood 1997). Thus, it is not merely the relationship between the focal organization and its stakeholders that is important; the concentration of power and the overarching network structure within which a stakeholder resides also determine the ability of a stakeholder to achieve a return on its investment as well as the ability of a community to sustain itself (Pfeffer and Salancik 1978; Rowley, Kupiec-Teahan, and Leeming 2007). This view suggests the importance of stakeholders and their structural positioning in their network for the sustainability (long-term maintenance) of the community.

To improve our understanding of the sustainability of open-source virtual world communities, we apply stakeholder theory to investigate the structures and resources by which different stakeholder groups share power and resources and self-organize in order to achieve community sustainability. In the following, we present the methodological issues that accompany our choice of theoretical approach.

OUR METHODOLOGICAL APPROACH

This section presents a set of three methods of analysis for our investigation: stakeholder analysis, content analysis, and social network analysis. For each of these methods, we provide a brief review of how they have been applied in previous research, before presenting our reasoning on how we applied them in our study. The first section discusses the possible methodologies that can be used to identify the stakeholders of an open source virtual world community and thus help to answer the following question: "Who are the stakeholders of an open source virtual world community and how can we identify them?" The next section discusses our choice of content analysis to answer the question, "What resources do the different stakeholders contribute to the open source virtual world community?" The last section introduces our social network analysis choices related to investigating the question, "How can we identify the relationships among the different stakeholders of an open source virtual world community?"

Stakeholder Analysis

Within the stakeholder literature, there is an ongoing discussion about how to identify stakeholders (e.g., Mitchell, Agle, and Wood 1997). Developers of stakeholder theory have found that classifying stakeholders into useful categories based on certain attributes facilitates the analysis (Frooman 1999; Rowley, Kupiec-Teahan, and Leeming 2007). Chevalier and Buckles (2008) proposed a list that can aid in the process of identifying key actors and stakeholders, including the following: identification by experts or other stakeholders, by self-selection (in response to advertisements or announcements), through written records or census data (which may provide information to categorize by age, gender, religion, and residence), through oral or written accounts of major events (identifying the people who were involved), or through using a checklist of likely stakeholder categories (Reed et al. 2009).

Reed et al. (2009) discussed the stakeholder identification process as an iterative process in which additional stakeholders are added as the analysis continues (such as using expert opinion, focus groups, semistructured interviews, snowball sampling, or a combination of these). Clarkson (1995) noted the risk that some stakeholders might be omitted during the identification process, resulting in not all relevant stakeholders of the phenomenon being identified. Clarke and Clegg (1998) assert that it is often not possible to include all stakeholders and a line must be drawn (such as demographic criteria: nationality or age) based on well-founded criteria established by the researcher. Reed et al. (2009) state that the decision about whom to include may depend on the method used for identifying stakeholders and on the purpose of the stakeholder analysis.

Social network analysis (SNA), which we discuss further in the following, is another method that can aid researchers in identifying stakeholders in different empirical settings. In an environmental application of SNA, Prell et al. (2008) demonstrate how knowledge gained from analyzing the social networks of stakeholders can be employed for selecting stakeholders. To identify stakeholders and issues, Prell et al. conducted an iterative stakeholder analysis involving focus groups and interviews. Their analysis identified more than two hundred relevant stakeholder organizations that were eventually placed into seven categories. These categories were later checked with participants from the earlier rounds of interviews and the focus group.

Turning to our study, in the initial stage we chose to conduct interviews to learn about the social dynamics of the OpenSimulator community and to help us to identify the stakeholders of the community. According to McNamara (1999), interviews are particularly useful for getting the story behind a participant's experiences, and they enable the interviewer to gain in-depth information on the topic under study. We employed a semistructured interview strategy that allowed us to develop a flexible interview structure that can be used in conjunction with a variety of other methods and theories (Longhurst 2003). The semistructured approach allows the researcher to present a general direction in terms of interview focus, but it allows participants to both adapt and change based on the responses given during the interview session. However, caution should be taken to ensure that the initial questions are carefully designed to elicit the interviewee's ideas and opinions on the topic of interest (as opposed to leading the interviewee toward preconceived choices). In addition to being an excellent discovery-stage method, interviews are valuable for validation feedback to determine whether the observations made by the researchers align with the historical context of the community. These interviews gave us an initial idea of the different categories of stakeholders involved in the OpenSimulator community.

Additionally, we conducted a literature review to find out how other scholars have identified the stakeholders of OSS communities. Existing literature on open-source communities has identified two groups of stakeholders who participate in such platforms: (1) individuals participating on their own behalf and (2) employees who participate on behalf of a firm (e.g., Dahlander and Wallin 2006; West and Gallagher 2006). However, our initial interviews revealed the existence of more diverse sets of actors such as community members who represent public organizations or individuals who make their living through selling their services by developing applications. Therefore, we wanted to take a more refined approach to identifying the members of the community than simply drawing on the two categories in the existing research literature. Similarly to a few previous studies (e.g., Dahlander and Wallin 2006), we chose to base our classification schema on an individual member's organizational affiliation and identify the stakeholders using the available information on the mailing lists, wiki postings, and a variety of social networking sites and webpages. We refer to this identification process as "tagging" in the rest of this chapter.

Content Analysis

Content analysis is a methodology used to investigate communication in the social sciences, and has been defined as a "systematic, replicable technique for compressing many words of text into fewer content categories based on explicit rules of coding" (Stemler, 2001). Research in OSS literature has used textual analysis mainly to interpret different aspects of technical communication and software contributions by community members. For example, Iivari (2009) outlines a textual approach for the analysis of the relationship among different actors in information technology production and incorporates the approach in the analysis of the role of users in the OSS development literature. In a study that examined how people advance, or progress, in a collectively managed open-source software project, Dahlander and O'Mahony (2011) coded the content of 137 mailing lists used by the GNOME community to distinguish different types of project activities in order to investigate technical communication. They sampled messages on each list to determine the list's focus of conversation and consolidated their codes into two basic categories of theoretical interest: technical discussions and coordination work. Furthermore, a few studies have also used textual analysis to investigate the social dynamics of virtual environments. Schwartz (2006) examined the virtual environments of four recent games by conducting textual analysis of the representation of fantasy, realism, and othering. Martin (2005) investigated the ways in which visual elements in online games affect the process of identifying with an online self through textual analysis of the online forums associated with the game World of Warcraft.

Although there are numerous textual analysis techniques offering various advantages to the researcher, for example, computational hermeneutics, concordance analysis, and conversational analysis, we decided to adopt content analysis as our technique in this study. Content analysis enables the quantitative analysis of a large number of texts through the identification of words or concepts used in the text. To date, content analysis has been met with limited success for a variety of reasons (see Carley 1993); however, recent developments have improved the method which we describe in the following.

Since our purpose in this study was to identify and characterize the various sets of stakeholders in the community, conducting a content analysis would enable us to identify words that were most representative of the various stakeholder groups and thus enable us to better understand the resources that each group was contributing to the community. Recent developments in the area of content analysis include the "word burst" technique, which identifies the words in a text that are most characteristic of a certain person or group (Kleinberg 2004). What is particular to word burst analysis is that it does not determine the absolute frequency of words used in the analyzed text, but instead it identifies the words that are most overrepresented in a portion of a text compared to the entire text using the "probabilistic generative model." This implies that words that are more characteristic of a person or a group rank more highly than do words that are less characteristic of a person or a group compared to the group as a whole.

A comparison of the word burst analysis technique with other techniques shows that word burst analysis produces results that are more refined than those produced using absolute or relative measures. Absolute measures tend to skew the results in favor of common words whereas relative measures give precedence to less common words (Kleinberg 2004). In the example of our study, the word burst analysis can provide insights into the different stakeholder groups involved in the OpenSimulator community by identifying the words that are most overrepresented by a particular stakeholder group in the communication compared to the communication by all stakeholder groups in the community. Moreover, we can identify the themes associated with each stakeholder group that depict the topical interests of that group.

Social Network Analysis

Social networks are constituted by actors or nodes that are connected to one another through socially meaningful relations that can be analyzed for structural patterns (Prell, Hubacek, and Reed 2009). Social network analysis (SNA) is the mapping and measuring of the structural patterns that emerge among these actors and represents "an analytic technique that researchers use to represent the relational data of networks and to investigate the nature and properties of these relations" (Teigland 2003, 115). Typically, nodes represent the people, resources, objects, organization units, and so on, whereas the links between nodes signify the relationships or ties between nodes. SNA helps researchers to understand the structural positioning and structural embeddedness of the stakeholders within a network. As a result, researchers can explore individual structural positions as well as the overall network structure in order to gain a contextual understanding of the relationships of a particular node and the network as a whole.

A small number of studies have applied SNA in Massively Multiplayer Online Game (MMOG) settings in order to understand the social structures of MMOGs. Shi and Huang (2004) derived certain social characteristics (e.g., popularity, influences, importance of avatar) and traits of avatar personality (e.g., trustworthiness of an avatar, leadership, selfishness, attraction, etc.) in an MMOG from SNA to reveal more about the social structure of these virtual environments. Ducheneaut et al. (2006) evaluated the social environment provided by a game guild (persistent association) in an MMOG by building social networks for each guild in order to assess the guild's potential for sociability and to quantify joint activities. In a later study, Ducheneaut et al. (2007) examined some of the factors that could explain the success or failure of a game guild based on more than a year of data collected from five MMOGs (World of Warcraft) servers by focusing on the structural properties of these groups as represented by their social networks and other variables. Similarly, Williams et al. (2006) interviewed a representative sample of players of World of Warcraft in order to map the social dynamics of guilds, using the time a player spent together in a group with his or her guild mates as the measure of the ties among participants.

Rosen and Corbit (2009) examined the structure of the communicative interactions within a Multiuser Virtual Environment (MUVE) through network analysis by mapping out the social networks from chatlogs of the IRC (Internet Relay Chat) interaction. They analyzed communication networks, defined as "the patterns of contact that are created by the flow of messages among communicators through time and space" by Monge and Contractor (2003, 3) in order to identify the communication structures and flows in a MUVE. By doing so, they presented a structural view of the communicative interaction within the MUVE.

In order to conduct a social network analysis, one must define the boundary for the network and then collect data on the nodes within this boundary. There are several challenges involved in conducting SNA in any environment. First, a response rate of at least 80 percent of the individuals in the entire network is required since holes in the network caused by nonrespondents can easily distort the results. Second, social network data tend to be more challenging to collect than are ordinary survey data because of their need to be dyadic (relating to or based on two nodes or actors). Finally, it is difficult for social network surveys to be anonymous because the method generally requires the identification of each individual. This often presents problems because it is quite common that individuals see this type of survey as a breach of their privacy, that is, posing questions about an individual's personal connections such as "With whom do you eat lunch?" Thus, it is not surprising that investigations using social network methods in relation to only one organization are quite common and that the majority of sociocentric network studies on individuals tend to be in smaller organizations or within organizational divisions or use some form of publicly available data (see Hansen 1996; Marsden 1990).

The intention in our study was that, once the stakeholders of the open source virtual world community had been identified, we wanted to look beyond the attributes of these individuals to examine the relations among them. This would shed light on how actors are positioned within the network and how relations are structured into overall network patterns (Scott 2000; Wasserman and Faust 1994; Wellman and Gulia 1999). Social network theory and social network analyses offer a wide range of analytical tools to describe and analyze emergent structures (Teigland 2003). Our starting point was that the application of social network theory and social network measures to an open-source virtual world community would improve our theoretical understanding and empirical knowledge of these emergent networks.

In order to conduct SNA, we surmised that the mailing list archives that were available on a community could be used to create the dyads needed for mapping the network structure. Because most of the development activity takes place on OSS mailing lists, we anticipated that they could give us a view of the structural relations among the developers of the community. However, we were aware of the fact that mailing lists do not include all the activity, so we might miss informal backchannel conversations as well as private discussions. Because we did not know how many of the discussions were actually taking place on the mailing list, clearly a limitation is attached to the method we are using. However, we performed follow-up interviews as a mitigation strategy to ensure that the network structure, its overall description, and our key findings concerning the structural network would be valid.

INTRODUCTION TO THE CASE STUDY

The OpenSimulator project (http://opensimulator.org) is an online open-source virtual world community that brings together organizations and individuals. We chose to use the OpenSimulator community as a focal community for our research for a number of reasons: (1) there has been continuous activity since its foundation in 2007, indicating that it has been sustainable to date; (2) it represents an OSS community with well-established firms participating (e.g., IBM and Intel), (3) it has a diverse membership in terms of demographics (e.g., age, educational and professional backgrounds, nationality, and geographical location); (4) it exhibits a number of characteristics raised in the literature on OSS communities that can accentuate the development of conflict, such as anonymity and intellectual property; and (5) it exists within a highly uncertain external environment due to the relative immaturity of the 3D Internet industry that can then have an impact on the supply of resources to the community.

OpenSimulator is an open-source multiplatform, multiuser 3D application server operating under the Berkeley Software Distribution license that enables individuals and firms across the globe to customize their virtual worlds based on their technology and use preferences. The project is powered by the efforts of the community members who devote their time and energy to the development processes. From its inception in 2007 to December 2011, at the time of our data collection, 101 developers had committed 16,056 submissions to the OpenSimulator project resulting in 338,467 lines of code in use and an estimated cost (based on the Constructive Cost Model (COCOMO)) of $4.99 million dollars (USD). The project has a global reach, crossing twenty-two time zones, and the community hosts a diverse group of members.

There are many ways for interested individuals to participate in and contribute to the OpenSimulator project: via IRC (Internet Relay Chat), mailing lists, Twitter hashtag (#OpenSim), and the OpenSimulator Wiki as well as through individual members' websites or blogs. Another way to participate is to create an OpenSimulator-related project hosted on SourceForge (http://forge.opensimulator.org/gf/) or elsewhere. With regard to the mailing lists, the community members can participate based on two generic roles. First, members who are *users* of the OpenSimulator platform can join the User mailing list that can be used to pose questions on usage, report bugs, and engage in conversation with like-minded individuals interested in utilizing OpenSimulator either personally or professionally. Second, members who are developers can participate in the Developer mailing list that discusses technical issues, project updates, and news announcements concerning modules and company actions as well as social communication to construct and embody a sense of community among the developers that is separate from the users.

Outline of Methods

Several data collection sources and analysis methods were used to conduct a multimethod case study of the OpenSimulator Developer community (http://opensimulator.org). Our decision to adopt a case study approach was based on the need to provide a highly contextualized and qualitatively rich description of how stakeholders interact with one another to obtain resources and develop the public good for the entire community (Benbasat, Goldstein, and Mead 1987; Yin 1994). Furthermore, because the existing literature did not adequately describe the phenomenon under investigation, theory construction was necessary in order to identify the relevant factors to private-collective communities (Eisenhardt 1989).

We conducted interviews with members of the community and scraped the relevant online sites and mailing lists for content analysis and relational tie data for the first four years and three months of the community. Furthermore, in order to investigate the dynamics of the community over time by comparing data sets, we chose to divide the data into two periods of (1) August 2007 to September 2009 and (2) October 2009 to October 2011.

This division was based on two factors: (1) an internal change in which the OpenSimulator code reached a relatively stable development level at the end of September 2009 and (2) an external change in which much of the hype and interest surrounding virtual worlds had faded (based on interviewee comments).

Interviews

We started our study by conducting interviews with members of the Open-Simulator community to get the "big picture" of what is going on in the community. First, we conducted ten unstructured and then twelve semistructured interviews with members of the OpenSimulator community. These interviews were all conducted virtually through the virtual world of Second Life, via OpenSimulator (Figure 8.2) or via Skype. Using the snowball technique, we conducted interviews with core developers and members of the OpenSimulator community while asking each interviewee to identify additional individuals to interview. Questions concerning the roles, resources, and motivations for contributing to the community were included in the

Figure 8.2   Conducting an interview with a member of the OpenSimulator community

interview questionnaire to ensure a rubric to assess resource contributions in our further analysis.

In order to secure interview appointments with members of the Open-Simulator, we sent them emails with background information on our study, requesting a one–hour interview. Almost everyone we contacted replied to us within a few days with a positive reaction. Once we conducted the interviews, we reflected on the very positive attitude of everyone we interviewed. Even though we had asked for a one-hour interview, in many cases the interviewees gave us two hours of their time, suggesting that many of the interviewees were passionate about their participation in the community and were interested in ensuring that all of the relevant information was included for our analysis to be complete. We also "gave back" to the community by sharing the results of our study as much as we could. Our research and its results were published in *Hypergrid Business* (a magazine for enterprise users of virtual worlds) twice.

Tagging

In our "tagging" of the different members of the OpenSimulator Community, we identified the following organizational affiliations: (1) Entrepreneur—self-employed or founder of a firm, (2) Academic—employed at a university, (3) Hobbyist—participating in OpenSimulator in own free time due to personal interests, (4) Large Firm Employee (>250 employees)[1], (5) Non-profit Employee, (6) Local Public Sector Employee, (7) Federal Public Sector Employee, and (8) SME1 (Small/Medium Enterprise) Employee (<250 employees). For those in groups 4 through 8, these individuals participated within OpenSimulator because of responsibilities assigned by their employer. Although this may be considered a fine-grained categorization (in contrast to grouping need-based individuals into one category or dividing members into firms and hobbyists), we maintained this view of stakeholder categories in order not to confound any findings by grouping together different organizations. In order to tag the different members of the community, we went through the mailing list names of the members (retrieved through Web scraping) to gather information and identified the organizational affiliations of individuals according to the categories listed earlier. We mainly used social networking sites such as LinkedIn, blogs, and corporate websites (all publicly available) in order to gather information on each community member. This tagging turned out to be quite significant in terms of the amount of time required per member because, on average, it took about fifteen to twenty minutes to ascertain each member's organizational affiliation. Because the assignment of members into stakeholder groups was a crucial part of our research, it was important that every member was tagged correctly. Therefore, two researchers conducted this coding independently and cross-checked each other's work.

Content Analysis

We used the OpenSimulator mailing lists for content analysis and relational tie data (to conduct the social network analysis described below) for the first four years and three months of the community—from the emergence of the community in August 2007 to the end of October 2011. We conducted the content analysis of the messages posted during each period by using Kleinberg's (2004) "probabilistic generative model," which—as noted earlier—identifies the words that are most overrepresented in a portion of a text compared to the entire text. This analysis generated a word burst for each stakeholder group that identified the words that were most overrepresented in the messages posted by a particular group compared to the sum of all messages by all groups during each period.

Social Network Analysis

We then used the relational tie data based on the mailing lists to perform SNA using UCINET version 6.181 (Borgatti et al. 2002) to determine the overall network structure of the OpenSimulator community as well as the structural positioning of different groups of stakeholders within the community. We discuss this analysis in detail in the following.

We validated the results of our social network analysis by interviewing several of the most central members of the community to determine whether the observations made by our research team aligned with the historical context of the community. However, as an ongoing research study, we will further use the SNA results to identify individuals to interview who may possess a unique perspective of the community due to his or her social interactions. This will allow additional validation of the archival data and provide additional descriptive and contextual information that can add depth to our findings.

ANALYSIS

The following sections discuss the use of the methodological framework as well as the methodological challenges we encountered during the stakeholder identification process and the content and social network analyses we used to investigate the OpenSimulator Community.

Anonymous Identities

During the tagging process, it was occasionally challenging to find information on some community members for stakeholder group classification. Interestingly, most of these individuals would represent themselves with their avatar identities on the OpenSimulator mailing lists. As mentioned earlier, it was vital for our analysis that we were able to correctly identify each active participant.

Quite a number of scholars have studied this aspect of anonymity in virtual worlds, and this helped us to reason why there are quite a few anonymous community members. Virtual worlds, as a communication medium, allow greater freedom to individuals in terms of expressing themselves more freely. Avatar-based interaction maintains real-world anonymity that results in participants not knowing the real-world identities of those with whom they interact (Fiedler and Haruvy 2009). Analyzing user goals in cyberspace, Jung and Kang's (2010) results showed that people join social virtual world platforms to satisfy their social and hedonic needs and to escape from real-world constraints. Similarly, Russell (2008: 1467) summarized the significance of the aspect of anonymity by saying, "The primary allure of virtual worlds, and no doubt a large part of their success, derives from the anonymity they afford their denizens. In the real world, people often tailor their behavior according to what they perceive as their society's norms of what is appropriate for people of their age, appearance, job, social skills, or social status. The physical remove of virtual worlds inspires people to speak and move about freely, uninhibited by a fear of real-world repercussions."

During our tagging process, we decided to identify the active individuals in the OpenSimulator community, those who made more than four posts—a total of 138 individuals in period 1. Our choice of more than four posts was based first on the average number of messages sent by *all* community members per year (five messages) and then on lowering this threshold to ensure that all relevant individuals were included in our data set. An additional investigation of the content of the messages by people posting four or fewer posts during these periods revealed that the majority of these messages were not relevant to the community and thus received no response (e.g., spam). Thus, we chose this cutoff because we did not consider those with four or fewer posts to be significantly contributing to the community. In total, we coded 119 individuals (86 percent) of the 138 active individuals with a "real" identity. Of the remaining nineteen coded individuals, fourteen (10 percent) had well-established online identities, such as through Second Life or a website and five (3.6 percent) acted truly anonymously whom we coded as Hobbyists because we found no evidence that they were affiliated with any particular stakeholder group. In cases when members used their real names on the mailing list, it was easier to get public information about them on the Web. One observation was that company employees in almost all cases used their real names. Entrepreneurs usually used Gmail, and most of them possessed multiple email addresses registered on the mailing list.

For people who used an avatar name on the mailing list, usually the avatar name was the same avatar name they had originally used in Second Life. Interestingly, some of these people, even on their blogs, never talked about their real names; it was interesting to observe how immersed these members were in their avatar identities. They were often members of avatar-based communities, for example, a platform in which people write about new developments that take place in Second Life, and they updated themselves very well on what was going on in these communities.

Because it was difficult to find information about these people, it was quite difficult to tag them. For instance, a member who founded a grid wrote on his Google+ profile that he or she was "born to create" the grid he or she founded. Because this member was so immersed in virtual worlds and because we were not able to get any information at all on the person's real identity, we tagged him or her as a Hobbyist.

Allocating Members to Stakeholder Groups: Methodological Challenges

Another methodological challenge that we encountered during the tagging process was how to allocate some of the members to a particular stakeholder group. The main obstacle here was that those individuals possessed multiple identities. One member defined herself as a "modern polymath with professional experience and distinction in virtual worlds, digital art and design, English literature, computer programming, engineering (bioengineering and structural engineering) and physics" on her personal webpages. On another page about herself, she said that she "is an artist and director and entrepreneur; her real life avatar is also a novelist, programmer, scholar, scientist, and writer." This member, for instance, has the characteristics of both an Entrepreneur and a Hobbyist. In this particular case, we ended up tagging her as an Entrepreneur because this was one way she defined herself and because she regards her role in Second Life as the executive producer and visual/creative director of an enterprise within Second Life.

For another member, when we searched for her name on Google images, the search engine displayed tens of photos of her avatar but only one real photo of her. Interestingly her avatar and the real person look very much alike, which indicates the strong immersion of this member in the virtual environment. This member also had the traits of both an Entrepreneur and a Hobbyist. She was mainly an "Avapreneur," an entrepreneur in virtual worlds (Teigland 2010), and had a business selling virtual furniture in Second Life. An observation we made about the avatars of members who were immersed in virtual worlds was that such members usually belonged either to the Avapreneur (therefore Entrepreneur) or to the Hobbyist category.

There were also members who represented themselves with their avatars, even in social media tools such as Facebook. In some cases, these members had presentations on Slideshare and shared personal pictures that all belonged to their avatars. Another issue that made it difficult to allocate individuals to stakeholder groups stemmed from the fact that some people used more than one email to communicate on the Developers mailing list. Especially in cases in which one email was a corporate email and the other one Gmail, it was difficult to decide on the stakeholder group of the community member.

Confusion in allocating members to stakeholder groups also resulted from the ways in which community members introduced themselves. Even prominent members of the community, sometimes introduced and/or defined themselves through their passions and hobbies rather than their occupation (e.g., "I am a passionate tennis player and a 3D artist"). In such cases, we had to be careful to allocate them to the correct stakeholder group.

Revealing the Social Dynamics of OpenSimulator through Content Analysis and Social Network Analysis

As noted earlier, we conducted content analysis and generated word burst lists (for each stakeholder group) of the messages posted to the mailing list during period 1 (Table 1, shown in Figure 8.3) in order to analyze the content of these messages. Content analysis helped us identify the theme associated with each stakeholder group that depicts the topical interest of that group. However, we encountered a few challenges when conducting the content analysis. The word burst generated naturally included every single word that the mailing lists included. This created a lot of "noise" in the word burst lists generated. For instance, one active member of the community included the following sentence right after his name in each email he sent to the Developer mailing list: "*There is no silver bullet. Plus, werewolves make better neighbors than zombies, and they tend to keep the vampire population down.*" This resulted in the words *werewolves, zombies,* and *vampire* ranking quite high up on the word bursts of the stakeholder group to which he belonged. We first had different hypotheses regarding why these words were ranked so high on the list. We even hypothesized that the people in this stakeholder group were interested in a particular fantasy grid of virtual worlds. However, after a collective reflection session with the team and further analysis, we uncovered the real reason behind the high rank of these words and thus removed these words from the list. We had similar encounters with other email signatures and extensions.

Thus, in order to make sure the words on a word burst list were actually representative of the particular stakeholder group, we went through all the lists and cleaned them. We always started the cleaning process from the top of the word burst list with the most frequently used words, and for each of these words, we went into the emails to see in which context the word was used. Words deemed irrelevant by the research team were removed from the list. On average, it took around forty-five to sixty minutes to clean each stakeholder word burst list. The results of the word burst analysis are discussed further in the following.

To conduct a content analysis for a stakeholder list, we investigated the top thirty words by clustering the words into categories. These categories were then confirmed through reading the individual mails in which the words were placed. Our content analysis gave us insights into the different focuses of stakeholder groups and the types of resources contributed by

Academics	Entrepreneur	Hobbyist	Large Firm	Non-profit
inventory	state	debug	availabletype	hints
user	join	osg	processing	help
really	obscures	saving	file	tested
servers	night	succeeded	worlds	internal
think	pages	osgrid	users	similar
server	scene	shape	mathematics	correctly
millions	region	guest	center	bitsystem
region	believe	functions	tree	sanded
addresses	physics	guests	wrote	people
different	prerouting	grid	next	understood
inventoryserver	core	value	approach	router
modules	currency	build	computer	map
grid	incoming	sims	rest	regions
agent	revision	project	attachments	viewer
service	opencurrency	allow	asset	computer
hypergrid	separate	regions	respond	host
search	model	assets	corp.	precious
registry	propose	fatal	math	programmers
set	sounds	notions	types	scripts
scenes	local	logins	printing	locally
people	joint	total	machines	next
register	application	running	utilization	instances
services	assigned	plazas	dissemination	priorities
session	points	vehicle	prohibited	Sim
system	tag	cba	privileged	configured
push	memory	mono	separate	software
cap	prim	perhaps	review	part
happy	think	patches	emulator	holding
regions	defaults	copyright	pervasive	website
security	objects	tester	vector	height
Stakeholder Topical Theme				
Infrastructure Development	Applied Development	Testing	Data Processing	Installation & Use

Local Public	Federal Public	Res Inst.	SME
stolen	currency	behaviour	portability
centos	money	geometry	openid
ceo	risk	states	metadata
info	losing	vehicle	asset
screen	chatrooms	phantom	userserver
sue	commerce	integer	inventoryserver
free	inworld	unit	regionserver
sued	owner	physics	script
terminal	legal	state	goods
ward	due	appenders	class
loss	educational	patch	executed
svn	solutions	everybody	assets
override	core	body	assetbase
release	monetary	collision	inform
viewing	argument	prim	cable
wrote	implementation	options	compiler
having	corruption	geometries	plugins
urge	devolve	independant	packet
readable	essential	zone	scriptengine
confirm.	opencurrency	logging	lock
current/trunk	scope	initialrotation	service
supportinformation	immature	printstatus	private
widows	plans	vehicles	lively
file	claims	hidden	neighbours
immediate	software	shapes	tests
copy	case	cultures	hack
flavored	samplemoney	initialposition	touch
lends	external	globally	return
wished	dollars	flag	servicebase
bandwidth	functions	initialization	creationdate
Stakeholder Topical Theme			
Legal & Financial Issues	Legal & Financial Issues	Modeling	Application Development

Figure 8.3   Table 1—Thirty most characteristic words per stakeholder group—period 1

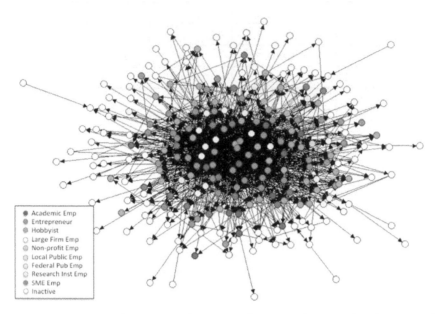

Figure 8.4   Network structure of OpenSimulator Developer mailing list—period 1

these stakeholder groups. For example, we found that Academics focused on the development of the technology infrastructure (e.g., inventory, servers, and regions) whereas Entrepreneurs tended to focus more on developing items related to user usage (e.g., night, region, and currency).

For the social network analysis, we generated the overarching network graphs using NetDraw based on an individual's replies to others in the community on the mailing lists. Figure 8.4 provides a snapshot of the network for the first period, depicting the relationship among the active members of the community.

Once we were able to obtain an idea of the structural composition of the community through the overarching network graphs, we calculated several individual scores for each stakeholder to understand his or her structural position and possible roles within the network. In social network theory, an actor's position determines his or her opportunities and constraints, and those actors who have more favorable network positions are those who generally have greater influence or power over others in the network (Hanneman and Riddle 2005). Although there is no single definition of what is a favorable position, network analysts have developed several measures such as degree, betweenness, closeness, eigenvector centrality, and structural holes to describe to what degree an actor holds certain positions in the network—see Figure 8.5 (Table 2).

Measure	Definition and Implication
Degree	The number of direct ties an actor has.
	The more ties an actor has, the more opportunities he/she has.
Closeness	Actors with a high closeness score have shorter average distances to all other nodes in the network.
	The closer an actor is to other actors, the more he/she can influence others.
Betweenness	How often an actor lies on the shortest paths between all other pairs of actors in the network.
	A high level of betweenness gives an actor the capacity to broker contacts among other actors.
Eigenvector	The degree to which an actor is connected to structurally important other individuals.
	Actors with a higher eigenvector score have a greater opportunity to influence others.
Structural hole	The degree to which an actor has a bridging position between groups.
	Actors with a greater degree of structural holes have an advantage in detecting and developing rewarding opportunities.

Figure 8.5 Table 2—Network structural position measures (Burt 2004; Hanneman and Riddle 2005)

For instance, individuals with high eigenvector scores indicate that individual was connected to other structurally important individuals (e.g., individuals who bridge structural holes, individuals with access to diverse subnetworks, etc.). Calculating these measures helped us to assess whether different stakeholders were structurally positioned within the network and whether this has an impact on stakeholders, as a group, within the larger network. We also calculated a structural hole measure to determine whether individuals positioned as bridges between subsets of the community associate with specific stakeholder groups. Figure 8.6 (Table 3) shows the network measures for the first period.

To determine whether the centrality measures were statistically different between stakeholder groups, we ran a means comparison test using SPSS (SPSS Inc., Chicago IL). The statistical test allows us to quantitatively demonstrate differences among the different groups and ensures that our interpretation of the key stakeholder groups holds in the light of the structural dynamics of the network. Our analyses thus led us to find that the stakeholder group of entrepreneurs had the highest degree of influence in the network relative to the other stakeholder groups, regardless of the measure.

The statistical analysis also lends support to our interest in collapsing the network based on stakeholder affiliation (Figure 8.7; Rowley, Kupiec-Teahan, and Leeming 2007). Because OpenSimulator is not an official organization with a focal organization, we ran two analyses: (1) all individual nodes were collapsed into one node based on stakeholder affiliation and (2) the separation of Core Developers at the end of each period to create a focal "organization" with the remaining network nodes connected

Group	Degree	Closeness	Betweenness	Eigenvector	Structural Hole
Entrepreneur	11.845	48.703	1.526	11.465	27.830
Large Firm	10.341	48.102	1.044	10.750	24.333
Pub Fed	9.957	47.433	1.079	9.697	23.000
Academic	9.560	46.770	0.896	9.297	22.667
Hobbyist	7.393	45.836	0.578	7.869	17.410
Non-profit	6.782	46.841	0.145	7.789	16.667
SME	6.465	45.641	0.541	7.228	15.133
Research	6.494	47.531	0.133	8.440	15.000
Pub Local	5.628	46.751	0.199	7.271	13.500
Periphery	1.069	37.784	0.033	1.372	2.511

Figure 8.6 Table 3—Network measures—period 1

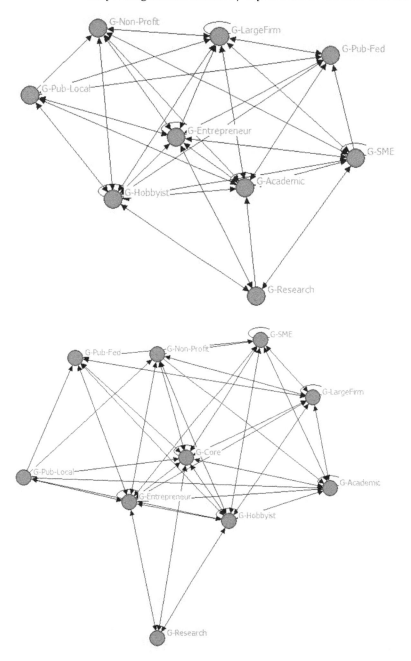

Figure 8.7 Collapsed node structure: Left without core and right with core—period 1

to each other and the core based on their collapsed stakeholder affiliation. Both figures indicate that there is a high degree of density in the overarching structure, with the stakeholder affiliation groups closely connected with one another.

DISCUSSION

Although stakeholder theory was originally developed for use by RL (real-life) firms and their managers, we found through our multimethod analysis that the concepts of stakeholders and resources also provide considerable insight into the investigation of open-source virtual world communities. Drawing on the OSS and stakeholder bodies of literature and our initial interviews, we developed a fine-grained stakeholder categorization scheme based on organizational affiliation. We were then able to categorize individual members of the OpenSimulator community into different stakeholder groups. Surprisingly, the most challenging aspect of this approach was the time commitment required to search and identify each individual. It was challenging to obtain publicly available information for a considerable number of individuals in order to classify them into our categorization matrix. Our content and social network analyses and final round of interviews further confirmed our categorization, revealing that these different stakeholder groups had quite differing norms, values, goals, and time frames despite their all being active in contributing to the development of the OpenSimulator community.

Our second task of identifying the resources contributed by the various stakeholder groups proved more challenging. The interviews and burst analyses enabled us to see which groups were most active in contributing certain resources, for example, entrepreneurs developing code and working with applied development; however, it took considerable time to clean the word burst lists in order to make sense of them. Furthermore, we found that resources related to issues other than pure code development, such as project management or talent recruiting skills, were much more difficult to attribute to certain stakeholder groups through our methods. In order to investigate this issue more thoroughly, a deeper qualitative data collection and analysis should be conducted.

Finally, regarding the relationships between the stakeholder groups, we were able to conduct social network analyses (despite the challenging tagging process) for at least 80 percent of the nodes in the network. Because we were able to tag almost all the active individuals easily, our data set was almost entirely complete. This enabled us to conduct various social network analyses at the individual, group, and community level. Our methods, data sources, challenges, and solutions are summarized in Figure 8.8 (Table 4).

With regard to lessons learned at a higher level of abstraction, we gained three significant insights into conducting research of phenomena that are

Method	Data Source	Challenge	Solution
Stakeholder analysis	Virtual world community sites	Identification/tagging of individuals due to anonymity issues	Use of secondary sources, e.g., social networking sites, blogs
Textual analysis / burst analysis	Mailing lists	Identification of non-relevant words	Use of secondary sources Collective reflection
Social network analysis	Mailing lists	Identification of nodes that are spammers and non-serious participants	Use of secondary sources, e.g., social networking sites, blogs Textual analysis of posts

Figure 8.8   Table 4—A multimethod approach, challenges, and solutions

emerging or in flux. First, we learned of the importance of *establishing a trusted relationship with the individuals* operating within the new phenomena. One of the researchers involved in this project had been active in virtual worlds for some years and had built not only an understanding of the phenomenon but also a credible reputation and significant network. This facilitated not only access to some of the key individuals within the community for interviews and access to other data, but also a deeper understanding of the phenomenon. Second, we learned of the importance of a *multidisciplinary team,* two of the researchers being from the field of marketing and strategy and the remaining one from the area of information systems. Although one of the researchers had an extensive understanding of virtual worlds, the other two were "newbies." Furthermore, the third researcher brought in new methodological insights due to her knowledge of word burst analysis. Third, we learned of the value of conducting *multimethod data collection and analyses* when applying concepts that are well established in the literature to new phenomena. Through our interviews, archival data, and various analytical methods, we were able to approach the investigation of our central concepts from various perspectives. The multidisciplinary team, combined use the trusting relationship built with key players within the community, enabled us to gather multiple sets of data.

CONCLUSION

A basic goal of the stakeholder approach is to understand who the stakeholders are and how they influence goal achievement (Freeman 1984). Our multimethod analysis of the OpenSimulator community revealed that this open-source virtual world community is similar to 2D communities and other face-to-face organizations in that it has a set of different stakeholders who contribute resources to the community to enable its sustainability. A noteworthy observation here is that an open-source community, be it based on developing virtual worlds or software applications, is not a traditional firm in the sense that it does not have a legal organization with paid employees producing products and/or services that are then sold on the market. As such, there is no formal boundary between the organization and any external stakeholders. Our analysis showed that the different stakeholder groups do indeed comprise the OpenSimulator community, and their interactions involving resource contribution and knowledge creation can be described through SNA. This provides insight into the relationships between the various stakeholder groups as well as into the overarching network structure within which each group is embedded. A thorough analysis of this structure and the relationships among the groups will enable a better understanding of the ability of the stakeholder groups to achieve a return on their investment in the community and thus for the community to sustain itself.

We look forward to continuing our research of the OpenSimulator community and of other virtual world communities as they emerge. Our intention with this chapter was to provide insights into our methodological approach and considerations for scholars interested in studying virtual world communities at the community or even the group or individual level.

ACKNOWLEDGMENTS

We would like to sincerely thank the members of the OpenSimulator community for their openness and helpfulness in conducting this study. It has been a real pleasure and extremely interesting to work with all of you! We would also like to thank Tomas Larsson, Christina Huitfeldt, Ayse Yetis Bayraktar, and Nuket Yetis for their support in our data collection and analysis.

REFERENCES

Benbasat, Izak, David K. Goldstein, and Melissa Mead. 1987. "The Case Research Strategy in Studies of Information Systems." *MIS Quarterly* 11:369–86.
Borgatti, S.P., Everett, M.G. and Freeman, L.C. 2002. "Ucinet for Windows: Software for Social Network Analysis." Harvard, MA: Analytic Technologies.
Burt, Ronald. 2004. "Structural Holes and Good Ideas." *American Journal of Sociology* 110 (2): 349–99.
Butler, Brian S. 2001. "Membership Size, Communication Activity, and Sustainability: A Resource-Based Model of Online Social Structures." *Information Systems Research* 12:346–62.
Carley, Kathleen. 1993. "Coding Choices for Textual Analysis: A Comparison of Content Analysis and Map Analysis." *Sociological Methodology* 23:75–126.
Chengalur–Smith, Indushobha, Anna Sidorova, and Sherae Daniel. 2010. "Sustainability of Free/Libre Open Source Projects: A Longitudinal Study." *Journal of the Association for Information Systems,* 11 (11): 657–83
Chevalier, Jaques M., and Daniel J. Buckles. 2008. *SAS2: A Guide to Collaborative Inquiry and Social Engagement.* London: Sage.

Clarke, Thomas, and Stewart Clegg. 1998. *Changing Paradigms: The Transformation of Management Knowledge for the 21st Century.* London: HarperCollins.

Clarkson, Max E. 1995. "A Stakeholder Framework for Analyzing and Evaluating Corporate Social Performance." *Academy of Management Review* 20:65–91.

Dahlander, Linus, and Siobhán O'Mahony. 2011. "Progressing to the Center: Coordinating Project Work." *Organization Science* 22 (4): 961–79.

Dahlander, Linus, and Martin W. Wallin. 2006. "A Man on the Inside: Unlocking Communities as Complementary Assets." *Research Policy* 35:1243–59.

Ducheneaut, Nicolas, Nicholas Yee, Eric Nickell, and Robert J. Moore. 2006. "'Alone Together?' Exploring the Social Dynamics of Massively Multiplayer Online Games." In *CHI '06: Proceedings of the SIGCHI Conference on Human Factors in Computing Systems*, edited by R. Grinter, T. Rodden, P. Aoki, E. Cutrell, R. Jeffries and G. Olson, 407–416. New York: Association of Computing Machinery.

Ducheneaut, Nicolas, Nicholas Yee, Eric Nickell, and Robert J. Moore. 2007. "The Life and Death of Online Gaming Communities: A Look at Guilds in World of Warcraft." In *CHI '07: Proceedings of the SIGCHI Conference on Human Factors in Computing Systems*, chaired by M. B. Rosson and D. Gilmour, 839–848. New York: Association of Computing Machinery.

Eisenhardt, Kathleen M. 1989. "Building Theories from Case Study Research." *Academy of Management Review* 14:532–50.

Fiedler, Marina, and Ernan Haruvy. 2009. "The Lab versus the Virtual Lab and Virtual Field—An Experimental Investigation of Trust Games with Communication." *Journal of Economic Behavior and Organization* 72 (2): 716–24.

Freeman, R. Edward. 1984. *Strategic Management: A Stakeholder Approach.* Boston: Pitman.

Frooman, Jeff. 1999. "Stakeholder Influence Strategies." *Academy of Management Review* 24:191–205.

Gartner. 2010. "Gartner Says More than 60 Percent of *Fortune* 1000 Companies with a Web Site Will Connect to or Host a Form of Online Community by 2010," *Gartner.com*, October 6, 2008. Accessed January 1, 2012. http://www.gartner.com/it/page.jsp?id=770914.

Ghosh, Rishab Aiyer. 2006. *Study on the Economic Impact of Open Source Software on Innovation and the Competitiveness of the Information and Communication Technologies (ICT) Sector in the EU.* Maastricht, the Netherlands: UNU-MERIT.

Hanneman, Robert A., and Mark Riddle. 2005. *Introduction to Social Network Methods.* Riverside: University of California.

Hansen, Morten. 1996. "Knowledge Integration in Organizations." Ph.D. diss., Graduate School of Business, Stanford University, Stanford, CA.

Iivari, Netta. 2009. "Empowering the Users? A Critical Textual Analysis of the Role of Users in Open Source Software Development." *AI & Society* 23 (4): 511–28.

Jung, Yoonhyuk, and Hyunmee Kang. 2010. "User Goals in Social Virtual Worlds: A Means-end Chain Approach." *Computers in Human Behavior* 26 (2): 218–25.

Kleinberg, Jon, 2004. "Temporal Dynamics of On-line Information Streams." In *Data Stream Management: Processing High-Speed Data Streams*, edited by M. Garofalakis, J. Gehrke, and R. Rastogi, Secaucus, NY: Springer-Verlag.

Longhurst, Robyn. 2003. "Semi-structured Interviews and Focus Groups." In *Key Methods in Geography*, edited by N. J. Clifford and G. Valentine, 117–32. London: Sage.

Madey, Greg, and Scott Christley. 2008. *F/OSS Research Repositories & Research Infrastructures. NSF Workshop on Free/Open Source Software Repositories and Research Infrastructures (FOSSRRI).* Irvine: University of California.

Marsden, Peter. 1990." Network Data and Measurement." *Annual Review of Sociology* 16:435–63.

Martin, Jennifer. 2005. "Virtually Visual: The Effects of Visual Technologies on Online Identification." In *Proceedings of DiGRA 2005 Conference: Changing Views—Worlds in Play*, Vancouver: DiGRA.

McNamara, Carter. 2009. "General Guidelines for Conducting Interviews." Accessed June 4, 2012. http://managementhelp.org/evaluatn/intrview.htm.

Mehra, Bharat, Kimberly Black, and Shu-Yueh Lee. 2010. "Perspectives of East Tennessee's Rural Public Librarians about the Need for Professional Library Education: An Exploratory Study." *Journal of Education for Library and Information Science* 51:142–57.

Mitchell, Ronald K., Bradley R. Agle, and Donna J. Wood. 1997. "Toward a Theory of Stakeholder Identification and Salience: Defining Principle of Who and What Really Counts." *Academy of Management Review* 22:853–86.

Monge, Peter R., and Noshir Contractor. 2003. *Theories of Communication Networks*. New York: Oxford University Press.

O'Mahony, Siobhán, and Fabrizio Ferraro. 2007. "The Emergence of Governance in an Open Source Community." *Academy Management Journal* 50:1079–106.

Pfeffer, Jeffrey. 1981. *Power in Organizations*. Marshfield, MA: Pitman.

Pfeffer, Jeffrey, and Gerald Salancik. 1978. *The External Control of Organizations: A Resource Dependence Perspective*. New York: Harper and Row.

Prell, Christina, Klaus Hubacek, Claire Quinn, and Mark Reed. 2008. "'Who's in the Network?' When Stakeholders Influence Data Analysis." *Systemic Practice and Action Research* 21:443–58.

Prell, Christina, Klaus Hubacek, and Mark Reed. 2009. "Stakeholder Analysis and Social Network Analysis in Natural Resource Management." *Society & Natural Resources* 22:501–18.

Ramirez, Ricardo. 1999. "Stakeholder Analysis and Conflict Management." In *Cultivating Peace: Conflict and Collaboration in Natural Resource Management*, edited by D. Buckles, 101–26. Washington, DC: World Bank Institute.

Reed, Mark, Anil Graves, Norman Dandy, Helena Posthumus, Klaus Hubacek, Joe Morris, Christina Prell, Claire H. Quinn, and Lindsay Stringer. 2009. "Who's in and Why? A Typology of Stakeholder Analysis Methods for Natural Resource Management." *Journal of Environmental Management* 90 (5): 1933–49.

Rice, Ronald E. 1982. "Communication Networking in Computer-conferencing Systems: A Longitudinal Study of Group Roles and System Structure." In *Communication Yearbook*, vol. 6, edited by M. Burgoomb, 925–44. Beverly Hills: Sage.

Rosen, Devan, and Margaret Corbit. 2009. "Social Network Analysis in Virtual Environments." In *Proceedings of the 20th ACM Conference on Hypertext and Hypermedia*, 317–22. New York: Association of Computing Machinery.

Rowley, Jennifer, Beata Kupiec-Teahan, and Edward Leeming. 2007. "Customer Community and Co-creation: A Case Study." *Marketing Intelligence & Planning* 25:136–46.

Russell, Gabrielle. 2008. "Pedophiles in Wonderland: Censoring the Sinful in Cyberspace." *The Journal of Criminal Law & Criminology*, 98 (4): 1467–99.

Schwartz, Leigh. 2006. "Fantasy, Realism, and the Other in Recent Video Games." *Space and Culture* 9 (3): 313–25.

Scott, John. 2000. *Social Network Analysis: A Handbook*. Newbury Park, CA: Sage.

Shi, Larry, and Weiyun Huang. 2004. "Applying Social Network Analysis and Data Mining to Dynamic Task Synthesis for Persistent MMORPG Virtual World." in *Proceedings of the Third International Conference on Entertainment Computing*, Eindhoven, The Netherlands, 2004, ser. Lecture Notes in Computer Science, edited by M. Rauterberg, vol. 3166. 204–215. Berlin Heidelberg, Springer.

SPSS Inc. (1999). SPSS Base 10.0 for Windows User's Guide. SPSS Inc., Chicago IL.

Stemler, Steve E. 2001. "An Overview of Content Analysis." *Practical Assessment, Research & Evaluation* 7 (17).

Stewart, Katherine J, David P. Darcy, and Sherae Daniel. 2006. "Opportunities and Challenges Applying Functional Data Analysis to the Study of Open Source Software Evolution." *Statistical Science,* 21 (2): 167–78.Teigland, Robin. 2003. "Knowledge Networking: Structure and Performance in Networks of Practice." Ph.D. diss., Stockholm: Institute of International Business, Stockholm School of Economics. Stockholm School of Economics Library Catalogue. http://urn.kb.se/resolve?urn=urn:nbn:se:hhs:diva-1958.

Teigland, Robin. 2010. "Born Virtuals and Avapreneurship: A Case Study of Achieving Successful Outcomes in Peace Train—A Second Life Organization." *Journal of Virtual Worlds Research* 2 (4): 1–24.

von Hippel, Eric, and Georg von Krogh. 2003. "Open Source Software and the 'Private-Collective' Innovation Model: Issues for Organization Science." *Organization Science,* 14: 209–23.

Wasserman, Stanley, and Katherine Faust. 1994. *Social Network Analysis: Methods and Applications.* Cambridge: Cambridge University Press.

Wellman, Barry, and Milena Gulia. 1999. "Net Surfers Don't Ride Alone." In *Communities in Cyberspace,* edited by P. Kollock and P. Smith, 167–94. New York: Routledge.

West, Joel, and Scott Gallagher. 2006. "Challenges of Open Innovation: The Paradox of Firm Investment in Open-source Software." *R&D Management* 36:319–31.

Williams, Dmitri, Nicolas Ducheneaut, Li Xiong, Yuanyuan Zhang, Nick Yee, and Eric Nickell. 2006. "From Tree House to Barracks: The Social Life of Guilds in World of Warcraft." *Games and Culture* 1 (4): 338–61.

Yin, Robert K., 1994. *Case Study Research: Design and Methods.* 2nd ed. Beverly Hills, CA: Sage.

Notes

NOTES TO CHAPTER 2

1. This chapter is based on research within a collaborative research project on Virtual Worlds, and draws on material, presentations, and personal communication from a number of workshops with developers and practitioners. Among these are the Virtual Worlds Workshop: Augmenting Reality in the Public Domain, Roskilde University, September 2010; Research Workshop, Making Sense of Virtual Worlds and User Driven Innovation Magleås, June 2010; Virtual Buildings and Cityscapes as Communication Technologies in the Making, Copenhagen Business School April 2010; Project meeting with partners on Innovation, Roskilde University, March 2010; and Seminar on Virtual Reconstruction October 2009.
2. David Sokol, "Wikitecture: From Licks to Bricks, Avatars to Architecture," *Architectural Record*, accessed May 13, 2011, http://archrecord.construction.com/archrecord2/work/0810/wikitecture.asp.
3. "Liquid Artifacts: Architecture in Virtual Worlds," *Metanomics.net*, http://www.metanomics.net/show/archive111708/.
4. Bengt Kalderén, interview, October 21, 2009.
5. "BIM-implementering starter indefra – ny miniguide viser vejen," *Det Digitale Byggeri*, http://www.detdigitalebyggeri.dk/news/bim-implementering-starter-indefra-%E2%80%93-ny-miniguide-viser-vejen.
6. Jacob Østergaard, architect and developer, interview, December 17, 2009.
7. Damon Hernandez of IDEAbuilder, interview, June 8, 2010.
8. Damon Hernandez of IDEAbuilder, interview, June 8, 2010.

NOTES TO CHAPTER 3

1. The chapter deals only with literature on virtual worlds. For an extensive discussion of presence in relation to media in general, see Bracken and Skalski (2009).
2. Here, the differences and contradictions within these approaches to presence have been glossed over. Further work might go into these differences and how they are dealt with by the actors involved. For the purposes of this analysis, presence is foregrounded as the prevailing frame of representation. Second Life, and virtual worlds more generally, are situated in additional imaginaires that call for exploration.

NOTES TO CHAPTER 4

1. Funding from the National Science Foundation, Grant IIS-0848692, made this research possible. Any opinions, findings, and conclusions or recommendations expressed in this material are those of the author and do not necessarily reflect the views of the National Science Foundation. I am deeply indebted to the research participants for fully embracing this study and sharing their experiences and insights openly.
2. In contrast to conceptions of cyborgs as biological organisms that are enhanced by the implantation of technologies (e.g., prostheses, pace makers), a more McLuhanesque (McLuhan 1964) notion of cyborg is adopted here as it is more appropriate in the era of social media. From this perspective, the cyborg is a dialectic synthesis between the individual and technology such that the users' naked senses are extended across space and time (e.g., making oneself present in a different space and time by means of a webpage or using a cell phone as an external memory).
3. Following Lee (2004), the term *actual* is used instead of *real* in this chapter. "Actual" refers to a situation that can be perceived, manipulated, and interacted with by the human body's sensory system alone, that is, unmediated by information technology.
4. All names are pseudonyms in order to protect the participants' anonymity.
5. Double quotes indicate reported speech taken from the interviews with Rene.
6. The compound acronym BDSM stands for B&D (Bondage & Discipline), D&S (Dominance & Submission), and S&M (sadomasochism).
7. To ensure the confidentiality of research participants, the photo-diary snapshot was converted into a pencil drawing using image-editing software.
8. The instructions included in the photo-dairy template for completing each snapshot's annotations are shown in italics.
9. According to *Webster's New Universal Unabridged Dictionary, Deluxe Second Edition (1979)*, being *content* means being "happy enough with what one has or is" and "not desiring something more or different." Additionally, as a transitive verb, contenting means "to satisfy the mind of" and "to stop complaint or opposition."

NOTES TO CHAPTER 6

1. This approach to visual anthropology is further elaborated in Pink's (2009b) latest book on sensory ethnography.
2. In Second Life, to "rezz" means to create or make a virtual object appear.
3. Machinima (*machine* and *cinema*) are movies and recordings of in-world activity and events. They are recorded with the in-world virtual camera. Machinimas are produced and captured by screen recording software.
4. The analytical software Advene (Annotate Digital Video and Exchange on the Net). http://liris.cnrs.fr/advene/. Accessed March 25, 2013.

NOTE TO CHAPTER 8

1. The European Union definition of an SME is fewer than 250 employees.

Contributors

Brenda Dervin is Professor Emeritus of Communication at Ohio State University, Columbus. She holds positions as Distinguished Visiting Scholar, Library and Information Science, University of South Carolina (Columbia); Adjunct Full Professor, Department of Communication Studies, Eastern Washington University (Cheney); and Associate Faculty, Department of Communication, Boise State University (Idaho). Now Director of the Sense-Making Methodology Institute (Meridian, Idaho), she has been working on Sense-Making Methodology for thirty-five years. She holds an honorary social science doctorate from the University of Helsinki (Finland) and earned her PhD in communication from Michigan State University (East Lansing).

Paul M. Di Gangi is Assistant Professor in the Information Systems and Operations Management Department at Loyola University Maryland, where he teaches information systems and security. His primary research interests are in social media, user-driven innovation, and knowledge management. His work has been published in *DSS*, *MISQ Executive*, *IJKM*, and *IJAIS* among others.

Sisse Siggaard Jensen, PhD, Dr. Phil. is Professor of Digital Communication at Roskilde University, Denmark. Her current research focus is on questions about how actors make sense of their chosen virtual world(s), their avatar figures, and the social relationships in which they take part. Her research aim is to produce new knowledge about the transformation of self and world by virtual world-making. She was the head of research of a large research project, "Sense-Making Strategies and User-Driven Innovation in Virtual Worlds: New Market Dynamics, Social and Cultural Innovation, and Knowledge Construction" (2008–12) (worlds.ruc.dk), which was supported by the Danish Strategic Research Council. The advanced doctoral dissertation, "Ways of Virtual World-making: Actors and Avatars" is one outcome of the research project. Sisse Siggaard Jensen is head of the Experience Lab RUC (experiencelab.ruc.dk) for experimental research on virtual world-making and games, multisensory, and mixed and augmented realities.

Louise Phillips (PhD, LSE) is Professor of Communication at the Department of Communication, Business and Information Technologies, Roskilde University, Denmark. Her current research is about dialogue-based and participatory approaches to communication theory and practice, including approaches to collaborative research. Her recent publications include *The Promise of Dialogue: The Dialogic Turn in the Production and Communication of Knowledge* (2011); *Knowledge and Power in Collaborative Research: A Reflexive Approach* with coeditors, M. Kristiansen, M. Vehviläinen, and E. Gunnarsson (2012); and *Citizen Voices: Performing Public Participation in Science and Environment Communication* with coeditors, A. Carvalho and J. Doyle (2012). She was the coordinator of the NordForsk Network for the Study of the Dialogic Communication of Research (2008–12) and former Chair of ECREA's Science and Environment Communication Section.

Ursula Plesner is associate professor at the Department of Organization, Copenhagen Business School. She holds a PhD in science communication and has done postdoctoral work on innovation communication. Her research focuses on how new information and communication technologies have an impact on the processes of organizing work relations and communication flows. She is interested in the role of discourses and expectations in innovation processes, and draws on the sociology of science and technology to make sense of the complex interplay among technology, discourses, and social organization. Some of her empirical studies have been published in *Information, Communication and Society*, *Public Understanding of Science*, and *Convergence: The International Journal of Research into New Media Technologies*, whereas some of her contributions to methodological discussions can be found in *Qualitative Inquiry* and *Journalism—Theory, Practice & Criticism*.

CarrieLynn D. Reinhard is an assistant professor in Communication Arts and Sciences at Dominican University, Chicago. After receiving her PhD in Communication from Ohio State University, she held a postdoctoral research position at Roskilde University, Denmark, as part of the collective research project, "Sense-Making Strategies and User-Driven Innovation in Virtual Worlds: New Market Dynamics, Social and Cultural Innovation, and Knowledge Construction" (2008–12). Her research focuses on the application of Dervin's Sense-Making Methodology to reception studies of newer media, such as the Internet, digital games, and virtual worlds, as well as the moment-by-moment sense-making and everyday appropriation of traditional media, such as film and television.

Minna Ruckenstein is Senior Researcher at the National Consumer Research Centre in Helsinki. She holds a PhD in anthropology and is currently doing research on everyday analytics, focusing on self-tracking technologies. Her research contributes to the study of childhood, consumption, and capitalism by looking at technology-enabled practices from the perspectives of materiality and economic developments. She has published in the *Journal of Consumer Culture, Childhood, Information, Communication and Society*, and *Children's Geographies* (forthcoming).

Ulrike Schultze is Associate Professor in Information Technology and Operations Management at Southern Methodist University (SMU; Dallas, Texas) and Visiting Associate Professor in Informatics at Lund University. Her research explores the work practice implications of information technology; it tends to rely on qualitative data and interpretive approaches. Her most recent project examines identity performance in a world increasingly infused by virtual others through the use of social media. Her research into the "avatar-self relationship" in the virtual world Second Life received National Science Foundation funding. She currently serves on the editorial boards of *EJIS, JIT, Information & Organizations*, Sense-Making Strategies and User-Driven Innovation in Virtual Worlds (2009-2011).

Dixi Louise Strand is currently Grants and Research Coordinator at the Department for Communication, Business, and Information Technologies at Roskilde University. She holds a PhD in Science and Technology Studies and has conducted research on systems development practices, collaborative work technologies, and virtual worlds. She has participated in several interdisciplinary research projects funded by the Danish Strategic Research Council, on IT design of web services (2000–2003), IT-based collaboration in health care (2004–2007), and Sense-Making Strategies and User-Driven Innovation in Virtual Worlds (2009-2011).

Robin Teigland is Associate Professor at the Center for Strategy and Competitiveness at the Stockholm School of Economics in Sweden, where she also is Program Director of the PhD in Business Administration and teaches strategy, marketing, and social networks. Robin's research interests focus on value creation through Internet-enabled networks in two-dimensional and three-dimensional spaces.

Zeynep Yetis is a PhD student at the Center for Strategy and Competitiveness at the Stockholm School of Economics in Sweden. Her research interests focus on the dynamics of open-source communities and user-driven innovation.

Index

Note: page numbers in *italics* indicate figures.